First edition August 2013

Edition 1.1 November 2013

Published by Design Community College Inc,

Design Community College Inc.
PO Box 1153
Topanga CA 90290 USA

info@curedale.com
Designed and illustrated by Robert Curedale

ISBN-10: 0989246868
ISBN-13: 978-0-9892468-6-6

Structured Workshops
The author presents workshops online and in person in global locations for executives, engineers, designers, technology professionals and anyone interested in learning and applying these proven innovation methods. For information contact: info@curedale.com

Service Design

250 essential methods

Robert Curedale

PUBLISHED BY DESIGN COMMUNITY COLLEGE LOS ANGELES

Dedicated to Aidan, Liam and Clayton

introduction

Design practice has changed. Design is no longer about only the aesthetics or surfaces of things. Today designers create diverse and complex experiences of products, services and spaces. This is a new approach to design practice. This book details the skills needed by a designer when working for companies that create services in order to drive business value, integrate new technologies and offer value to end users.

We are immersed in services every day. We use the internet, we watch television, we travel on public transport, we shop, we drink coffee and eat at restaurants, we use government services. we go to movies. We live in a service economy. The majority of companies now deliver services. In the United States employment in service industries has steadily risen from around 60% of the overall population in the 1950s to around 90% today. Service design has growing significance for economies. In most Western countries approximately 70% of GDP is currently generated by services.

"There been a lot of focus on product innovation over the years, but very little discussion or thought on innovation in the service sector despite the vast growth of that part of the economy" *John Byrne, editor Fast Company*

Services are different to products because they are not physical, they change over time, they cannot be owned in the same way that physical products are owned, and they cannot be stored. Delivering successful service design means learning new methods and mind sets. Service design involves research, innovation and the application of design tools that are relatively new. The production and consumption of services often occurs in the same place, Effective design of new services requires a step-by-step approach towards a complete understanding of people and their context. Service design is a multidisciplinary area of design. Service design involves creating complex interactive experiences and systems.

Many design methods have been developed by private organizations and so is proprietary. It is my aim to make these methods more widely available to designers. I describe around 250 methods for service design. This book is the tenth in a series outlining new methods in design that are being quickly adopted by global design organizations. Good service design delivers tangible benefits to organizations, the people they are providing services to and to designers. Good service design can give organizations considerable competitive advantage.

contents

contents

Chapter 5
Service design methods

contents

Chapter 1
What is Service Design?

some definitions of service design

"Service design is an interdisciplinary approach that combines different methods and tools from various disciplines. It is a new way of thinking as opposed to a new stand-alone academic discipline. Service design is an evolving approach, this is particularly apparent in the fact that, as yet, there is no common definition or clearly articulated language of service design."
Mark Stickdorn Service Design Thinking

1. "When you have two coffee shops right next to each other, that each sell the exact same coffee at the exact same price. Service Design is what make you walk into the one and not the other." *Marc Fonteijn 31 volts*

2. "Services is a process consisting of a series of more or less intangible activities that normally, but not necessarily always, take place in interactions between the customer and service employees and /or physical resources or goods and/or systems of the service provider, which are provided as solutions to customer problems/ needs." *Christian Grönroos Prof*

3. "Service design is all about making the service you deliver useful, usable, efficient, effective and desirable." *UK Design Council*

4. "It [service design] is a creative and practical way to improve existing services and innovate new ones. *"Live / Work*

5. "Service Design is a design discipline involving the application of design methods to create new, valuable services. Working from the perspective of the user, Service Design projects focus not only on the design of new services, but also on optimizing the general experience and value of a service." *Jeneanne Rae*

6. "Service design is a holistic way for a business to gain a comprehensive, empathic understanding of customer needs." *Frontier Service Design*

7. "Service design is a design specialism that helps develop and deliver great services. Service design projects improve factors like ease of use, satisfaction, loyalty and efficiency right across areas such as environments, communications and products – and not forgetting the people who deliver the service."*Engine Service Design*

8. "Service Design helps to innovate (create new) or improve (existing) services to make them more useful, usable, desirable for clients and efficient as well as effective for organisations. It is a new holistic, multidisciplinary, integrative field.*"Stephan Moritz*

9. "Good service cannot be reduced to nothing more than an efficient operation: its value lies in the less tangible sense that the service is supporting you, meeting your needs, working for and on behalf of you." *Parker & Heapy*

10. "Service Design is an emerging field focused on the creation of well thought through

experiences using a combination of intangible and tangible mediums. It provides numerous benefits to the end user experience when applied to sectors such as retail, banking, transportation, & healthcare consciously designed services that incorporate new business models are empathetic to user needs and attempt to create new socio-economic value in society. Service design is essential in a knowledge driven economy." *Copenhagen Institute of Interaction Design.*

11. "Service Designers visualize, formulate and choreograph solutions that are not yet available. They watch and interpret needs and behaviours and transform them into potential future services. In the process, exploring, generating and evaluating approaches are used similarly and a redesign of existing services is just as much a challenge as the development of new innovative services." *Birgit Mager*

12. "Service design is about creating and taking decisive and deliberate actions that will promote, support, and sustain positive service experiences in order to strengthen provider-customer relationships. "*Susan Spraragen*

13. "Service Design is the design of value creating offerings by aligning intangible processes and incorporating tangible products to create remarkable customer experiences. "*Bernhard*

14. ":Service Design allows us to create personal enjoyable user centred experiences, that will sustain over, without creating unnecessary products that will obsolete and end up in a landfill." *Eilidh Dickson*

15. "Service Design is the thinking and designing of every interaction that a service organisation has with its customers, in such a way that the organisation delivers both a dramatically improved customer experience and increased profitability."*Damian Kernahan*

16. "Good service design is the process of deliberately crafting our experience and delivery of services, to make them more valuable for the people that use and provide them "*Nick Marsh*

17. "Service is everything that can't fall on your feet. "*The Economist*

18. "Developing the environments, tools, and processes that help employees deliver superior service in a way that is proprietary to the brand ".*Design Continuum*

history of service design

Service design is a relatively new field of expertise: it has mostly developed over the past 20 years. Designers and other professionals have been doing service design without knowing it by that name. The development of the field of service design has been connected to Design Thinking

3rd century BC Porphry of Tyros develops mind maps.

1877 Georg von Mayr invents radar charts.

1879 Louis Emile Javal develops eye tracking.

1880 John Venn invents Venn Diagrams

1890s Credit Agricole pioneer co-creation methods.

1909 E.B. Titchener invented the word empathy in an attempt to translate the German word "Einfühlungsvermögen".

1921 Robert Bruere first uses the terms primary research and secondary research.

1928 Margaret Mead develops ethnographic field studies.

1929 Bonislaw Malinowski develops ethnographic field studies.

1940s 2nd World War from which came operational research methods and management decision-making techniques

1940 Robert Merton develops focus groups.

1942 Gordon Allport, may have been the first to describe diary studies.

1944 Alex Bavelas develops Fly on the wall method.

1948 Edward Tolman invents Cognitive Maps

1950 Herman Kahn Rand develops Scenarios method.

1950s Development of creativity techniques

1953 Term brainstorming was popularized by Alex Faickney Osborn in the 1953 book Applied Imagination

1958 Michael Polanyi uses the term Tacit Knowledge.

1960s Designers explore models for design methodology, and "design research" to better understand and improve design processes and practices This movement marked the beginning of a debate over the process and methodology of design.

1960 Affinity diagram was devised by Jiro Kawakita

1960 Allan Collins, Northwestern University USA develops mind maps.

1961 Gordon The first creativity books start to appear

1962 The First 'Conference on Design Methods,.

1962 Archer, L. Bruce. Systematic Method for Designers.

1962 Ernest Becker Behavioral Maps
Service design is a relatively new field of

3rd century BC Porphry of Tyros develops mind maps.

1877 Georg von Mayr invents radar charts.

1879 Louis Emile Javal develops eye tracking.

1880 John Venn invents Venn Diagrams

1890s Credit Agricole pioneer co-creation methods.

1909 E.B. Titchener invented the word empathy in an attempt to translate the German word "Einfühlungsvermögen".

1921 Robert Bruere first uses the terms primary research and secondary research.

1928 Margaret Mead develops ethnographic field studies.

1929 Bonislaw Malinowski develops ethnographic field studies.

1940s 2nd World War from which came operational research methods and management decision-making techniques

1940 Robert Merton develops focus groups.

1942 Gordon Allport, may have been the first to describe diary studies.

1944 Alex Bavelas develops Fly on the wall method.

1948 Edward Tolman invents Cognitive Maps

1950 Herman Kahn Rand develops Scenarios method.

1950s Development of creativity techniques

1953 Term brainstorming was popularized by Alex Faickney Osborn in the 1953 book Applied Imagination

1958 Michael Polanyi uses the term Tacit Knowledge.

1960s Designers explore models for design methodology, and "design research" to better understand and improve design processes and practices This movement marked the beginning of a debate over the process and methodology of design.

1960 Affinity diagram was devised by Jiro Kawakita

1960 Allan Collins, Northwestern University USA develops mind maps.

1961 Gordon The first creativity books start to appear

history of service design

1962 The First 'Conference on Design Methods,.

1962 Archer, L. Bruce. Systematic Method for Designers.

1962 Ernest Becker Behavioral Maps Service design is a relatively new field of

1963 Osborn, Alex F. Applied Imagination: Principles and Procedures of Creative Thinking. New York: Scribner,

1964 Alexander The first design methods or methodology books start appearing:

1965 Archer, L. Bruce. Systematic Method for Designers. Council of Industrial Design, H.M.S.O.

1965 SWOT Analysis developed by Albert Humphrey Stanford University

1968 Kaoru Ishikawa develops fishbone diagram.

1968 Professor Bernd Rohrbach pioneers 635 Brainstorming Method

1969 Bill Gaver Royal College of Art cultural probes

1970 Jones, John Christopher. Design Methods. New York: John Wiley & Sons

1973 Robert McKim's publishes Experiences in Visual Thinking The class McKim creates, "ME101: Visual Thinking,"in the design

program at Stanford University is still taught today.

1979 Bruce Archer "There exists a designerly way of thinking and communicating that is both different from scientific and scholarly ways of thinking and communicating, and as powerful as scientific and scholarly methods of inquiry when applied to its own kinds of problems."

1980s The term first emerged prominently in the with the rise of human-centered design. Rolf Faste building on McKim's work in his teaching at Stanford,

1981 Koberg, Don, and Jim Bagnall. The All New Universal Traveller: a Soft-systems Guide To: Creativity, Problem-solving and the Process of Reaching Goals. Los Altos, CA: Kaufmann

1981 The American Society of Mechanical Engineers conference on Design Theory and Methodology. The rise of human-centered design and the rise of design-centered business management.

1982 G. Lynn Shostack proposed design that integrates material components (products) and immaterial components (services).

1982 Cross, Nigel. "Designerly Ways of Knowing." Design Studies 3.4 (1982): 221-27.

1983 Schön, Donald. The Reflective

Practitioner: How Professionals Think In Action. New York: Basic Books, 1983.

1983 Lyn Shosack develops service blueprinting method.

1984 Jay Conrad Levinson guerilla ethnography

1985 Edward de Bono Six Thinking Hats.

1986 Six Sigma emerges to streamline the design process for quality control and profit. 1987 Peter Rowe professor at the Harvard Graduate School of Design, book Design Thinking was the first significant usage of the term "Design Thinking" in literature. Rowe, G. Peter (1987). Design Thinking. Cambridge: The MIT Press. ISBN 978-0-262-68067-7.

1988 Rolf Faste, director of the design program at Stanford, publishes "Ambidextrous Thinking,"

1988 Whiteside, Bennet, and Holtzblatt Contextual Inquiry

1990s Human-centered design evolves from a technology driven focus to a human one.

1991 The consulting company IDEO. design process, is influenced by the Stanford curriculum.

1991. Service design was first introduced as a "disciplinary" field of

design by Profes sor Dr. Michael Erlhoff at Köln International School of Design (KISD)

1991 Rowe popularized the phrase "design thinking" referring to the ways in which designers approach design problems,

1991 Mood boards first used by Terence Conran.

1992 Richard Buchanan's article "Wicked Problems in Design Thinking," Design Issues, vol. 8, no. 2, Spring 1992. adopts a broader view of Design Thinking

1994 Rolf Faste, "Ambidextrous Thinking", Innovations in Mechanical Engineering Curricula for the 1990s, American Society of Mechanical Engineers, November 1994

1994 Matthew Van Horn invents the term Wireframe the term in New York.

1995 Ikujiro Nonaka expands the ideas of Michael Polanyi on tacit versus explicit knowledge.

1999 IDEO Design Thinking approach was the featured on ABC's Nightline in 1999 in an episode called "The Deep Dive."

2000 Brandt and Grunnet develop Empathy Tools.

2000 The Rotman School of Management develops a new model for business

history of service design

education based on Dean Roger Martin's integrative thinking for solving wicked problems.

2001 The first service design consultancy, live | work, opened for business in London

2002 Florida, Richard L. The Rise of the Creative Class: and How It's Transforming Work, Leisure, Community and Everyday Life. New York, NY: Basic, 2002.

2002 William McDonough Cradle to Cradle.

2000 Bodystorming Buchenau and Fulton.

2003 Misuse Scenario method developed by Ian Alexander.

2004, The Service Design Network was launched by Köln International School of Design, Carnegie Mellon University, Linköpings Universitet, Politecnico di Milano, and Domus Academy in order to create an international network for Service Design academics and professionals. Nowadays the network extends to service design professionals worldwide as well as design consultancies who have started offering service design."

2005 The Hasso Plattner Institute of Design or the d.school is established at Stanford.

2005, SAP co-founder Hasso Plattner made a donation of U.S. $35 million to fund the d.school, which is named the "Hasso Plattner Institute of Design" at Stanford."

2006 Lawson, Bryan. "How Designers Think." Oxford UK: Architectural Press Elsevier, 2006

2006 Pink, Daniel H. A Whole New Mind: Why Right-brainers Will Rule the Future. New York: Riverhead, 2006

2006 Jeff Howe uses the term Crowd Sourcing.

2007 Cross, Nigel. Designerly Ways of Knowing. London UK and Boston MA: Birkhauser Verlag AG, 2007.

2007 The d-school at the HPI in Potsdam, Germany, was founded and took up operation

2007 Martin, Roger L. The Opposable Mind: How Successful Leaders Win through Integrative Thinking. Boston, MA: Harvard Business School, 2007.

2008, the HPI at Potsdam and Stanford University launched a joint research program on innovation, which is jointly led by Leifer and Christoph Meinel.

2009 Tim Brown of IDEO, and is the author of Change by Design: How Design Thinking Transforms Organizations and Inspires Innovation

2009 Design Thinking authored by Plattner, Meinel, and Weinberg

2009 Roger Martin, Dean of the Rotman School of Management in Toronto, authors The Design of Business: Why Design Thinking is the Next Competitive Advantage

2009 Brown, Tim. "The Making of a Design Thinker." Metropolis Oct. 2009: 60-62. Pg 60: "David Kelley... said that every time someone came to ask him about design, he found himself inserting the word thinking to explain what it is that designers do. The term design thinking stuck."

2010 Lockwood, Thomas. Design Thinking: Integrating Innovation, Customer Experience and Brand Value. New York, NY: Allworth, 2010

2011 Faste, Rolf. "The Human Challenge in Engineering Design." International Journal of Engineering Education, vol 17, 2001.

2011 Dorst discusses how a core element of expert design is framing dealing with the paradoxes that arise from conflicting considerations in order to create value.

2011 A number of schools begin teaching design thinking in classrooms and community projects

2011 Cross, N (2011) Design Thinking: Understanding How Designers Think and Work, Berg, Oxford and New York.

some types of services

Accident & Health Insurance
Accommodation
Accommodation for the Aged
Accountants
Accounting Services
Acoustic Consultants
Advertising Services
Air Delivery & Freight Services
Amusement and Theme Parks
Amusement Arcades and Centres
Apparel Stores
Architectural Services
Asset Management
Audiology Services
Auto Dealerships
Auto Parts Stores
Auto Parts Wholesale
Banks
Basic Materials Wholesale
Biotechnology
Bookbinding Services
Botanic Gardens
Broadcasting - Radio
Broadcasting - TV
Building Materials Wholesale
Business Events Venues
Business Management Services
Business Services
Cafes and Restaurants
Casinos
Catalogue & Mail Order Houses
Catering and food service
Catering Engineers
Child care companies?
Child Care Services
Chiropractic Services
Cleaning Services
Clubs, Pubs, Taverns and Bars
Commercial Art Galleries
Commercial Cleaning Services
Computers Wholesale
Construction Services
Consulting Engineering Services
Consumer Services
Convention, trade show, concert and other

Crane Hire Services Crane Repairs
Credit Services
Cultural and Recreational Services industry
Dental Services
Department Stores
Design
Discount, Variety Stores
Diversified Investments
Drain Unblocking Services
Drilling Services
Drug Stores
Drugs Wholesale
Ecological Consultancy
Electrical Engineering Companies
Education & Training Services
Electric Utilities
Electrical Supplies Services
Electronic Design Services
Electronics Equipment Testing Services
Engineering Consultants
Electronics Stores
Electronics Wholesale
Employment Placement and Contract Staff
Services
Engineering Designers
Entertainment
Event organisers
Film and Video Production and Distribution
Financial services
Food Wholesale
Funeral Directors, Crematoria and
Cemeteries
Gambling Services
Gaming Activities
Gardening Services
Gas Utilities
General Entertainment
General Practices and Specialist Services
Grocery Stores
Hairdressing and Beauty Salons
Health and Community Services Industry
Health Care Plans
Healthcare
Healthcare Information
Home Furnishing Stores

10

Home Health Care
Home Improvement Stores
Horse and Dog Racing
Hospitality & Travel
Hospitals
Human resources
Industrial Cleaning Services
Industrial Equipment
Information & Delivery
Information Technology
Insurance Brokers
Internet Information Providers
Internet Service Providers
Internet Software & Services
Investment Brokerage
Jewellery Stores
Landscape care
Laser Specialist Services
Laundries and Dry-Cleaners
Laundry Services
Legal Services
Libraries,
Lodging
Long Distance Carriers
Long-Term Care Facilities
Lotteries
Major Airlines
Management Services
Market Research Services
Marketing Services
Medical Appliances & Research
Medical Equipment Wholesale
Medical Practitioners
Microfilming Services
Model Making Services
Motion picture
Motion Picture Exhibition
Motor Vehicle Hire
Movie Production, Theatres
Multimedia & Graphics
Museums
Museums
Music & Video Stores
Music and Theatre Productions
Music publishing

Networking & Communication
Nursing Homes
Optometry and Optical Dispensing Services
Other Allied Health Services
Other Recreation Services
Packing Services
Pathology Services
Performing Arts Festivals
Performing Arts Venues
Household Goods Hiring
Personal and Other Services Industry
Personal Services
Photographic activities
Photographic Film Processing
Physiotherapy Services
Plant & Machinery Repairs
Plant Hiring and Leasing
Plumbing and Heating (2)
Pneumatics Services
Powder Coating Services
Power Transmission Services
Practice of law?
Printing Suppliers
Property and Business Services Industry
Protective Coating Services
Public Libraries
Publishing - Books
Publishing - Newspapers
Publishing - Periodicals
Pump Repair Services
Radio Services
Railroads
Real Estate Services
Real estate
Recreational Parks and Gardens
Recycling Schemes
Refrigerated storage suppliers
Refrigerators & Freezers - Servicing
Regional Airlines
Rental & Leasing Services
Repair of computers
Research
Research Services
Residential and Non-Residential Care
Resorts & Casinos

some types of services

Restaurants, cafes and bars
Retail
Rope Access Services
Scrap Metal Recycling
Security & Protection Services
Security and investigation activities
Security Guards
Services to the Arts
Shipping
Shot Blasting Services
Software publishing
Sound Recording Studios
Specialized Health Services
Sporting Activities
Sporting Goods Stores
Sports and Services to Sports
Sports Grounds and Facilities
Staffing & Outsourcing
Steel Erection Services
Stocktaking & Inventory Services
Surveying Services
Taxis
Technical Services
Television programme activities
Television Services
Tourism?
Toy & Hobby Stores
Transport and Storage Industry
Travel Agency Services
Trucking
Veterinary Services
Video Hire Outlets
Warehousing and storage
Waste Disposal Services
Waste Management Services
Water Suppliers Services
Water transport
Water Treatment Services
Water Utilities
Wholesale Trade Industry
Wholesale, Other Technology
Zoos

related design movements

YEAR	DESIGN MOVEMENT	DESIGN APPROACHES	PEOPLE
2010s	Design Thinking	Experience design	David Kelley
		Creative class	Tim Brown
			Roger Martin
			Bruce Nussbaum
			Rolf Faste
2000s	Service Design	Human Centered Design	Lucy Kimbell
1990s	Process Methods	Meta Design	Ezio Manzini
			William Rause
			Richard Buchanan
1980s	Cognitive Reflections	User Centered Design	Don Norman
			Donal Schon
			Nigel Cross
			Peter Rowe
			Bryan Lawson
1970s			Robert McKim
1960s	Design Science	Participatory Design	Horst Rittel
		Design Methods	Herbet Simon
			Bruce Archer
1950s	Creativity Methods	Brainstorming	Alex Osborn

service design addresses human needs

Service design takes a people-centric approach. Service design seeks to uncover unmet needs and desires and respond with innovative design solutions. By not referencing existing products services and experiences this approach can lead to design solutions that are differentiated or unique and have a competitive advantage. Here is a list of some human needs that you could consider when developing a design solution.

"There's a hexagram in the I Ching, The Well, that says, "...the well is the symbol of that social structure which, evolved by mankind in meeting its primitive needs, is independent of all political forms. Political structures change, as do nations, but the life of man with its needs remains eternally the same this cannot be changed. The key to designing for eternity is to design for unchanging needs."
Jim Lewis

Physical Sustenance
1. Air
2. Food
3. Health
4. Movement
5. Physical Safety
6. Rest / sleep
7. Shelter
8. Touch
9. Water

Security
1. Consistency
2. Order/Structure
3. Peace
4. Peace of mind
5. Protection
6. Safety
7. Stability
8. Trusting

Leisure/Relaxation
1. Humor
2. Joy
3. Play
4. Pleasure

Affection
1. Appreciation
2. Attention
3. Closeness
4. Companionship
5. Harmony
6. Intimacy
7. Love
8. Nurturing
9. Sexual Expression
10. Support
11. Tenderness
12. Warmth

Understanding
1. Awareness
2. Clarity
3. Discovery
4. Learning

Autonomy
1. Choice
2. Ease
3. Independence
4. Power
5. Self-responsibility
6. Space
7. Spontaneity

Meaning
1. Aliveness
2. Challenge
3. Contribution
4. Creativity
5. Effectiveness
6. Exploration
7. Integration
8. Purpose

Mattering
1. Acceptance
2. Care
3. Compassion
4. Consideration
5. Empathy
6. Kindness
7. Mutual Recognition
8. Respect
9. To be heard, seen
10. To be known, understood
11. To be trusted
12. Understanding others

Community
1. Belonging
2. Communication
3. Cooperation
4. Equality
5. Inclusion

6. Mutuality
7. Participation
8. Partnership
9. Self-expression
10. Sharing

Sense of self
1. Authenticity
2. Competence
3. Creativity
4. Dignity
5. Growth
6. Healing
7. Honesty
8. Integrity
9. Self-acceptance
10. Self-care
11. Self-knowledge
12. Self-realization
13. Mattering to myself

Transcendence
1. Beauty
2. Celebration of life
3. Communion
4. Faith
5. Flow
6. Hope
7. Inspiration
8. Mourning
9. Peace (internal)
10. Presence

Sources: MarshallRosenberg, ManfredMax-Neef, Miki and Arnina Kashtan

15

COMPONENTS OF SERVICES

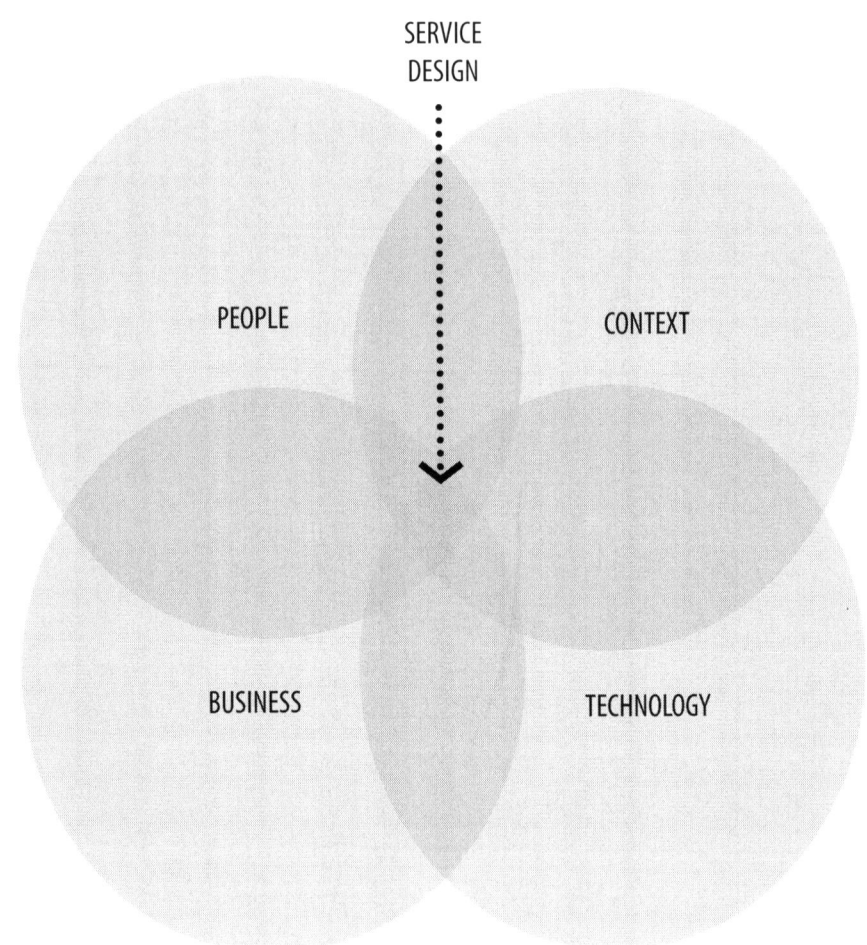

SERVICE
DESIGN

PEOPLE

CONTEXT

BUSINESS

TECHNOLOGY

components of services

Service design seeks to find an optimal balance between four components or factors.

1. Business needs, including
   - Return on investment,
   - Growth,
   - Price point,
   - Competitive advantage
   - Cash flow.
   - Management
   - Negotiation
2. Technology.
   - Internet
   - Travel
   - Methods
   - Analytical tools
   - Communications
3. People.
   - Usability
   - Stakeholders
   - End Users
   - Perspectives
   - Cultures
   - Values
   - Tacit knowledge
   - Experiences
   - Interactions
   - Behaviors
4. Context. Value creation for services depends on context.

THE PERCENTAGE OF US WORKERS IN SERVICES IS GROWING

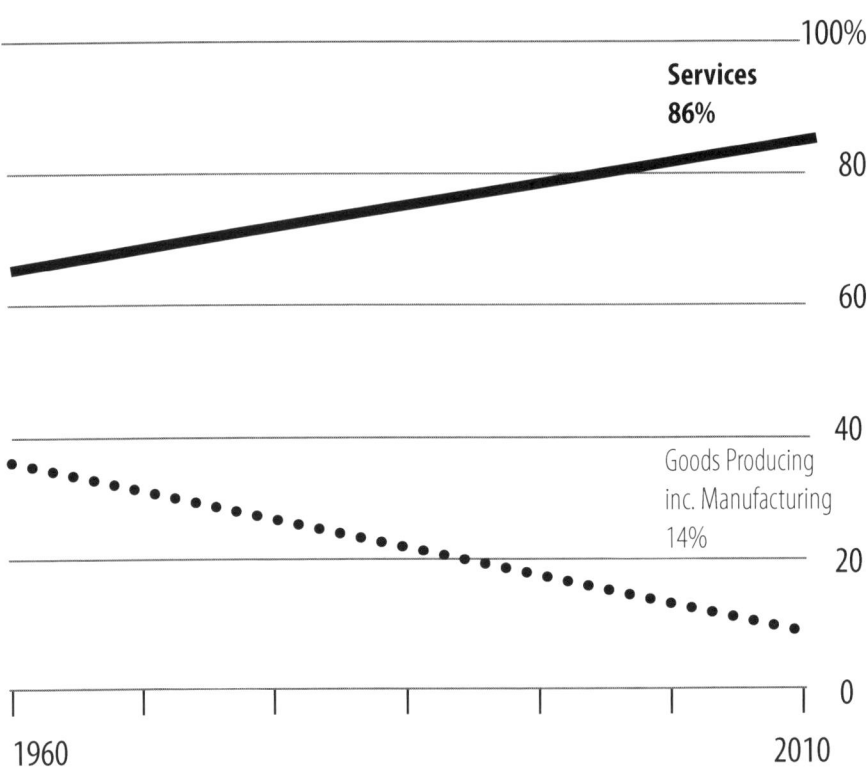

Source: New York Times

customer insights

PEOPLE AND HUMAN VALUES

Service design identifies and addresses human needs. Design Thinking attempts to balance business requirements, human needs, the application of technologies and environmental sustainability.

Designers research how the end user has adapted their environment with their own designs or workarounds. Human needs are investigated throughout the design process and the solution is refined through repetitive iterative steps with physical and behavioral prototypes. Service design adapts the solution to the end user through understanding the end user.

UNRECOGNIZED NEEDS

The methods of service design are capable of identifying and developing design solutions to meet human needs sometimes even before people know that they have needs. Testing prototypes and interactions with real people and observing their responses can lead designers to innovative solutions that are not yet recognized.

HOW DO YOU DO IT?

The ISO standard (ISO 9241-210, 2010) describes 6 key principles that will ensure a design is user centred:

1. The design is based upon an explicit understanding of users, tasks and environments.
2. Users are involved throughout design and development.
3. The design is driven and refined by user-centred evaluation.
4. The process is iterative.
5. The design addresses the whole user experience.
6. The design team includes multidisciplinary skills and perspectives.

SOME QUESTIONS TO ASK

1. Who are the users?
2. What are the users' tasks and goals?
3. What are the users' experience levels?
4. What functions do the users need from the design?
5. What information will be needed by end-users?,
6. In what form do they need it?
7. How do users think the design should work?
8. What are the extreme environments?
9. Is the user multitasking?
10. Does the interface utilize different inputs modes such as touching, spoken, gestures, or orientation?

PERCENTAGE OF US WORKFORCE BY DECADE

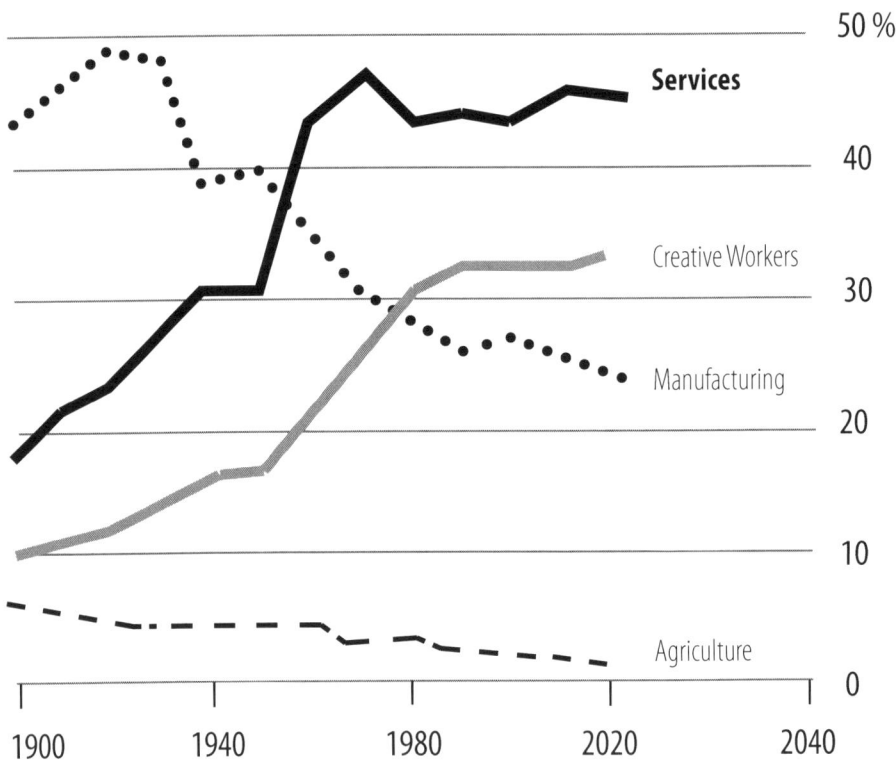

Source: Richard Florida/ Kevin Stolarick

what differentiates services

1. Services are not physical or tangible.
2. Services are a type of consumption
3. Services cannot be stored and may have no value if not used. For example a seat in a theater.
4. Services are used rather than owned.
5. Economies of scale may be less for services than manufactured objects.
6. Growth in services not be a miracle solution to the problem of sustainability, because agricultural and industrial growth are also necessary to meet the needs of the growing world population
7. Value creation for services depends on context.
8. Services may require more educated workers
9. Services require relatively less natural capital and more human capital than producing agricultural or industrial goods. Conserving natural capital and building up human capital help global development become more environmentally and socially sustainable.
10. Many products are sold as part of a system of products and services. For example vehicles need fuel and maintenance. The value of the services over time may be more than the value of the product at purchase. For example the cost of printer ink over the life of a printer may be more than the cost of a printer at the time of purchase
11. Services are often sold to enhance commodity products
12. The production and consumption of services for example a haircut, often occurred in the same place

why do service design

The main drivers for a company to establish or optimize its service management practices are varied:

1. To give an organization an understanding of changing market needs and desires.
2. To create more value with existing resources
3. To create more effective services
4. To create more efficient services
5. To create higher quality service experiences
6. To differentiate services from competitors
7. To better align services and brand.
8. To plan future service offerings
9. Costs can be reduced, by integrating the service and products
10. Increasing service revenue.
11. Improved forecasting.
12. Improve customer satisfaction levels.
13. To ensure that new services are consistent with other services.
14. To ensure that technology and management systems are consistent with new services.
15. To ensure that roles responsibilities and skills are able to support new services.

service touchpoints

Service touchpoints are the tangibles, for example, spaces, objects, people or interactions, that make up the total experience of using a service. *"Moritz 2005*

"Touchpoints can take many forms, from advertising to personal cards; web-, mobile phone- and PC interfaces; bills; retail shops; call enters and customer representatives. In service design, all touchpoints need to be considered in totality and crafted in order to create a clear, consistent and unified customer experience. *"Live/work 2008*

FRONTOFFICE/FRONTSTAGE
"The time and place in which customers come in contact with the service," *Morelli 2002*

LINE OF INTERACTION/VISIBILITY
When the customer is experiencing the service she/ he is facing the line of interaction for example the receptionist at a hotel

BACKOFFICE/BACKSTAGE
How services are facilitated inside the organisation: for example, the food production chain inside the restaurant not visible to the customer. The design of the service may involve a re-organisation of these back office activities performed by the service provider. *Morelli 2002*

1960 Largest US private employers

Goods Producing

GM
Ford
General Electric
US Steel
Esso
Bethlehem Steel
ITT
Westinghouse
General Dynamics
Chrysler
Sperry Rand
International Harvester

Service Providing

Bell System
Sears Roebuck
AP

2010 Largest US private employers

Goods Producing

HP
PepsiCo
General Electric

Service Providing

Walmart
Kelly Services
IBM
UPS
McDonald's Corp
Yum
Target
Kroger
Home Depot
Sears
Bank Of America
Cvs Pharmacy

Source: New York Times

the growth of the service economy

Service industries increased their share of the world economy during the past two decades, while the relative shares of agriculture and industry shrank in most developing regions" *The World Bank 1*

Service industries account for 68 percent of U.S. GDP and four out of five U.S. jobs. In 2011 the United States exported $606 billion dollars in services with a trade surplus of $179 billion.

A look at the largest employers shows how America's economy has changed. Over the last 50 years, the country has shifted from creating goods to providing services. Today, about a tenth of Americans work in manufacturing, while service providers and retailers like Walmart and temp firms like Kelly Services employ about six in seven of the nation's workers.

The majority of developed countries' gross national product (GNP) is already derived from services. And the majority of employees work in services businesses. These service businesses span all industry sectors and range from a one-person laundry service, through medium-size retail outlets, to large IT service companies.
The 2011 World Development Indicators show that the services sector accounted for almost 71% of global GDP in 2010 and is expanding at a quicker rate than the agriculture and the manufacturing sectors. Moreover, trade in services is growing at a pace faster than trade in goods since the 1980s. In 2011, commercial services exports grew 11% to US$ 4.1 trillion(3) — 29'82% coming from developing countries and 2.85% from transition economies

According the Organization for Economic Co-operation and Development (OECD), post industrial economies (i.e. Western developed economies) are now solidly 'service' oriented. By some estimates over 75% of US GDP is composed of services, the UK comes in at 71.6%, Switzerland at 72.1%, and Luxembourg at 79.4%.

Indeed, the casual observer wouldn't be inaccurate in concluding that the U.S. is a post-industrial, services based economy. However, it's only relatively recently that services have become an important source of export growth as well as these services that are integral to the U.S. economy are increasingly sought out by foreign buyers overseas.

Between 1995 and 2005, the US economy lost 3 million manufacturing jobs and created 17 million service sector jobs.

GROWTH OF SERVICES DURING ECONOMIC DEVELOPMENT

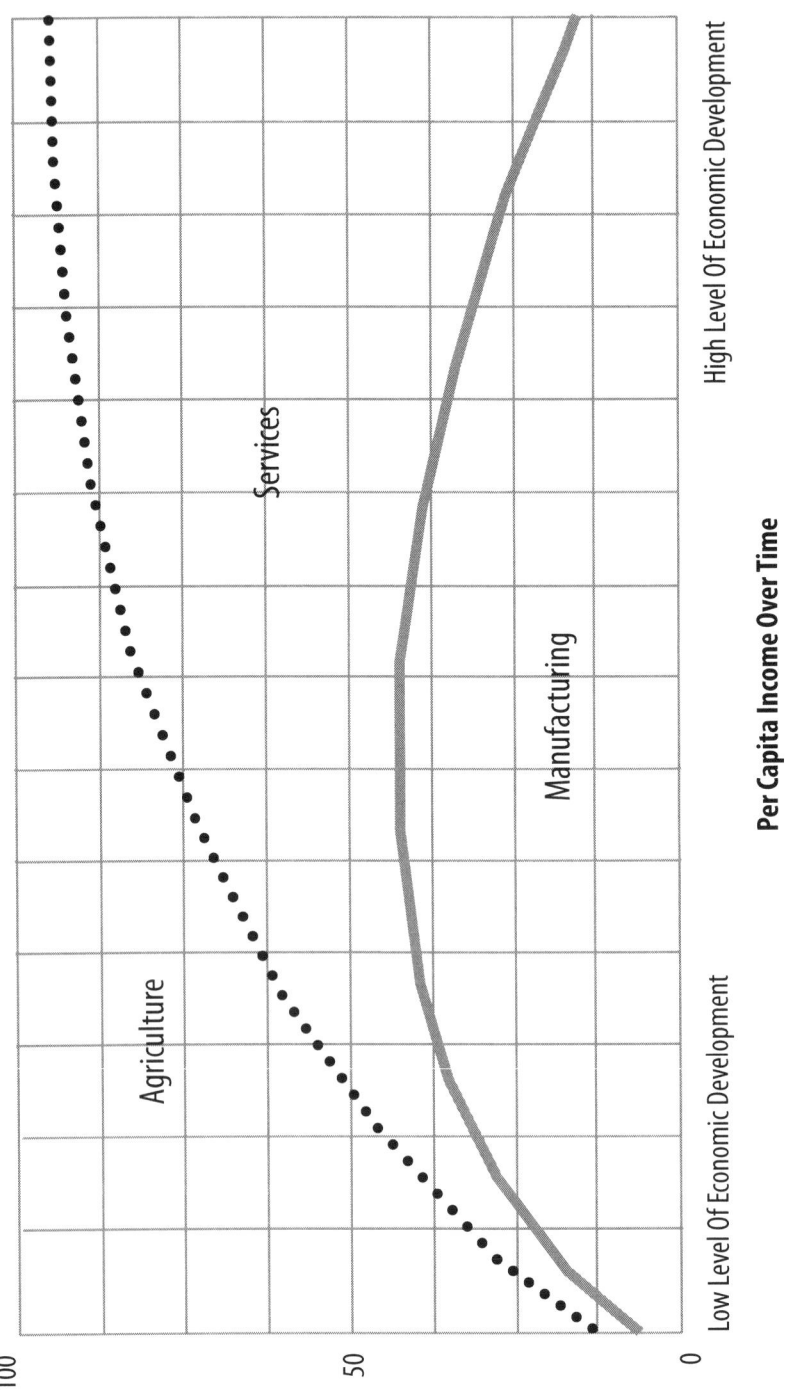

Source: World Bank 2004

postindustrial economies

Most economies go through three stages of economic development:

1. Primary,
The primary stage is driven by labor and natural resource-intensive agriculture.

2. Secondary,
The secondary stage is driven by capital-intensive industry

3. Tertiary.
"The tertiary stage is driven by knowledge-intensive services. As incomes continue to rise, people's material needs are satisfied and their needs become less "material" and they begin to demand more services such as health, education, entertainment. Meanwhile, labor productivity in services does not grow as fast as it does in agriculture and industry because most service jobs cannot be filled by machines. This makes services more expensive relative to agricultural and industrial goods, increasing the share of services in GDP."

"The economies of the developed nations have been moving from the primary to secondary and to tertiary economies over the past century. Eventually the service sector replaces the industrial sector as the leading sector of the economy. "

"Most high-income countries today are post-industrializing—becoming less reliant on industry—while most low income countries are industrializing— becoming more reliant on industry But even in countries that are still industrializing, the service sector is growing relative to the rest of the economy. By the mid- 1990s services accounted for almost two-thirds of world GDP up from about half in the 1980s."

"Conserving natural capital and building up human capital may help global development become more environmentally and socially sustainable. Growth of the service sector will not, however, be a miracle solution to the problem of sustainability, Because agricultural and industrial growth are also necessary to meet the needs of the growing world population."

Source Growth of the Service Sector World Bank

what is design thinking

Design Thinking is a people centered way of solving difficult problems. It follows a collaborative, team based cross disciplinary process. It uses a toolkit of methods and can be applied by anyone from the most seasoned corporate designers and executives to school children

Design Thinking is an approach that seeks practical and innovative solutions to problems. It can be used to develop products, services, experiences and strategy. It is an approach that allows designers to go beyond focusing on improving the appearance of things to provide a framework for solving complex problems. Design Thinking combines empathy for people and their context with tools to discover insights. It drives business value. Companies such as GE, Target, Procter and Gamble IDEO and Intuit have successfully applied this approach to design. Design Thinkers observe users and their physical environments, interact with them with prototypes, and feed the outcomes of their experiences back into the design. In this chapter I will explore what Design Thinking is about.

In this chapter we will discuss what Design Thinking is and how it differs from a traditional approaches to design. We will discuss some of the characteristics of Design Thinking and some ideas that underlie each of these characteristics:

I will discuss how design thinking is:
1. People focused
2. Collaborative
3. About building doing and testing things.
4. That it is an iterative process
5. That it has an agile perspective.
6. That it follows a tested and successful process
7. That it has a wide range of tools and methods that can help overcome traditional problems with design process to create more usable and innovative designs.

Design Thinking starts by thinking about people rather than by thinking about things. It is important to stand in those people's shoes, to see through their eyes, to uncover their stories, to share their worlds. Start each design by identifying a problem that real people are experiencing. Use the methods in this book selectively to gain empathy, understanding. and to inform your design. Good process needs to be supported by talented and skilled and collaborative people on your design team.

Design Thinking is an approach to designing products, services, architecture, spaces and experiences that seeks to overcome some of the problems that have been associated with design since the beginning of the industrial revolution.

These problems include:

1. That the finished design often reflects the perspective of the designer more than the perspective of the group of people who may use the design.
2. That design problems have been becoming slowly more complex and that a solution must involve the knowledge of specialists in many areas beyond the expertise of the designer.
3. That designer training has evolved form art training which has stressed satisfying the designer's need for creative expression more than the needs and desires of the people who may use the design.
4. That the designer's training has not stressed collaboration of the designer with others during the design process to find a balanced design.
5. That designers tend to be stronger at creative thinking rather than analytical thinking but that analytical and creative thinking are required to find the most successful balanced solution.
6. That the design process used by designers needs to be more agile and adaptive to deal with increasing uncertainty, complexity and change.

In this chapter we will discuss why design thinking can help address these issues

"The "Design Thinking" label is not a myth. It is a description of the application of well-tried design process to new challenges and opportunities, used by people from both design and non-design backgrounds. I welcome the recognition of the term and hope that its use continues to expand and be more universally understood, so that eventually every leader knows how to use design and design thinking for innovation and better results. " *Bill Moggridge, 2010.*

design thinking

WHAT IS IT?

Design Thinking is a methodology or approach to designing that should help you be more consistently innovative. It involves methods that enable empathy with people, it focuses on people. It is a collaborative methodology that involves iterative prototyping. It involves a series of divergent and convergent phases. It combines analytical and creative thinking approaches. It involves a toolkit of methods that can be applied to different styles of problems by different types of people. Anyone can use Design Thinking. It can be fun.

WHO INVENTED IT?

The origins of new design methods date back to before the 1950s. 1987 Peter Rowe, Professor at the Harvard Graduate School of Design, published "Design Thinking"the first significant usage of the term "Design Thinking" in literature. After 2000 the term became widely used.

CHALLENGES

1. There has been little research to validate claims about Design Thinking by advocates.
2. Some critics of Design Thinking suggest that it is a successful attempt to brand a set of existing concepts and frameworks with a appealing idea.

WHY USE DESIGN THINKING?

Design Thinking is useful when you have:
1. A poorly defined problem.
2. A lack of information.
3. A changing context or environment
4. It should result in consistently innovative solutions.

Design Thinking seeks a balance of design considerations including:
1. Business.
2. Empathy with people.
3. Application of technologies.
4. Environmental consideration.

Design Thinking seeks to balance two modes of thinking:
1. Analytical thinking
2. Creative Thinking

Advocates of Design Thinking believe that the approach results in consistently innovative design solutions oriented towards people.

Design Thinking takes a cross disciplinary team approach. It rejects the idea of a designer being a lone expert artist working in a studio remote from people in favor of an approach where a designer collaborates with a multidisciplinary team. Design Thinking advocates making informed decisions based on evidence gathered from the people and context in place of designers working on a hunch.

WHEN TO USE DESIGN THINKING

Design Thinking is an approach that can be applied throughout the design process:

1. Define intent
2. Know Context
3. Know User
4. Frame insights
5. Explore Concepts
6. Make Plans
7. Deliver Offering

RESOURCES

1. Paper
2. Pens
3. Camera
4. Notebook
5. Post-it-notes
6. Cardboard
7. White board
8. Dry-erase markers

REFERENCES

1. Martin, Roger L. The Opposable Mind: How Successful Leaders Win through Integrative Thinking. Boston, MA: Harvard Business School, 2007.

2. Buchanan, Richard, "Wicked Problems in Design Thinking," Design Issues, vol. 8, no. 2, Spring 1992

3. Cross, Nigel. "Designerly Ways of Knowing." Design Studies 3.4 (1982): 221-27.

4. Brown, Tim, and Katz, Barry. Change by Design: How Design Thinking Transforms Organizations and Inspires Innovation. New York: Harper Business, 2009.

5. Florida, Richard L. The Rise of the Creative Class: and How It is Transforming Work, Leisure, Community and Everyday Life. New York, NY: Basic, 2002 Basic, 2002

6. Jones, John Christopher. Design Methods. New York: John Wiley & Sons, 1970.

design thinking

FOCUS ON PEOPLE:

Design is more about people than it is about things. It is important to stand in those people's shoes, to see through their eyes, to uncover their stories, to share their worlds. Start each design by identifying a problem that real people are experiencing. Use the methods in this book selectively to gain empathy and understanding. and to inform your design. Good process is not a substitute for talented and skilled people on your design team.

GET PHYSICAL

Make simple physical prototypes of your ideas as early as possible. Constantly test your ideas with people. Do not worry about making prototypes beautiful until you are sure that you have a resolved final design. Use the prototypes to guide and improve your design. Do a lot of low cost prototypes to test how Your Ideas physically work. using cardboard, paper, markers, adhesive tape, photocopies, string and popsicle sticks. The idea is to test your idea, not to look like the final product. Expect to change it again. Limit your costs to ten or twenty dollars. Iterate, test and iterate. Do not make the prototype jewelry. It can stand in the way of finding the best design solution. In the minds of some a high fidelity prototype is a finished design solution rather than a tool for improving a design. You should make your idea physical as soon as possible. Be the first to get your hands dirty by making the idea real.

BE CURIOUS

Ask why? Explore and Experiment. Go outside your comfort zone. Do not assume that you know the answer. Look for inspiration in new ways and places. Christopher Columbus and Albert Einstein followed their curiosity to new places.

SEEK TEAM DIVERSITY

A diverse design team will produce more successful design than a team that lacks diversity. Innovation needs a collision of different ideas and approaches. Your team should have different genders, different ages, be from different cultures, different socioeconomic backgrounds and have different outlooks to be most successful. With diversity expect some conflict. Manage conflict productively and the best ideas will float to the surface. Have team members who have lived in different countries and cultures and with global awareness. Cross cultural life experience enables people to be more creative.

TAKE CONSIDERED RISKS

Taking considered risks is helps create differentiated design. Many designers and organizations do not have the flexibility or courage to create innovative, differentiated design solutions so they create products and services that are like existing products and services and must compete on price. "It takes a lot of courage to release the familiar and seemingly secure, to embrace the new, but there is no real security in what is no longer meaningful." *Alan Cohen*

USE THE TOOLS

To understand the point of view of diverse peoples and cultures a designer needs to connect with those people and their context. The tools in this book are an effective way of seeing the world through the eyes of those people.

LEARN TO SEE AND HEAR

Reach out to understand people. Interpret what you see and hear. Read between the lines. Make new connections between the things you see and hear.

COMBINE ANALYTICAL AND CREATIVE THINKING

Effective collaboration is part of effective design. Designers work like members of an orchestra. We need to work with managers, engineers, salespeople and other professions. Human diversity and life experience contribute to better design solutions.

LOOK FOR BALANCE

Design Thinking seeks a balance of design factors including:
1. Business.
2. Empathy with people.
3. Application OF technology.
4. Environmental consideration.

TEAM COLLABORATION

Design today is a more complex activity than it was in the past. Business, technology, global cultural issues, environmental considerations, and human considerations all need careful consideration. Design Thinking recognizes the need for designers to be working as members of multidisciplinary multi skilled teams.

The need for creative self expression for designers is important. For an artist the need for creative self expression is a primary need. For a designer this need must be balanced by an awareness and response to the needs of others. Balanced design needs analytical as well as creative thinking. The methods in this book balance a designer's creative thinking with analytical thinking. This balance comes most effectively from a team rather than from an individual. Designers must respond to the needs of the design team, the needs of the business needs of those who employ us to design and the needs of those people that we design for.

primary research

WHAT IS IT?

Primary research also called field research is collecting data that is created during the time of study. Primary research techniques include, questionnaires, interviews and direct observations.

WHO INVENTED IT?

Robert W. Bruere of the Bureau of Industrial Research 1921 may have been the first to use the term

WHY USE THIS METHOD?

You can collect this information yourself. There may be no secondary research available. It may be more reliable than secondary research.
It may be more up to date than secondary research

CHALLENGES

1. May be more expensive than secondary research.
2. Information may become obsolete
3. Large sample can be time-consuming

WHEN TO USE THIS METHOD

1. Define intent
2. Know Context
3. Know User
4. Frame insights
5. Explore Concepts
6. Make Plans
7. Deliver Offering

HOW TO USE THIS METHOD

Methods such as:
1. Diaries
2. E-mail
3. Interviews
4. News footage
5. Photographs
6. Raw research data
7. Questionnaires
8. Observation

RESOURCES

1. Camera
2. Notebook
3. Pens
4. Digital Voice recorder
5. Diaries
6. E-mail

REFERENCES

1. Creswell, John. Research Design: Qualitative, Quantitative, and Mixed Methods Approaches. 3rd ed. Sage publications, 2008. Print.
2. Rubin, Herbert and Irene Rubin. Qualitative Interviewing: The Art of Hearing Data. 2nd edition. Thousand Oaks, CA: Sage Publications, 2004. Print.
3. Sanger, Jack. Compleat Observer? A Field Research Guide to Observation. New York: Routledge, 1996. Print.

secondary research

WHAT IS IT?
Secondary research is research that is existing and has been collected by others. Secondary research is the most widely used method for data collection. Secondary research accesses information that is already gathered from primary research.

WHO INVENTED IT?
Robert W. Bruere of the US Bureau of Industrial Research 1921 may have been the first to use the term secondary research.

WHY USE THIS METHOD?
1. Ease of access
2. Low cost
3. May be the only resource, for example historical documents
4. useful for studying trends.

CHALLENGES
1. Secondary resources always have some bias.
2. Secondary research has been collected in the past so it may not be as current as primary research.
3. May not be aligned with research goals
4. Lack of consistency of perspective
5. Biases and inaccuracies
6. Data affected by context of its collection

WHEN TO USE THIS METHOD
1. Define intent
2. Know Context
3. Know User
4. Frame insights
5. Generate Concepts
6. Create Solutions

HOW TO USE THIS METHOD
1. Define goals.
2. Define the context of the problem to be researched.
3. Frame research questions.
4. Develop procedure.
5. Select and retrieve appropriate data.
6. Analyze the data.
7. Review your findings by comparing them with other studies.
8. Summarize your insights.

RESOURCES
1. Books
2. Internet
3. Online search engines
4. Magazines
5. E-books
6. Bibliographies
7. Biographical works
8. Commentaries, criticisms
9. Dictionaries, Encyclopedias
10. Histories;
11. Newspaper articles
12. Web site

REFERENCES
1. Secondary Research: Information Sources and Methods. David W. Stewart, Michael A. Kamins Sage Publications, Inc; 2nd edition (December 18, 1992) ISBN-10: 0803950373 ISBN-13: 978-0803950375

qualitative research

WHAT IS IT?

Qualitative research seeks to understand people in the context of their daily experiences. Uses ethnographic methods including observation and interviews. Seeks to understand questions like why and how. Obtains insights about attitudes and emotions. Often uses small sample sizes. Seeks to see the world through the eyes of research subjects. Methods are flexible. Used to develop an initial understanding.

WHO INVENTED IT?

Bronisław Malinowski 1922

WHY USE THIS METHOD?

Methods commonly used by designers to gain empathy for the people they are designing for.

CHALLENGES

1. Concerned with validity
2. Subjective
3. Hard to recreate results
4. People may behave differently to the way they say they behave
5. Experiences can not be generalized.

WHEN TO USE THIS METHOD

1. Define intent
2. Know Context
3. Know User
4. Frame insights
5. Explore Concepts
6. Make Plans

HOW TO USE THIS METHOD

1. Define research question
2. Select research subjects and context to study.
3. Collect data
4. Interpret data.
5. Study data for insights
6. Collect more data
7. Analyze data

RESOURCES

1. Camera
2. Video camera
3. Note pad
4. Pens
5. Digital voice recorder
6. White board
7. Post-it-notes
8. Blank cards

REFERENCES

1. Holliday, A. R. (2007). Doing and Writing Qualitative Research, 2nd Edition. London: Sage Publications
2. Denzin, N. K., & Lincoln, Y. S. (2011). The SAGE Handbook of qualitative research (4th ed.). Los Angeles: Sage Publications.
3. Malinowski, B. (1922/1961). Argonauts of the Western Pacific. New York: E. P. Dutton.

quantitative research

WHAT IS IT?

Quantitative research uses mathematical and statistical methods. Sample sizes are often large. Findings may be expressed as numbers or percentages. Uses methods such as surveys and questionnaires. Asks questions like "How many?" Used to recommend a final course of action.

WHO INVENTED IT?

The Royal Statistical Society founded in 1834 pioneered the use of quantitative methods.

WHY USE THIS METHOD?

1. High level of reliability
2. Minimum personal judgement.
3. It is objective.

CHALLENGES

1. Methods are static. Real world changes.
2. Structured methods
3. Difficult to control the environment
4. Can be expensive if studying a large numb Er of people.

WHEN TO USE THIS METHOD

1. Define intent
2. Know Context
3. Know User
4. Frame insights
5. Explore Concepts
6. Make Plans
7. Deliver Offering

HOW TO USE THIS METHOD

1. Research design
2. Devise ways to measure hypothesis
3. Select subjects and context
4. Undertake research
5. Process data
6. Analyze data
7. Conclusions

REFERENCES

1. Bernard, H (1994) Research Methods in Anthropology: Qualitative and Quantitative Approaches, London, Sage
2. Creswell, J. W. (2009). Research design: Qualitative, quantitative, and mixed methods approaches (3rd ed.). Thousand Oaks, CA: Sage.

core attributes of design thinking

Ambiguity	Being comfortable when things are unclear or when you do not know the answer	Design Thinking addresses wicked = ill-defined and tricky problems.
Collaborative	Working together across disciplines	People design in interdisciplinary teams.
Constructive	Creating new ideas based on old ideas, which can also be the most successful ideas	Design Thinking is a solution-based approach that looks for an improved future result.
Curiosity	Being interested in things you do not understand or perceiving things with fresh eyes	Considerable time and effort is spent on clarifying the requirements. A large part of the problem solving activity, then, consists of problem definition and problem shaping.
Empathy	Seeing and understanding things from your customers' point of view	The focus is on user needs (problem context).
Holistic	Looking at the bigger context for the customer	Design Thinking attempts to meet user needs and also drive business success.
Iterative	A cyclical process where improvements are made to a solution or idea regardless of the phase	The Design Thinking process is typically non-sequential and may include feedback loops and cycles (see below).
Non judgmental	Creating ideas with no judgment toward the idea creator or the idea	Particularly in the brainstorming phase, there are no early judgments.
Open mindset	Embracing design thinking as an approach for any problem regardless of industry or scope	The method encourages "outside the box thinking" ("wild ideas"); it defies the obvious and embraces a more experimental approach.

Core Attributes of Design Thinking from Baeck & Gremett, 2011

process of service design

The process of service design has six phases.

1. DEFINE THE VISION
What are we looking for? Why do we need to design something?

2. KNOW THE PEOPLE AND THEIR CONTEXT
Who are we designing it for? What is their point of view. What is their context? What else is out there?

3. FRAME INSIGHTS
What have we learned and why is it important?

4. EXPLORE IDEAS
How is this for starters?

5. PROTOTYPE AND ITERATE
How does it work? How can we make it better?

6. IMPLEMENT
Make your developed vision a reality. Make it and sell it.

GOOD SERVICE DESIGN INVOLVES

1. Flexibility
2. Parallel work
3. Collaboration
4. Shaping experiences rather than form.
5. Engaging and interacting with people and context
6. Constant and clear communication
7. Efficiency
8. Synergy
9. Multiple iterations
10. Rapid low fidelity prototyping
11. Smart,human centered solutions
12. Risk management
13. Predictability through following a process

INDUSTRY SHARE OF TOTAL EMPLOYMENT

UK

USA

Japan

China

Korea

Adapted from "China's Future in the Knowledge Economy" by Peter Sheehan

ΔNote: scale condensed before 1900

Industry percentage share of total employment

40

Chapter 2
Service Design Methods
Define the intent

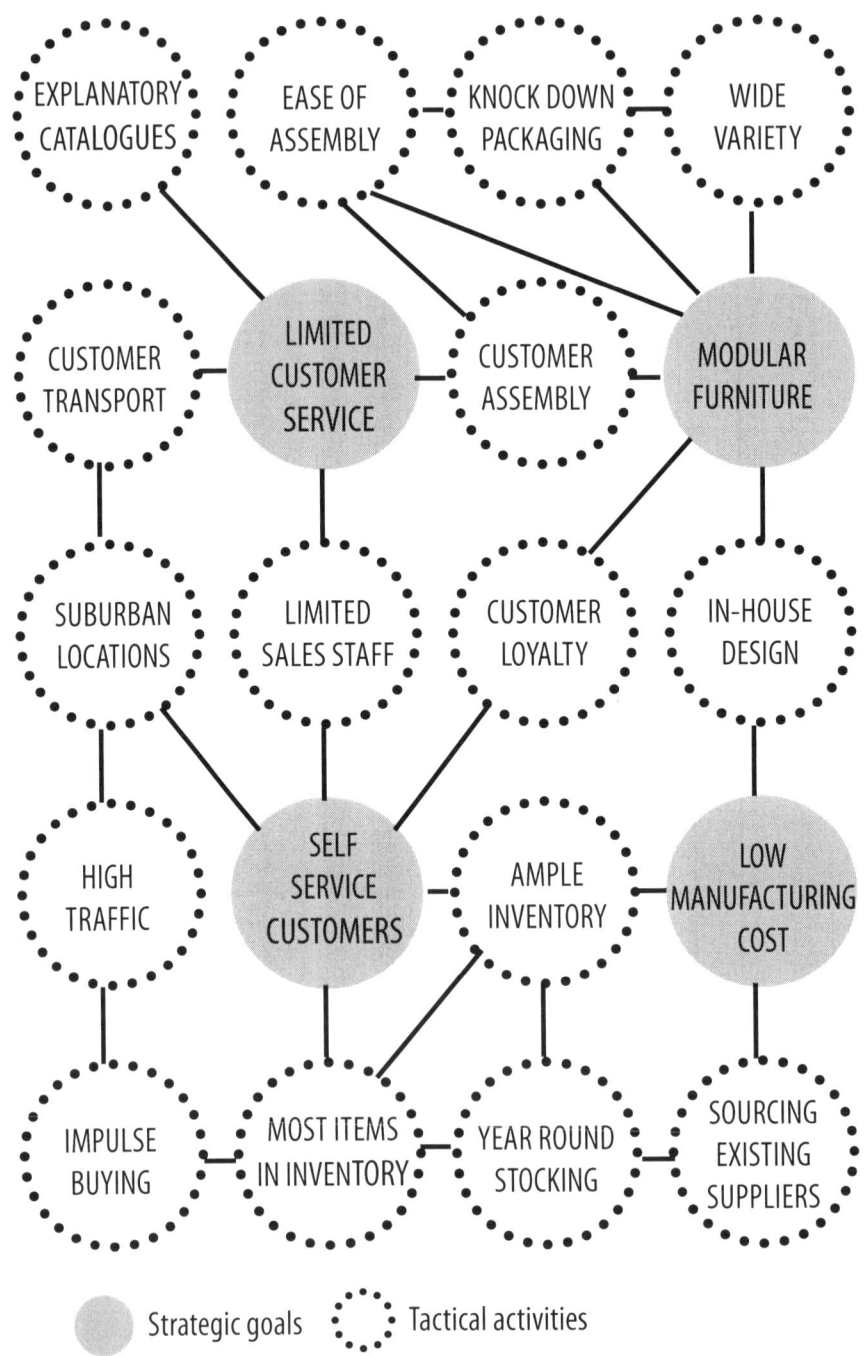

EXPLANATORY CATALOGUES

EASE OF ASSEMBLY

KNOCK DOWN PACKAGING

WIDE VARIETY

CUSTOMER TRANSPORT

LIMITED CUSTOMER SERVICE

CUSTOMER ASSEMBLY

MODULAR FURNITURE

SUBURBAN LOCATIONS

LIMITED SALES STAFF

CUSTOMER LOYALTY

IN-HOUSE DESIGN

HIGH TRAFFIC

SELF SERVICE CUSTOMERS

AMPLE INVENTORY

LOW MANUFACTURING COST

IMPULSE BUYING

MOST ITEMS IN INVENTORY

YEAR ROUND STOCKING

SOURCING EXISTING SUPPLIERS

Strategic goals   Tactical activities

Activity map for Ikea (after Porter)

activity map

WHAT IS IT?

An activity map is a map that show a company's strategic position in relation to company activities. A number of higher order strategic themes are implemented through linked activities.

WHO INVENTED IT?

Walt Disney Corporation 1957

WHY USE THIS METHOD?

1. Activity maps are useful for understanding and strengthening organizational strategy.
2. The value of individual activities cannot be separated from the system of activities.
3. Helps develop a unique competitive position.
4. Helps align activities with strategy
5. Helps understand trade off and choices.

WHEN TO USE THIS METHOD

1. Define intent
2. Know Context
3. Know User
4. Frame insights

HOW TO USE THIS METHOD

1. Is each activity contributing positively to the overall strategy, and customer needs?
2. Are there ways of making the activities and the relationships of activities support strategy better?

REFERENCES

1. Michael E Porter. What is Strategy? Harvard Business Review November-December 1996

anthropopump

WHAT IS IT?

This method involves the research videotaping one or more participant's activities. The videos are replayed to the participants and they are asked to explain their behavior.

WHO INVENTED IT?

Rick Robinson, John Cain, E- Lab Inc.,

WHY USE THIS METHOD?

1. Used for collecting data before concept and for evaluating prototypes after concept phases of projects,

CHALLENGES

1. Best conducted by someone who has practice observing human interactions in a space.

RESOURCES

1. Video camera
2. Video projector
3. Note pad
4. White board
5. Dry erase markers

WHEN TO USE THIS METHOD

1. Know Context
2. Know User
3. Frame insights

HOW TO USE THIS METHOD

1. People are first captured on video while interacting with products.
2. The participants are then asked to watch the tapes while researchers question them about what they see, how they felt, etc. In effect, research subjects analyses their own actions and experiences.
3. The company invites people who have been captured on video to watch their tapes as researchers pose questions about what's happening.
4. E Lab videotapes and dissects these follow-up sessions, analyzing research subjects analyzing themselves.

Source: [1]

REFERENCES

1. http://www.fastcompany.com/magazine/05/october-november-96

autoethnography

WHAT IS IT?

This is research where the researcher studies their own activities and behavior rather than others. May also refer to research of the cultural group that the researcher is part of.

WHO INVENTED IT?

Duncan 1993

WHY USE THIS METHOD?

1. Easy access to self
2. Inexpensive

CHALLENGES

1. Some quantitative researchers consider this method unscientific and unreliable.
2. The study may be too personal
3. May be difficult for the researcher to be objective when studying self.

WHEN TO USE THIS METHOD

4. Know Context
5. Know User
6. Frame insights

RESOURCES

1. Camera
2. Video camera
3. Note pad

HOW TO USE THIS METHOD

1. Be objective
2. Record data while the activity is being undertaken or soon after
3. Analyze and summarize data "
4. Create Reflexive journal summary

REFERENCES

1. Chang, Heewon. (2008). Autoethnography as method. Walnut Creek, CA: Left Coast Press.
2. Duncan, M., Autoethnography: Critical appreciation of an emerging art. International Journal of Qualitative Methods, 3, 4, (2004), Article 3,
3. Ellis, Carolyn. (2004). The Ethnographic I: A methodological novel about autoethnography. Walnut Creek: AltaMira Press.
4. Maréchal, Garance. (2010). Autoethnography. In Albert J. Mills, Gabrielle Durepos & Elden Wiebe (Eds.), Encyclopedia of case study research (Vol. 2, pp. 43-45). Thousand Oaks, CA: Sage Publications.

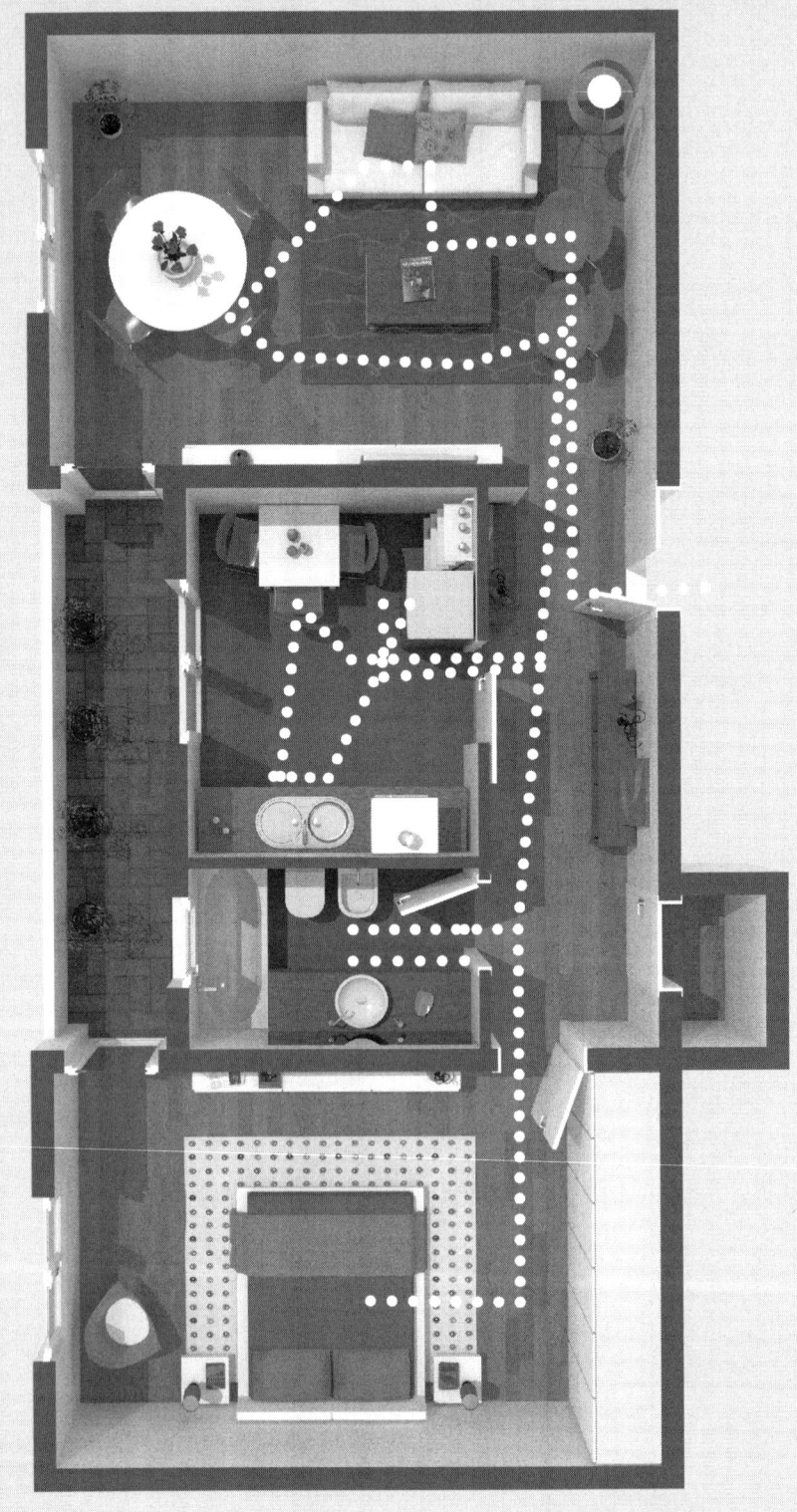

behavioral map

WHAT IS IT?

Behavioral mapping is a method used to record and analyze human activities in a location. This method is used to document what participants are doing and time spent at locations and travelling. Behavioral maps can be created based on a person or a space

WHO INVENTED IT?

Ernest Becker 1962

WHY USE THIS METHOD?

1. This method helps develop an understanding of space layouts, interactions and experiences and behaviors.
2. Helps understand way finding.
3. Helps optimize use of space.
4. A limitation of this method is that motivations remain unknown.
5. Use when you want to develop more efficient or effective use of space in retail environments, exhibits, architecture and interior design.

WHEN TO USE THIS METHOD

1. Know Context
2. Know User

HOW TO USE THIS METHOD

1. Decide who are the users.
2. Ask what is the purpose of the space?
3. Consider what behaviors are meaningful.
4. Consider different personas.
5. Participants can be asked to map their use of a space on a floor plan and can be asked to reveal their motivations.
6. Can use shadowing or video ethnographic techniques.
7. Create behavioral map.
8. Analyze behavioral map.
9. Reorganize space based on insights.

RESOURCES

1. A map of the space.
2. Video camera
3. Digital still camera
4. Notebook
5. Pens

REFERENCES

1. Nickerson 1993: Bnet. Understanding your consumers through behavioral mapping.
2. A Practical Guide to Behavioral Research Tools and Techniques. Fifth Edition Robert Sommer and Barbara Sommer ISBN13: 9780195142099ISBN10: 0195142098

   Aug 2001

Image: © Memendesig. | Dreamstime.com

CRITERIA	A	B	C	D	E	F	G	H	I
USABILITY	1	2	3	1	4	1	1	2	3
SPEED TO MARKET	2	1	1	2	2	4	2	1	4
BRAND COMPATIBILITY	3	3	4	1	3	0	3	1	2
RETURN ON INVESTMENT	3	3	5	3	0	3	2	1	3
FITS STRATEGY	2	3	1	1	4	1	1	3	3
AESTHETIC APPEAL	1	1	1	4	0	3	1	2	2
DIFFERENTIATION	2	4	0	2	2	4	0	4	4
TOOLING COST	2	2	2	0	1	1	3	3	0
FITS DISTRIBUTION	2	2	1	1	1	2	0	4	3
USES OUR FACTORY	2	2	3	1	2	1	4	0	3
FITS TRENDS	1	3	2	2	1	3	4	3	2
TOTAL	21	26	23	18	20	23	21	24	29

Sample benchmarking matrix for products

benchmarking

WHAT IS IT?

Benchmarking is a method for organizations to compare their products, services or customer experiences with other industry products, services and experiences in order to identify the best practices.

WHO INVENTED IT?

Robert Camp Xerox, 1989
Benchmarking: the search for industry best practices that lead to superior performance.

WHY USE THIS METHOD?

1. A tool to identify, establish, and achieve standards of excellence.
2. A structured process of continually searching for the best methods, practices, and processes and either adopting them
3. The practice of measuring your performance against world-class organizations.

WHEN TO USE THIS METHOD

1. Define intent
2. Know Context
3. Know User
4. Frame insights

CHALLENGES

1. Can be expensive
2. Organizations often think their companies were above the average for the industry when they are not.

HOW TO USE THIS METHOD

1. Identify what you would like to be bench marked,
2. Define the process,
3. Identify potential partners
4. Identify similar industries and organizations.
5. Identify organizations that are leaders.
6. Identify data sources
7. Identify the products or organizations to be bench marked
8. Select the benchmarking factors to measure.
9. Undertake benchmarking
10. Visit the "best practice" companies to identify leading edge practices
11. Analyze the outcomes
12. Target future performance
13. Adjust goal
14. Modify your own product or service to conform with best practices identified in benchmarking process.

RESOURCES

1. Post-it-notes
2. Pens
3. Dry-erase markers
4. White board
5. Paper

REFERENCES

1. Benchmarking for Competitive Advantage. Robert J Boxwell Jr, New York: McGraw-Hill. 1994. pp. 225. ISBN 0-07-006899-2.
2. Beating the competition: a practical guide to Benchmarking. Washington, DC: Kaiser Associates. 1988. pp. 176. ISBN 978-1-56365-018-5.

BENEFITS MAP

HIGH BENEFIT

ACTIVITY B

ACTIVITY A

ACTIVITY I

ACTIVITY C

ACTIVITY H

EASY TO IMPLEMENT

DIFFICULT TO IMPLEMENT

ACTIVITY F

ACTIVITY E

ACTIVITY D

ACTIVITY G

LOW BENEFIT

benefits map

WHAT IS IT?

The benefits map is a simple tool that helps your team decide what will give you the best return on investment for time invested

WHY USE THIS METHOD?

1. Aids communication and discussion within the organization.
2. It is human nature to do tasks which are not most urgent first.
3. To gain competitive advantage,
4. Helps build competitive strategy
5. Helps build communication strategy
6. Helps manage time effectively

CHALLENGES

1. Can be subjective

WHEN TO USE THIS METHOD

1. Define intent

HOW TO USE THIS METHOD

1. Moderator draws axes on whiteboard or flip chart.
2. Worthwhile activity at the start of a project.
3. Map individual tasks.
4. Interpret the map.
5. Create strategy.
6. Tasks which have high benefit with low investment may be given priority.

RESOURCES

1. Pen
2. Paper
3. White board
4. Dry erase markers

boundary shifting

WHAT IS IT?

Boundary shifting involves identifying features or ideas outside the boundary of the system related to the defined problem and applying to them to the problem being addressed.

WHY USE THIS METHOD?

1. It is fast and inexpensive.

RESOURCES

1. Pen
2. Paper
3. White board
4. Dry-erase markers

WHEN TO USE THIS METHOD

1. Know Context
2. Know User
3. Frame insights

HOW TO USE THIS METHOD

1. Define the problem.
2. Research outside systems that may have related ideas or problems to the defined problem.
3. Identify ideas or solutions outside the problem system.
4. Apply the outside idea or solution to the problem being addressed.

REFERENCES

1. Walker, D. J., Dagger, B. K. J. and Roy, R. Creative Techniques in Product and Engineering Design. Woodhead Publishing Ltd 1991. ISBN 1 85573 025 1

BOWMAN'S STRATEGY CLOCK

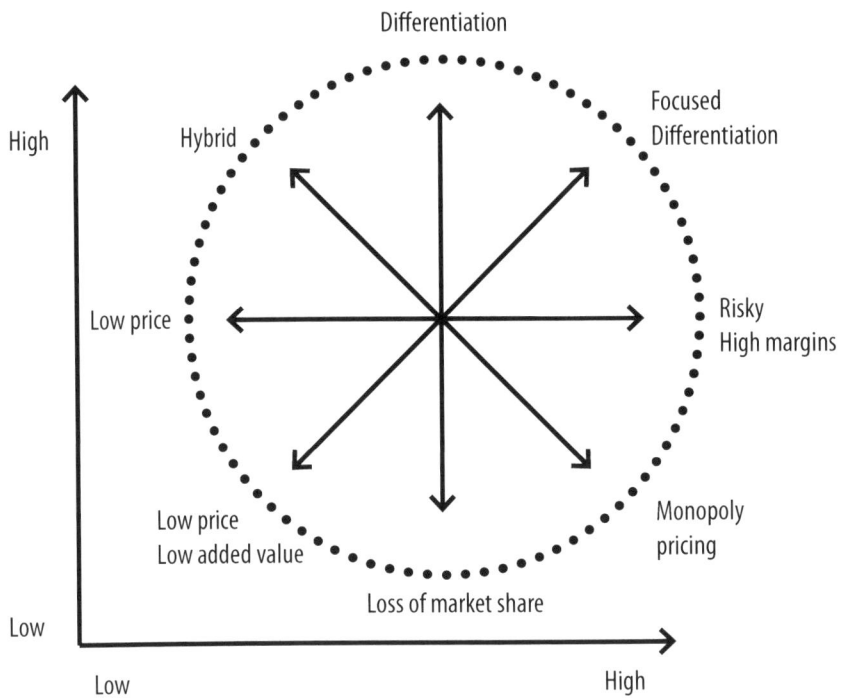

bowman's strategy clock

WHAT IS IT?

This is a method for analyzing the possibility of success for a number of different strategies. It identifies the cost and perceived value of different approaches. Bowman's Strategy Clock has eight alternative strategies in four quadrants.

WHO INVENTED IT?

Cliff Bowman and David Faulkner 1996

WHY USE THIS METHOD?

1. Helps develop a strategy of competitive advantage.
2. Can be used to analyze current strategy and strategies of competitors.

RESOURCES

1. Pen
2. Paper
3. White board
4. Dry erase markers

WHEN TO USE THIS METHOD

1. Define intent

HOW TO USE THIS METHOD

1. Graph competing options on a two axis chart
2. The x axis is high low price
3. The y axis is high low perceived value to the consumer
4. The 8 types of strategy are
- Low price low value
- Low price
- Moderate price and differentiation
- Differentiation
- Focused differentiation
- Increased price and standard product
- High price low value
- Low value and standard price.
- Some of these alternatives are not viable strategies in a competitive environment.

REFERENCES

1. Bowman, C. and Faulkner, D. (1997), "Competitive and Corporate Strategy", Irwin, London.

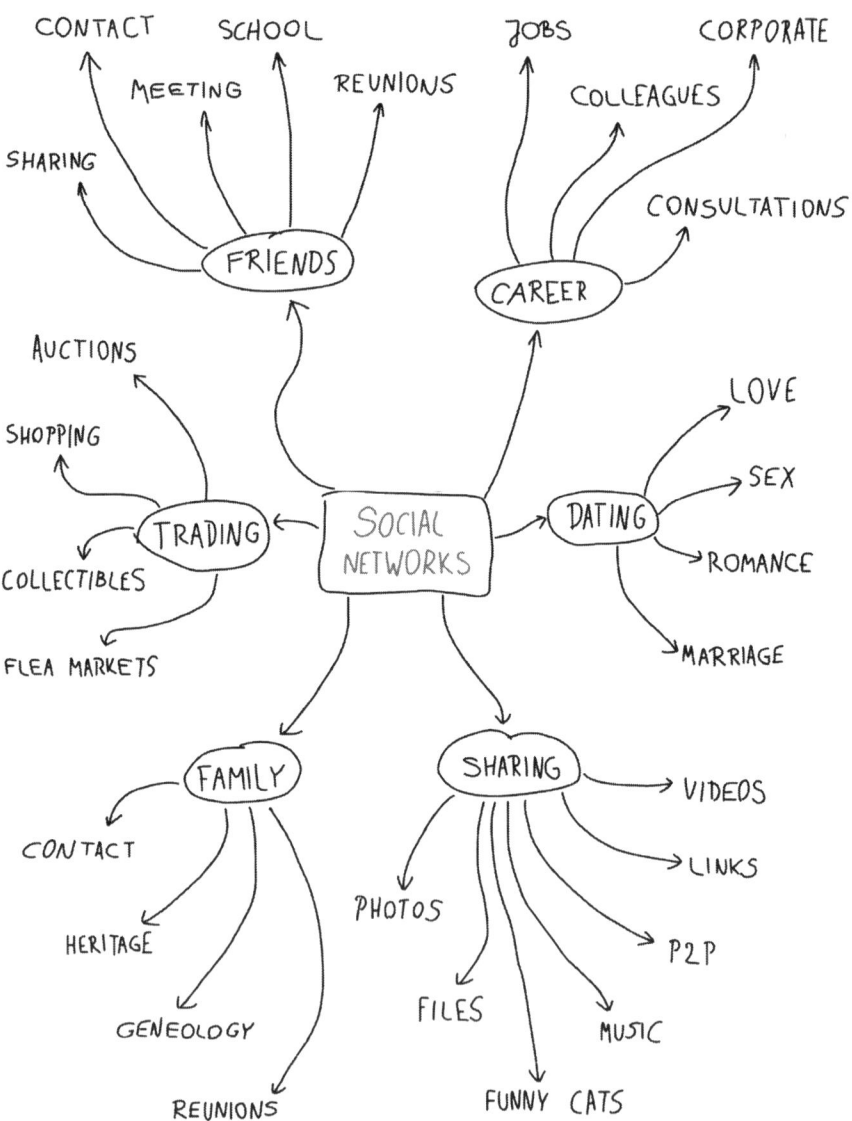

mind map

WHAT IS IT?

A mind map is a diagram used to represent the affinities or connections between a number of ideas or things. Understanding connections is the starting point for design. Mind maps are a method of analyzing information and relationships.

WHO INVENTED IT?

Porphry of Tyros 3rd century BC.
Allan Collins, Northwestern University 1960, USA

WHY USE THIS METHOD?

1. The method helps identify relationships.
2. There is no right or wrong with mind maps. They help with they help with memory and organization.
3. Problem solving and brainstorming
4. Relationship discovery
5. Summarizing information
6. Memorizing information

CHALLENGES

Print words clearly, use color and images for visual impact.

WHEN TO USE THIS METHOD

1. Define intent
2. Know Context
3. Know User
4. Frame insights
5. Explore Concepts
6. Make Plans

HOW TO USE THIS METHOD

1. Start in the center with a key word or idea. Put box around this node.
2. Use images, symbols, or words for nodes.
3. Select key words.
4. Keep the key word names of nodes s simple and short as possible.
5. Associated nodes should be connected with lines to show affinities.
6. Make the lines the same length as the word/image they support.
7. Use emphasis such as thicker lines to show the strength of associations in your mind map.
8. Use radial arrangement of nodes.

RESOURCES

1. Paper
2. Pens
3. White board
4. Dry-erase markers

REFERENCES

1. Mind maps as active learning tools', by Willis, CL. Journal of computing sciences in colleges. ISSN: 1937-4771. 2006. Volume: 21 Issue: 4
2. Mind Maps as Classroom Exercises John W. Budd The Journal of Economic Education, Vol. 35, No. 1 (Winter, 2004), pp. 35-46 Published by: Taylor & Francis, Ltd.

cradle to cradle

WHAT IS IT?
Cradle-to-Cradle is is a biometic approach to the design of products and systems proposed by the authors William McDonough and Michael Braungart based on the intelligence of natural systems. it is an industrial and social framework that proposes systems that are efficient and waste free.

The basis for the Cradle-to-Cradle approach involves three guiding principles:
1 Use current solar income.
2 Waste equals Food.
3 Celebrate diversity.

WHO INVENTED IT?
William McDonough and Michael Braungart 2002

WHY USE THIS METHOD?
1. The Cradle-to-Cradle approach is a framework for global economic and natural stainability

CHALLENGES
1. Cradle to Cradle is often criticized for its lack of attention to energy.
2. Some critics see the approach as utopian.
3. Even the highest Cradle to cradle certification requires only 50 % of energy for production to come from solar sources.

WHEN TO USE THIS METHOD
1. Define intent
2. Know Context
3. Know User
4. Frame insights
5. Explore Concepts
6. Make Plans
7. Deliver Offering

HOW TO USE THIS METHOD
1. Do not specify environmentally damaging materials processes and systems.
2. Follow informed personal preferences.
3. Create a 'passive positive' list of substances known to be healthy and safe for use.
4. Eliminate waste
5. Use solar energy.
6. Respect human and natural systems.
7. Design the product from beginning to end to become food for either biological or technical metabolisms.
8. Reinvent. Recast the design assignment. Towards environmentally sustainable ends.

REFERENCES
1. Braungart, Michael; & McDonough, William (2002). Cradle to Cradle: Remaking the Way We Make Things. North Point Press. ISBN 0-86547-587-3.

six thinking hats

WHAT IS IT?

Six thinking hats is a tool for thinking described in a book by the same name by Edward de Bono. It can help a design team understand the effects of decisions from different viewpoints.

1. White Hat thinking is information, numbers, data needs and gaps.
2. Red Hat thinking is intuition, desires and emotion.
3. Black Hat thinking is the hat of judgment and care.
4. Yellow Hat thinking is the logical positive.
5. Green Hat thinking is the hat of creativity, alternatives, proposals, provocations and change.
6. Blue Hat thinking is the overview or process control.

WHO INVENTED IT?

Edward de Bono 1985

CHALLENGES

1. When describing your concept, be specific about your goal.
2. Utilize your thinking for practical solutions.
3. Always think in the style of the hat you're wearing.
4. Stick to the rules.

WHY USE THIS METHOD?

The key theoretical reasons to use the Six Thinking Hats are to:
1. Encourage Parallel Thinking
2. Encourage full-spectrum thinking
3. Separate ego from performance
4. Encourage critical thinking.

WHEN TO USE THIS METHOD

1. Define Intent
2. Know Context
3. Know User
4. Frame insights
5. Generate Concepts
6. Create Solutions

HOW TO USE THIS METHOD

1. Optimum number of participants is 4 to 8.
2. Present the facts White Hat.
3. Generate ideas on how the issue should be handled Green Hat.
4. Evaluate the ideas. Yellow Hat.
5. List the drawbacks Black Hat.
6. Get the feelings about alternatives Red Hat.
7. Summarize and finish the meeting. Blue Hat.
8. Time required 90 minutes.

RESOURCES

1. Paper and
2. Pens,
3. Descriptions of different hats
4. Symbols of hats
5. Space to sit in the circle

REFERENCES

1. de Bono, Edward (1985). Six Thinking Hats: An Essential Approach to Business Management. Little, Brown, & Company. ISBN 0-316-17791-1 (hardback) and 0316178314 (paperback).

CONTEXT MAP

TRENDS	POLITICAL	ECONOMIC	USER NEEDS	TECHNOLOGY	UNCERTAINTIES	TRENDS

context map

WHAT IS IT?

A context map is a tool for representing complex factors affecting an organization or design visually. Context maps are sometimes used by directors or organizations as a tool to enable discussion of the effects of change and related interacting business, cultural and environmental factors in order to create a strategic vision for an organization. A context map can be used to analyze trends

WHO INVENTED IT?

Joseph D. Novak Cornell University 1970s.

WHY USE THIS METHOD?

Uses include:
1. New knowledge creation
2. Documenting the knowledge existing informally within an organization.
3. Creating a shared strategic vision

WHEN TO USE THIS METHOD

1. Define intent
2. Know Context
3. Know User
4. Frame insights

RESOURCES

1. Template
2. White board
3. Paper flip chart
4. Pens
5. Dry-erase markers
6. Post-it-notes

HOW TO USE THIS METHOD

1. Put together a team of between 4 and 20 participants with diverse backgrounds and outlooks.
2. Appoint a good moderator
3. Prepare a space. Use a private room with a white board or large wall.
4. Distribute post-it notes to each participant.
5. Brainstorm the list of factors one at a time.
6. These can include Trends, technology, trends, political factors, economic climate customer needs, uncertainties.
7. Each participant can contribute.
8. All contributions are recorded on the white board or on the wall with the post-it-notes.
9. When all factors have been discussed prioritize each group of contributions to identify the most critical.
10. This can be done by rearranging the post-it-notes or white board notes.
11. Video the session and photograph the notes after the session.
12. Analyze the map and create strategy.

REFERENCES

1. Context Map: A Method to Represent the Interactions Between Students' Learning and Multiple Context Factors written by Gyoungho Lee and Lei Bao Physics Education Research Conference 2002

61

CRITICAL SUCCESS FACTOR CHART

BRAND

FACTOR	A			B			C			D		
	-	+	++	-	+	++	-	+	++	-	+	++
Cost		X			X				X	X		
Brand			X			X	X					X
Technology		X		X				X		X		
Employees	X				X		X				X	
Customer service		X				X			X		X	
Distribution			X	X				X		X		
Speed to market			X			X	X					X
Design		X		X			X				X	
Reliability		X			X				X			X

critical success factor

WHAT IS IT?

The critical success factor is the factor that is necessary for a project to achieve it's goal or mission. In order to be profitable and survive, a company needs to have a critical success factor.

WHO INVENTED IT?

The term success factor was developed by D. Ronald Daniel of McKinsey & Company in 1961.
John F. Rockart further developed the concept of critical success factors between 1979 and 1981

WHY USE THIS METHOD?

1. It is a method of graphically representing a company's critical success factors so they can be the focus for discussion and refinement.
2. It is a method of comparing competitors

CHALLENGES

1. The method can be subjective

RESOURCES

1. Pen
2. Paper
3. Computer
4. Graphics software

WHEN TO USE THIS METHOD

1. Define intent

HOW TO USE THIS METHOD

1. Ask your team: 'Why would customers choose us?'."What do we need to do well to win business?" The answer is typically a critical success factor.
2. Create a matrix and rate each identified critical success factor an a 3 point scale.
3. Graph each score and connect the scores for each company being assessed with a line.

REFERENCES

1. Boynlon, A.C., and Zmud, R.W. 1984. "An Assessment of Critical Success Factors," Sloan Management Review (25:4), pp. 17-27.
2. Rockart, John F. "A Primer on Critical Success Factors" published in The Rise of Managerial Computing: The Best of the Center for Information Systems Research, edited with Christine V. Bullen. (Homewood, IL: Dow Jones-Irwin), 1981, OR, McGraw-Hill School Education Group (1986)
3. Johnson, James A. and Michael Friesen (1995). The Success Paradigm: Creating Organizational Effectiveness Through Quality and Strategy New York: Quorum Books. ISBN 978-0-89930-836-4

critical thinking

WHAT IS IT?
Critical thinking is the discipline of rigorously and skillfully using information, experience, observation and reasoning to guide your decisions, actions and beliefs.

WHO INVENTED IT?
Socrates, Buddhist kalama sutta and Abhidharma.

WHY USE THIS METHOD?
1. More effective decisions
2. More efficient use of time
3. Rational rather than emotion-driven decisions.

WHEN TO USE THIS METHOD
1. Define intent
2. Know Context
3. Know User
4. Frame insights
5. Explore Concepts
6. Make Plans
7. Deliver Offering

HOW TO USE THIS METHOD
Critical thinking skills include:
1. Recognizing and solving problems.
2. Information gathering.
3. Interpreting information.
4. Recognizing relationships.
5. Drawing sound conclusions.
6. Leaning from experience
7. Recognizing assumptions.
8. Self criticism.
9. Self awareness.
10. Reflective thought.
11. Understanding meaning.

REFERENCES
1. Title: Critical Thinking Handbook: K-3rd Grades. A Guide for Remodelling Lesson Plans in Language Arts, Social Studies, and Science. Author: Richard W. Paul, A.J.A. Binker, Daniel Weil. Publisher: Foundation for Critical Thinking. ISBN: 0-944583-05-9
2. Paul, Richard; and Elder, Linda. The Miniature Guide to Critical Thinking Concepts and Tools. Dillon Beach: Foundation for Critical Thinking Press, 2008, p. 4. ISBN 978-0-944583-10-4
3. Ennis, R.H., "Critical Thinking Assessment" in Fasko, Critical Thinking and Reasoning: Current Research, Theory, and Practice (2003). ISBN 978-1-57273-460-9

critical thinking

"Critical thinking is independent thinking for oneself. Many of our beliefs are acquired at an early age, when we have a strong tendency to form beliefs for irrational reasons (because we want to believe, because we are praised or rewarded for believing). Critical thinkers use critical skills and insights to reveal and reject beliefs that are irrational.

In forming new beliefs, critical thinkers do not passively accept the beliefs of others; rather, they try to figure things out for themselves,

They are not limited by accepted ways of doing things. They evaluate both goals and how to achieve them. They do not accept as true, or reject as false, beliefs they do not understand. They are not easily manipulated."

Source: The critical thinking Handbook.
Richard W. Paul

AFFECTIVE STRATEGIES
1. Thinking independently
2. Developing insight into egocentricity or sociocentricity
3. Exercising fair-mindedness
4. Exploring thoughts underlying feelings and feelings underlying thoughts
5. Developing intellectual humility and suspending judgment
6. Developing intellectual courage
7. Developing intellectual good faith or integrity
8. Developing intellectual perseverance
9. Developing confidence in reason

Source: The critical thinking Handbook.
Richard W. Paul

65

DEMING CYCLE

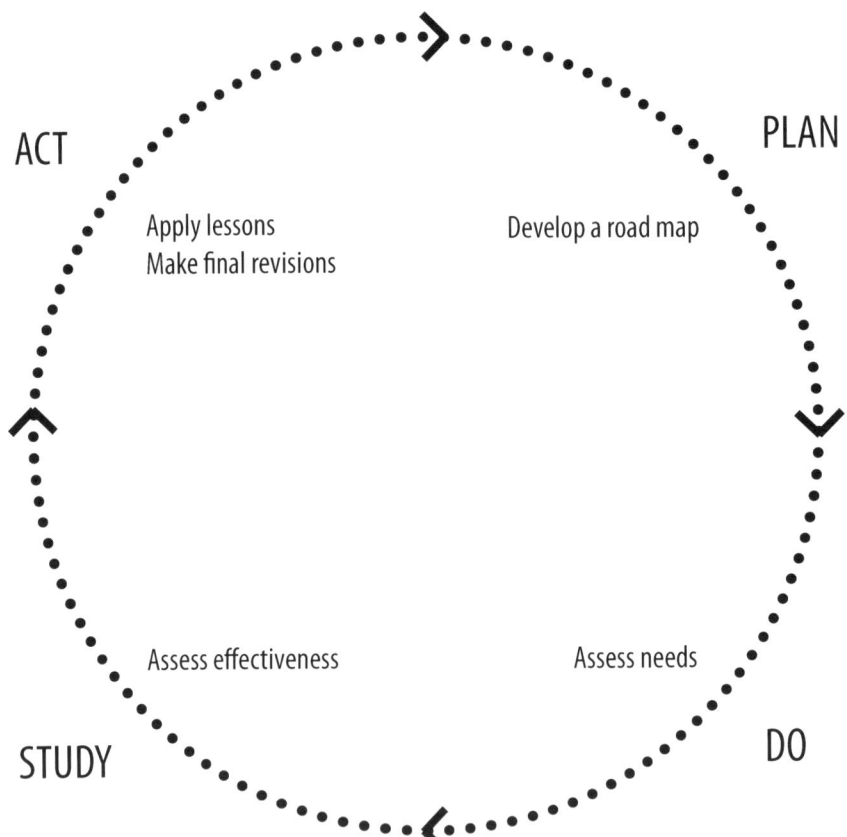

ACT

PLAN

Apply lessons
Make final revisions

Develop a road map

Assess effectiveness

Assess needs

STUDY

DO

deming cycle

WHAT IS IT?

The Deming Cycle is a method to test information before making a decision for the continuous improvement of systems and products. Also known as PDCA and Shewhart cycle. A principal of the method is iteration.

WHO INVENTED IT?

Made popular by Dr. W. Edwards Deming based on the "scientific method"of Francis Bacon *Novum Organum, 1620*

WHY USE THIS METHOD?

1. To assess proposed problem solutions
2. To identify and measure the effects and outcomes of initial, trial efforts.

RESOURCES

1. Paper
2. Pens
3. White board
4. Dry erase markers

WHEN TO USE THIS METHOD

1. Frame insights
2. Explore Concepts

HOW TO USE THIS METHOD

Plan. Establish objectives.
Do. Implement the plan.
Check. Study the results and compare to the expected results.
Act. On differences between planned and actual results.

REFERENCES

1. Rother, Mike (2010). Toyota Kata. Chapter 6: MGraw-Hill. ISBN 978-0-07-163523-3.

FUTURE WHEEL

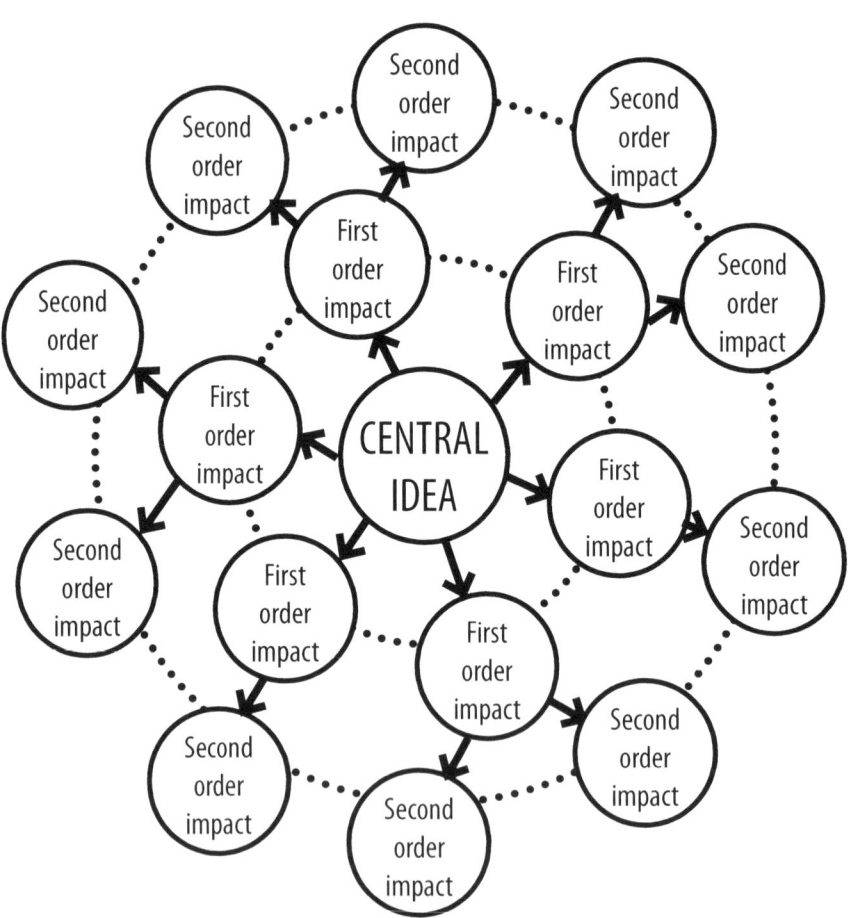

future wheel

WHAT IS IT?

The future wheel is a method to graphically represent and analyze the direct and indirect outcomes of a proposed change.

WHO INVENTED IT?

Jerome Glenn 1972

WHY USE THIS METHOD?

1. A method of envisioning outcomes of decisions.
2. Can be used to study possible outcomes of trends.
3. Helps create a consciousness of the future.

CHALLENGES

1. Can be subjective

WHEN TO USE THIS METHOD

1. Define intent

HOW TO USE THIS METHOD

1. Define the proposed change
2. Identify and graph the first level of outcomes
3. Identify and graph the subsequent level of outcomes
4. Link the dependencies
5. Identify insights
6. Identify the actions
7. Implement the actions

RESOURCES

1. Pen
2. Paper
3. White board
4. Dry erase markers

REFERENCES

1. Futures Wheel, Futures Research Methodology Version 3.0, The Millennium Project, Washington, DC 2009

mood board

WHAT IS IT?

A mood board is a collage made of images and words and may include sample of colors and fabrics or other materials. They are used to convey the emotional communication of an intended design

WHO INVENTED IT?

Possibly Terence Conran 1991

WHY USE THIS METHOD?

1. A mood board helps convey complex emotional ideas at an early stage in design project
2. Provides a focus for team discussion and alignment.
3. It is fast
4. Inexpensive
5. A form of visual prototype of a perceptual experience

CHALLENGES

1. It is subjective,

WHEN TO USE THIS METHOD

1. Define intent

HOW TO USE THIS METHOD

A mood board can include
1. Colors
2. Forms
3. Cultures
4. Materials
5. Finishes
6. Textures

RESOURCES

1. Graphic programs
2. Print Magazines
3. Digital images
4. Fabric swatches
5. Color swatches
6. Graphics software
7. Computer

REFERENCES

1. Kathryn McKelvey, Janine Munslow Fashion Forecasting :Page 150 2008
2. Product Design: Practical Methods for systematic Development of New Products By Mike Baxter 1995

image: © -kuba- | Dreamstime.com

PROBLEM TREE

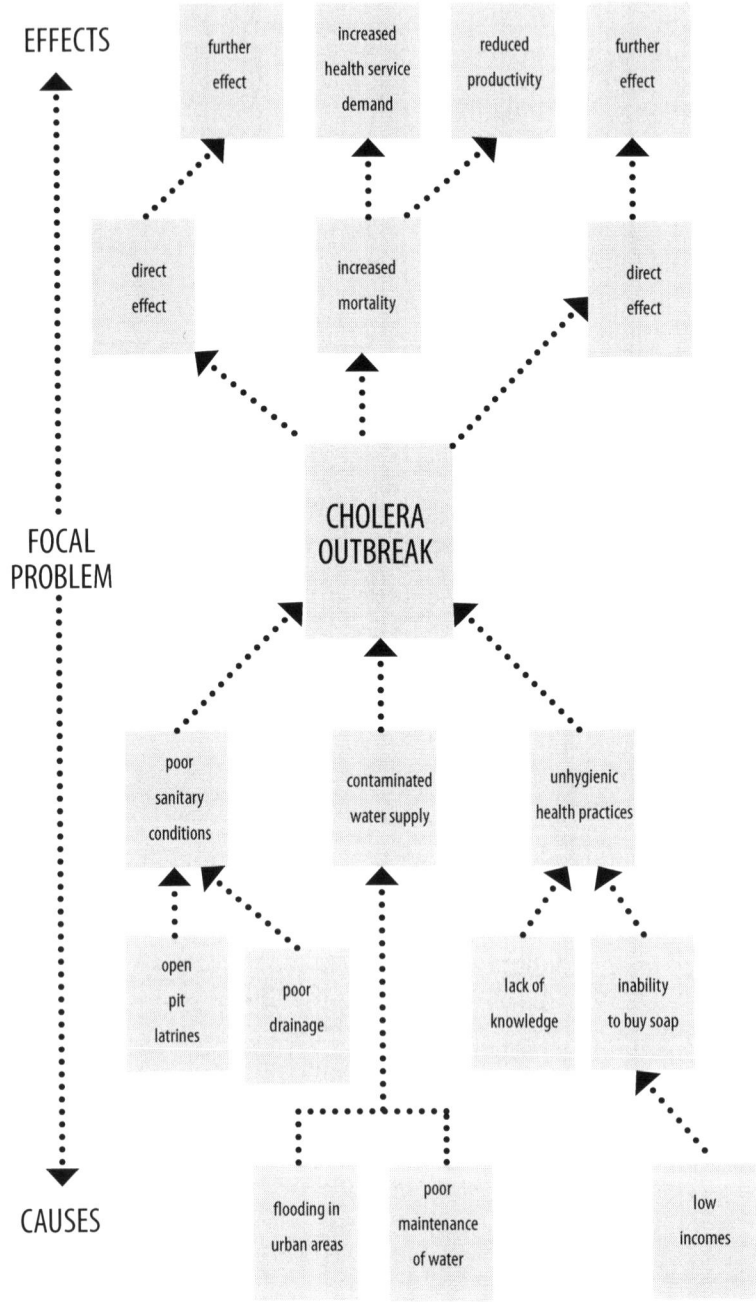

Source: Adapted from Water Supply and Sanitation Collaborative Council

problem tree

WHAT IS IT?

A problem tree is a tool for clarifying the problems being addressed by a design project.

The problem tree shows a structured hierarchy of problems being addressed with higher level problems branching into related groups of sub-problems.

WHY USE THIS METHOD?

1. A problem tree is a visual way of mapping your design problems so that you can discuss and refine them.
2. It is useful for identify a core problem and it's and root causes
3. It is a way to refine vague problems into more concrete and solvable goals.
4. The problem tree often helps build a shared sense of understanding, purpose and action.

CHALLENGES

1. Consider the likely stakeholders and constraints.
2. It may be difficult to understand all effects and causes of a problem early in a project.

WHEN TO USE THIS METHOD

1. Define intent

HOW TO USE THIS METHOD

1. Imagine a large tree with its trunk, branches, leaves, primary and secondary roots.
2. Write the main problem/concern in the center of a large flip chart (trunk).
3. Add the causes of the main problem onto the chart below the main problem, with arrows leading to the problem (primary roots).
4. For each of the causes, write the factors that lead to them, again using arrows to show how each one contributes (secondary roots).
5. Draw arrows leading upwards from the main problem to the various effects/consequences of that problem (branches).
6. For each of these effects, add any further effects/consequences (leaves).

Source: Adapted from Water Supply and Sanitation Collaborative Council

RESOURCES

1. Pen
2. Paper
3. White board

REFERENCES

1. Campbell, K.l.i.; Garforth, C.; Heffernan, C.; Morton, J.; Paterson, R.; Rymer, C. ; Upton, M. (2006): The Problem Tree. Analysis of the causes and effects of problems. The Problem Tree. Analysis of the causes and effects of problems.

73

OBJECTIVES TREE

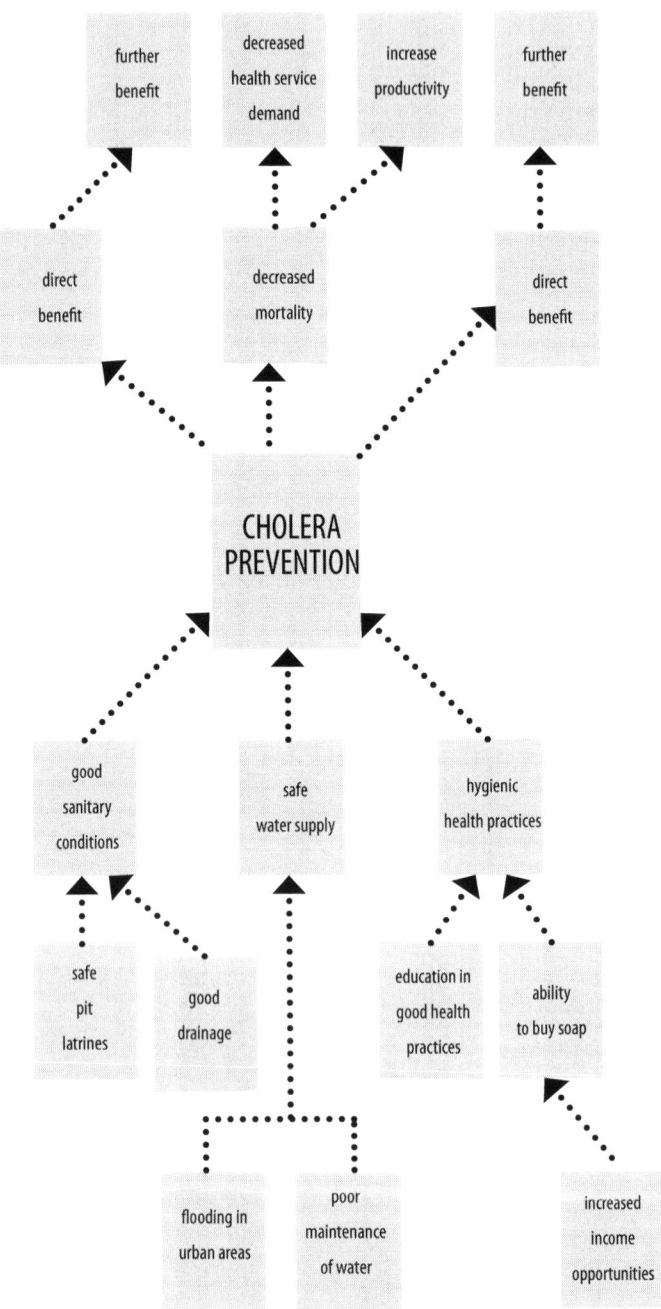

Source: Adapted from Water Supply and Sanitation Collaborative Council

objectives tree

WHAT IS IT?

Objective Tree method, also known as decision tree, is a tool for clarifying the goals of a project.

The objective tree method shows a structured hierarchy of goals with higher level goals branching into related groups of sub goals.

WHY USE THIS METHOD?

1. An objectives tree is a visual way of mapping your design objectives so that you can discuss and refine them.
2. Building a better understanding of the project objectives.
3. It is a way to refine vague goals into more concrete and achievable goals.
4. Build stakeholder consensus.
5. Identify potential constraints

CHALLENGES

1. Consider the likely stakeholders and constraints.
2. Be precise

SEE ALSO

1. Decision tree
2. Concept tree
3. Problem tree

WHEN TO USE THIS METHOD

1. Define intent

HOW TO USE THIS METHOD

1. Prepare a list of design objectives. This can be done by brainstorming within your team and by undertaking research of your customers, their needs and desires. You can create an objective tree from a problem tree. Convert each problem into an objective.
2. Create a written list of objectives.
3. Create lists of higher and lower level objectives by sorting your original list of objectives. This can be done with an affinity diagram.
4. Create an objectives tree, showing hierarchical relationships and interconnections
5. Place each task in a box.
6. Connect the boxes with lines show associations.
7. Iterate.
8. Make the task descriptions as simple as possible

RESOURCES

1. White board
2. Dry-erase markers.

REFERENCES

1. Campbell, K.l.i.; Garforth, C.; Heffernan, C.; Morton, J.; Paterson, R.; Rymer, C. ; Upton, M. (2006): The Problem Tree. Analysis of the causes and effects of problems. The Problem Tree. Analysis of the causes and effects of problems.

REFRAMING MATRIX

PRODUCT PERSPECTIVE

1. Is there something wrong with the product or service?
2. Is it priced correctly?
3. How well does it serve the market?
4. Is it reliable?

PLANNING PERSPECTIVE

1. Are our business plans, marketing plans, or strategy at fault?
2. Could we improve these?

POTENTIAL PERSPECTIVE

1. How would we increase sales?
2. If we were to seriously increase our targets or our production volumes, what would happen with this problem?

PEOPLE PERSPECTIVE

1. What are the people impacts and people implications of the problem?
2. What do people involved with the problem think?
3. Why are customers not using or buying the product?

DESIGN PROBLEM ....

....

reframing matrix

WHAT IS IT?

The reframing matrix is a method of approaching a problem by imagining the perspectives of a number of different people and exploring the possible solutions that they might suggest.

WHO INVENTED IT?

Michael Morgan 1993

WHY USE THIS METHOD?

1. This is a method for assisting in empathy which is an important factor in gaining acceptance and creating successful design.

CHALLENGES

1. The reframing is not done with stakeholders present or in context so may be subjective

RESOURCES

1. Pens
2. Paper
3. Post it notes
4. White board
5. Dry erase markers

WHEN TO USE THIS METHOD

1. Define intent

HOW TO USE THIS METHOD

1. Define a problem.
2. On a white board or paper draw a large square and divide it into four quadrants.
3. Select 4 different perspectives to approach the problem. They could be four professions or four people or four other perspectives that are important for your problem.
4. With your team brainstorm a number of questions that you believe are important from the perspectives that you have selected.
5. The moderator writes the questions in the relevant quadrants of the matrix.
6. The group discusses each of these questions.
7. The answers are recorded and the perspectives are incorporated into the considerations for design solutions.

REFERENCES

1. Morgan, M. Creating Workforce Innovation: Turning Individual Creativity into Organizational Innovation. Publisher: Business & Professional Pub (October 1993) ISBN-10: 1875680020 ISBN-13: 978-1875680023

PERCENTAGE OF CHINA'S GDP FROM SERVICES

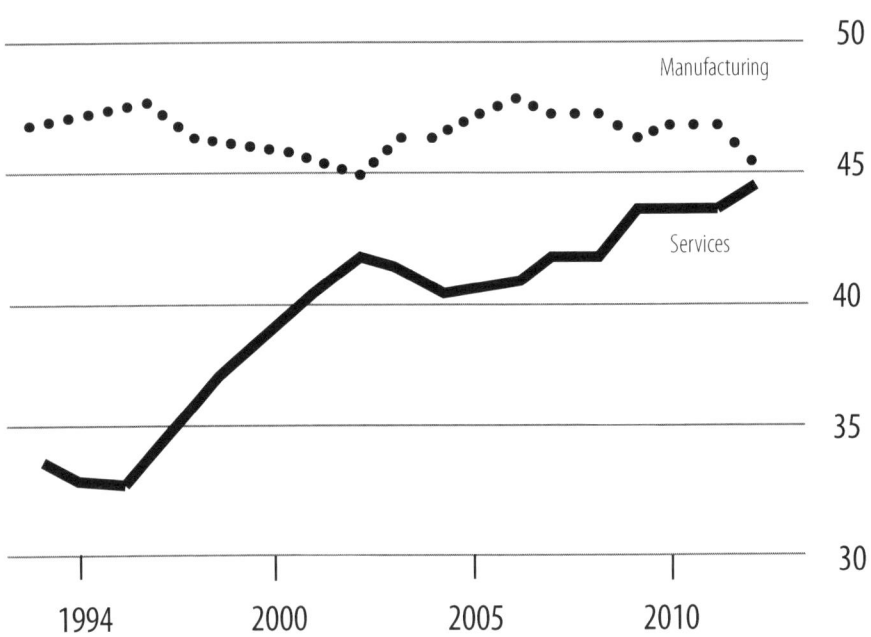

Source: Wind Info

Chapter 3
Service Design Methods
Frameworks

a(x4)

WHAT IS IT?

One of a number of ethnographic frameworks have been developed to give structure to observations and to ensure that the researcher doesn't miss important data.

1. Actors
2. Artifacts
3. Atmosphere
4. Actions

WHO INVENTED IT?

Paul Rothstein, Arizona State University 2001

WHY USE THIS METHOD?

1. To give structure to research
2. In order to collect most important information.
3. To provide some certainty in the uncertain environment of fieldwork

HOW TO USE THIS METHOD

Actors

Who are the people you are observing? Tell us through:

a. Photographs
b. Stories of them, their past
c. Simple data such as age, ethnicity,

Artifacts

Show us with photographs, and some annotation:

a. What kinds of objects do they choose to surround themselves with?
b. What objects are important to them? (why?)c. What do they use on a daily basis?

c. Are there objects that they are dependent on?
d. Take a close look objects that you might be designing or redesigning, and show us through annotated image(s) how that object works or does not work. What does it look like, what needs does it meet? Or not?

Atmosphere

Spending on your project, this becomes more or less important/detailed. You can choose from a variety of approaches:

a. A floor plan of the space if this is relevant.
b. The general environment that you will be designing for (e.g. photographs of their home/work/travel experience).

Actions

This is very detailed. Some firms, advocate doing as second-by-second analysis of all of the steps involved in the activity you will be designing for. Consider the following methods for presenting the information:

a. Video or selected frames from a video
b. Series of photographs (numbered & timed)c. Re-enactment
c. Written list of steps along with noted times

Source: Rothstein, P. (2001). a(x 4): A user-centered method for designing experience. 2001

REFERENCES

1. Rothstein, P. (2001). a(x 4): A user-centered method for designing experience. 2001

aeiou

WHAT IS IT?

One of a number of ethnographic frameworks have been developed to give structure to observations and to ensure that the researcher doesn't miss important data.

Activities: Goal directed sets of actions which people want to accomplish.
Environments: where activities take place
Objects: located in an environment. Their use, function, meaning and context.
Users: The people and their behaviors, preferences and needs.

Source Recording ethnographic observations: palojono

WHO INVENTED IT?

The Doblin Group Elab 1997

WHY USE THIS METHOD?

1. To give structure to research
2. In order to collect most important information.
3. To provide some certainty in the uncertain environment of fieldwork

WHEN TO USE THIS METHOD

1. Know Context
2. Know User
3. Frame insights

RESOURCES

1. Computer
2. Notebook
3. Pens
4. Video camera
5. Digital camera
6. Digital voice recorder
7. Release forms
8. Interview plan or structure
9. Questions, tasks and discussion items

bringing the outside in

WHAT IS IT?

One of a number of ethnographic frameworks have been developed to give structure to observations and to ensure that the researcher doesn't miss important data.

1. Territory
2. Stuff
3. People
4. Authority
5. Talk

WHO INVENTED IT?

Patty Sotirin 1999

WHY USE THIS METHOD?

1. To give structure to research
2. In order to collect most important information.
3. To provide some certainty in the uncertain environment of fieldwork

WHEN TO USE THIS METHOD

1. Know Context
2. Know User
3. Frame insights

REFERENCES

1. Sotirin, P. (1999). Bringing the Outside In: Ethnography in/beyond the Classroom, Presented at the 85th Annual Meeting of the National Communication Association Conference, Ethnography Division, Chicago, Illinois, November 4-7, 1999

Territory:
How are work areas decorated? How are non-work areas designated?
How do people protect their own space?
Architecture: How is space arranged? Who gets more or less?
Stuff:
Who has what? What are private and what are communal possessions?
Furniture: what kinds and how is it arranged?
Visual signs: describe any graphics: what. Where, who looks at it. Who put it !here?
Technology: Who is using what for what purposes? How are access and use controlled and by whom?
People:
What categories do you observe? What flows of people do you observe Press: What are the consistencies and variations'? What patterns do you observe? Bodies: How are different bodies accommodated? Or not? What nonverbal behaviours do you observe?
Authority:
Who has it? Who is subjected to it and when/why? What interactions indicate differences in authority? Challenges to authority (subtle or not)? Affection: how. where, and between whom is it expressed? How often and intensely.,
Talk:
What is said and what vocabularies are in use?
Vocabularies: what technical or colloquial words are distinct to this group? What words and names are used frequently?
Source: Soitrin, P. (1999). Bringing the outside in

nine dimensions

WHAT IS IT?

One of a number of ethnographic frameworks have been developed to give structure to observations and to ensure that the researcher doesn't miss important data.

Space: Layout of the physical setting, rooms outdoor spaces etc.
Actors: The names and details of the people involved
Activities: the various activities of the actors
Objects: Physical elements: furniture etc
Acts: Specific Individual actions
Events: Particular occasions Eg meetings
Time: The sequence of events
Goals: What actors are attempting to accomplish
Feelings: Emotions in particular contexts

Source Recording ethnographic observations: palojono

WHO INVENTED IT?

Spradley, J. P. 1980

WHY USE THIS METHOD?

1. To give structure to research
2. In order to collect most important information.
3. To provide some certainty in the uncertain environment of fieldwork

WHEN TO USE THIS METHOD

1. Know Context
2. Know User
3. Frame insights

RESOURCES

1. Computer
2. Notebook
3. Pens
4. Video camera
5. Digital camera
6. Digital voice recorder
7. Release forms
8. Interview plan or structure
9. Questions, tasks and discussion items

REFERENCES

1. Spradley, J. P. (1980). Participant Observation. New York: Holt, Rinehart & Winston.

poems

WHAT IS IT?

One of a number of ethnographic frameworks have been developed to give structure to observations and to ensure that the researcher doesn't miss important data. the poems framework tags data in order to organize user observations.

1. People
2. Objects
3. Environments
4. Messages
5. Services

WHO INVENTED IT?

Kumar and Whitney 2003

WHY USE THIS METHOD?

1. To give structure to research
2. In order to collect most important information
3. The POEMS framework is able to be nonlinear in time and can cross domains for larger projects.
4. To provide some certainty in the uncertain environment of fieldwork

WHEN TO USE THIS METHOD

1. Know Context
2. Know User
3. Frame insights

RESOURCES

1. Computer
2. Notebook
3. Pens
4. Video camera
5. Digital camera
6. Digital voice recorder
7. Release forms
8. Interview plan or structure
9. Questions, tasks and discussion items

REFERENCES

1. Kumar, V. & Whitney, P. (2003). Faster, Cheaper, Deeper User Research. Design Management Journal, Spring 2003, 50-57. Design Management Institute.

posta

WHAT IS IT?

One of a number of ethnographic frameworks have been developed to give structure to observations and to ensure that the researcher doesn't miss important data.

1. People
2. Objects
3. Environments
4. Messages
5. Services

WHO INVENTED IT?

May have been invented by Pat Sachs Social Solutions and Gitte Jordan Institute for Research on Learning

WHY USE THIS METHOD?

1. To give structure to research
2. In order to collect most important information
3. To provide some certainty in the uncertain environment of fieldwork

WHEN TO USE THIS METHOD

1. Know Context
2. Know User
3. Frame insights

HOW TO USE THIS METHOD

Observe participant in the work setting around, observing what they do and how they interact with other people and tools in their environment. Or they may focus on key objects or artifacts in the environment, with special attention to the various roles that they play (functional, psychological and social). During another observation, the team may take notes and photo-graphs of the work setting and try to understand how the configuration of space mediates the work. Finally, they chart activities, including both formal workflow and informal work practices.

RESOURCES

1. Computer
2. Notebook
3. Pens
4. Video camera
5. Digital camera
6. Digital voice recorder
7. Release forms
8. Interview plan or structure
9. Questions, tasks and discussion items

latch

WHAT IS IT?

One of a number of ethnographic frame-works have been developed to give structure to observations and to ensure that the researcher doesn't miss important data.

1. Location
Compare information sources.
2. Alphabet
Used for very large volume of data.
3. Time
Used for events that occur over a measurable duration of time.
4. Category
Grouped by similarity of characteristics.
5. Hierarchy
Information is organized on a scale

WHO INVENTED IT?

Richard Saul Wurman, 1996

WHY USE THIS METHOD?

6. To give structure to research
7. In order to collect most important information.
8. To provide some certainty in the uncertain environment of fieldwork

WHEN TO USE THIS METHOD

1. Know Context
2. Know User
3. Frame insights

RESOURCES

1. Notebook
2. Pens
3. Video camera
4. Digital camera
5. Digital voice recorder
6. Release forms

SHARE OF SERVICES IN GDP

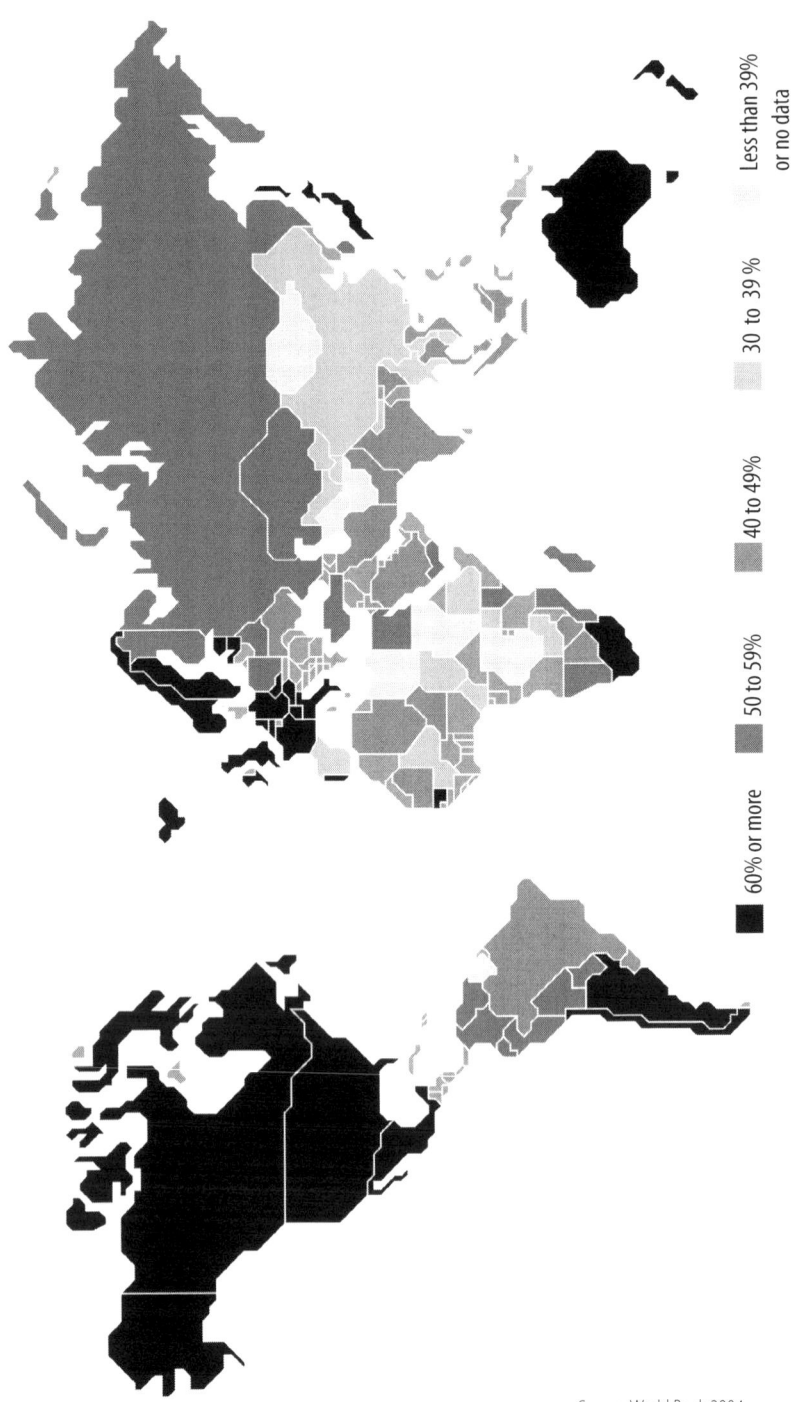

Source: World Bank 2004

Chapter 4
Service Design Methods
Know people and context

active listening

WHAT IS IT?

Active listening is a communication method where the listener repeats what they understand to the speaker.

WHO INVENTED IT?

Thomas Gordon coined the term
Carl Rogers 1980

WHY USE THIS METHOD?

1. The ability to listen is an important skill for a designer to demonstrate empathy.

CHALLENGES

1. Listening and hearing or understanding are not the same
2. People give meaning to what they hear.
3. Listening constructs meaning from verbal and non verbal observations.

WHEN TO USE THIS METHOD

1. Know Context
2. Know User

HOW TO USE THIS METHOD

1. The listener observes the speakers body language.
2. This helps the listener understand the speaker's message
3. The listener paraphrases the speakers words to demonstrate understanding of the message.
4. The listener summarizes the issues.

Active listening skills include

1. Posture showing engagement
2. Eye contact
3. Environment that does not distract
4. Appropriate gestures and facial expressions.

REFERENCES

1. Reed, Warren H. (1985). Positive listening: learning to hear what people are really saying. New York: F. Watts. ISBN 0-531-09583-5
2. Atwater, Eastwood (1981). I Hear You. Prentice-Hall. p. 83. ISBN 0-13-450684-7.
3. Novack DH, Dube C, Goldstein MG. Teaching medical interviewing. A basic course on interviewing and the physician-patient relationship. Arch Intern Med 1992;152:1814–2.

activity analysis

WHAT IS IT?

Activity analysis is a method involving observing people in the context of their work.

WHO INVENTED IT?

Thomas Moran

WHY USE THIS METHOD?

1. Observation can reveal ways to make work more effective, efficient and valuable.

CHALLENGES

1. Medium level of cost and time required
2. Analysis may be difficult

WHEN TO USE THIS METHOD

1. Know Context
2. Know User
3. Frame insights

HOW TO USE THIS METHOD

1. Observe work in context
2. Undertake contextual interviews of workers
3. Analyze data
4. Create insights
5. Create Recommendations

RESOURCES

1. Note pad
2. Pens
3. Camera
4. Video camera
5. Digital voice recorder
6. Post-it notes

REFERENCES

1. Garrigou, A., Daniellous, F., Carballeda, G., Ruaud, S. Activity analysis in participatory design and analysis of participatory design activity.1995.

ACTORS MAP

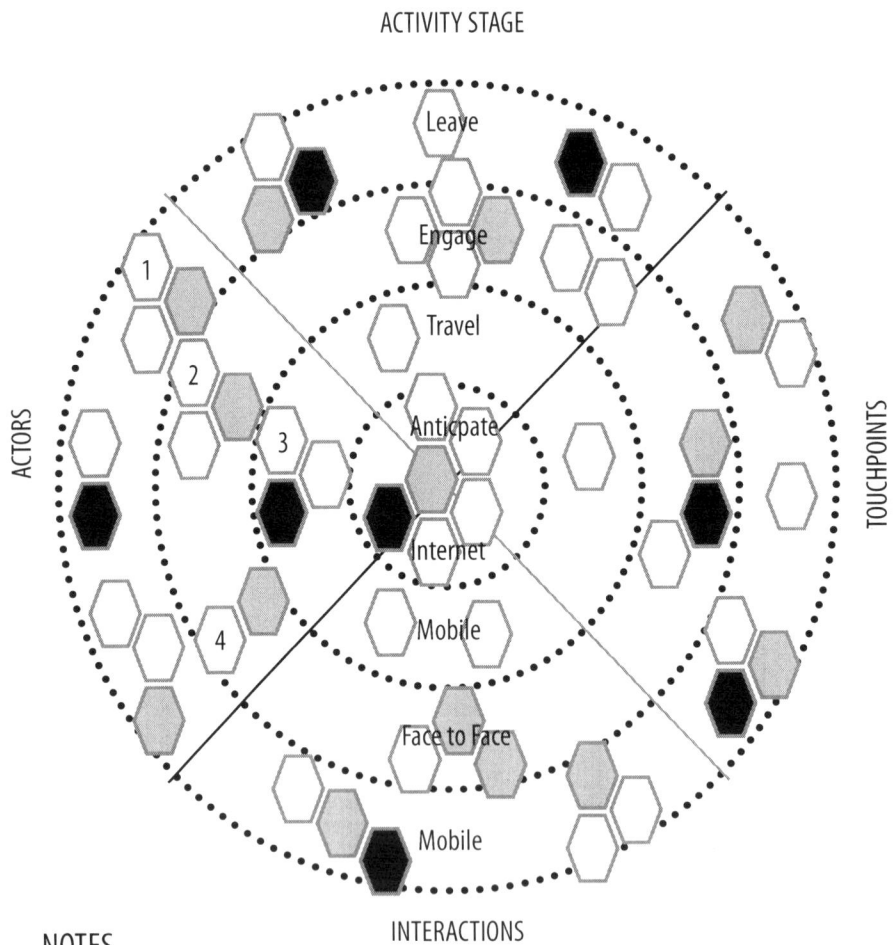

ACTIVITY STAGE

Leave

Engage

Travel

Anticpate

Internet

Mobile

Face to Face

Mobile

ACTORS

TOUCHPOINTS

INTERACTIONS

NOTES

1. **Activity Stage.** This is the timeline of stages in the activity that you are presenting

2. **Actors.** Each icon represents a person or stakeholder or group or organization involved in the activity at that particular stage

3. **Interactions.** This is the type of interaction such as face to face, mobile or online.

4. **Touchpoints.** Customer interaction channels such as call centers, web sites, automated teller machines and web kiosks.

actors map

WHAT IS IT?

The Actors Map represents the system of stakeholders and their relationships. It is a view of the service and its context. Stakeholders are organized by their function.

WHY USE THIS METHOD?

1. Understanding relationships is an important aspect of service design.

CHALLENGES

1. This is not a user centered method

WHY USE THIS METHOD?

1. Inexpensive and fast.
2. Connects to existing research tools and methods
3. Makes implicit knowledge explicit
4. Structures complex reality
5. Flexible for use in different contexts.

WHEN TO USE THIS METHOD

1. Know Context
2. Know User
3. Frame insights

SEE ALSO

1. Network map.

REFERENCES

1. (2007) Nicola Morelli, New representation techniques for designing in a systemic perspective, paper presented at Design Inquires, Stockholm.

93

AFFINITY DIAGRAM

Put individual answers or ideas on post-it-notes Spread post-it-notes or cards on a wall or large table.

Group similar items and name each group with a different colored card or Post-it-note above the group.

affinity diagram

WHAT IS IT?

Affinity diagrams are a tool for analyzing large amounts of data and discovering relationships which allow a design direction to be established based on the affinities. This method may uncover important hidden relationships.

Affinity diagrams are created through consensus of the design team on how the information should be grouped in logical ways.

WHO INVENTED IT?

Jiro Kawaita, Japan, 1960

WHY USE THIS METHOD?

Traditional design methods are less useful when dealing with complex or chaotic problems with large amounts of data. This method helps to establish relationships of affinities between pieces of information. From these relationships insights and relationships can be determined which are the starting point of design solutions. It is possible using this method to reach consensus faster than many other methods.

RESOURCES

1. White board
2. Large wall spaces or tables
3. Dry-erase markers
4. Sharpies
5. Post-it notes
6. Digital camera

WHEN TO USE THIS METHOD

1. Know Context
2. Know User
3. Frame insights

HOW TO USE THIS METHOD

1. Select your team
2. Place individual opinions or answers to interview questions or design concepts on post-it-notes or cards.
3. Spread post-it-notes or cards on a wall or large table.
4. Group similar items.
5. This can be done silently by your design team moving them around as they each see affinities. Work until your team has consensus.
6. Name each group with a different colored card or Post-it-note above the group.
7. Repeat by grouping groups.
8. Rank the most important groups.
9. Photograph results
10. Analyze affinities and create insights.
11. 5 to 20 participants

REFERENCES

1. Brassard, M. (1989). The Memory Jogger Plus +, pp. 17 - 39. Methuen, MA:
   Goal/QPC.
2. King, R. (1989). Hoshin Planning, The Developmental Approach, pp. 4-2 - 4-5. Methuen, MA: Goal/QPC.

ACTIVITY PHASE	ACTIVITY PHASE	ACTIVITY PHASE	ACTIVITY PHASE	ACTIVITY PHASE	ACTIVITY PHASE

CUSTOMER ACTIONS

What does user do?

TOUCHPOINTS

moments places customer contact

LINE OF INTERACTION

DIRECT CONTACT

What your Staff do

LINE OF VISIBILITY

BACK OFFICE

What your Staff do

EMOTIONAL EXPERIENCE

service blueprint

WHAT IS IT?

A blueprint is a process map often used to describe the delivery of services information is presented as a number of parallel rows of activities. These are sometimes called swim lanes. They may document activities over time such as:

1. Customer Actions
2. Touch points
3. Direct Contact visible to customers
4. Invisible back office actions
5. Support Processes
6. Physical Evidence
7. Emotional Experience for customer.

WHO INVENTED IT?

Lynn Shostack 1983

WHEN TO USE THIS METHOD

1. Know Context
2. Know User
3. Frame insights

WHY TO USE THIS METHOD

1. Can be used for design or improvement of existing services or experiences.
2. Is more tangible than intuition.
3. Makes the process of service development more efficient.
4. A common point of reference for stakeholders for planning and discussion.
5. Tool to assess the impact of change.

HOW TO USE THIS METHOD

1. Define the service or experience to focus on.
2. A blueprint can be created in a brainstorming session with stakeholders.
3. Define the customer demographic.
4. See though the customer's eyes.
5. Define the activities and phases of activity under each heading.
6. Link the contact or customer touchpoints to the needed support functions
7. Use post-it-notes on a white board for initial descriptions and rearrange as necessary drawing lines to show the links.
8. Create the blueprint then refine iteratively.

RESOURCES

1. Paper
2. Pens
3. White board
4. Dry-erase markers
5. Camera
6. Blueprint templates
7. Post-it-notes

REFERENCES

1. (1991) G. Hollins, W. Hollins, Total Design: Managing the design process in the service sector, Trans Atlantic Publications

97

bodystorming

WHAT IS IT?

Bodystorming is method of prototyping experiences. It requires setting up an experience - complete with necessary artifacts and people - and physically "testing" it. A design team play out scenarios based on design concepts that they are developing. The method provides clues about the impact of the context on the user experience.

WHO INVENTED IT?

Buchenau, Fulton 2000

WHY USE THIS METHOD?

1. You are likely to find new possibilities and problems.
2. Generates empathy for users.
3. This method is an experiential design tool. Bodystorming helps design ideation by exploring context.
4. It is fast and inexpensive.
5. It is a form of physical prototyping
6. It is difficult to imagine misuse scenarios

CHALLENGES

1. Some team members may find acting a difficult task.

RESOURCES

1. Empathy tools
2. A large room
3. White board
4. Video camera

WHEN TO USE THIS METHOD

1. Know Context
2. Know User
3. Frame insights
4. Explore Concepts

HOW TO USE THIS METHOD

1. Select team.
2. Define the locations where a design will be used.
3. Go to those locations and observe how people interact. the artifacts in their environment.
4. Develop the prototypes and props that you need to explore an idea. Identify the people, personas and scenarios that may help you with insight into the design directions.,
5. Bodystorm the scenarios.
6. Record the scenarios with video and analyze them for insights.

REFERENCES

Understanding contexts by being there: case studies in bodystorming. Personal and Ubiquitous Computing, Vol. 7, No. 2. (July 2003), pp. 125-134, doi:10.1007/s00779-003-0238-7 by Antti Oulasvirta, Esko Kurvinen, Tomi Kankainen

dramaturgy

WHAT IS IT?

Dramaturgy is a method that uses drama techniques to help understand user behaviors and needs. It a form of prototyping.

WHO INVENTED IT?

Robert, Benford D., and Scott A. Hunt

WHY USE THIS METHOD?

1. Created to make personas more dynamic.

CHALLENGES

1. Some team members may be uncomfortable with drama based activity.
2. The method is not in context
3. The method may be subjective as it does not involve the people being designed for,

WHEN TO USE THIS METHOD

4. Know Context
5. Know User
6. Frame insights
7. Explore Concepts

HOW TO USE THIS METHOD

1. Choose a character
2. Create groups of 2 or 3 members of your design team
3. Ask your teams to write monologues for the characters based on public, private and intimate levels.
4. Ask your team to discuss the rituals of the character's lives
5. Ask your team to create maps of the stakeholders
6. Create scenes exploring crucial moments in your character's experiences or interactions.
7. Present these scenarios with groups of actors.
8. Explore the problems and challenges of the character's experiences and interactions.

REFERENCES

1. Robert, Benford D., and Scott A. Hunt. "Dramaturgy and Social Movements: The Social Construction and Communication of Power." Social Inquiry 62.1 (2007): 36-55. Wiley Online Library.

99

empathy

WHAT IS IT?

Empathy is sometimes defined as 'standing in someone else's shoes' or 'seeing through someone else's eyes'. It is The ability to identify and understand another's situation, feelings and motives. In design it may be defined as: identifying with others and, adopting their perspective. Empathy is different to sympathy. Empathy does not necessarily imply compassion. Empathy is a respectful understanding of what others are experiencing and their point of view.

WHO INVENTED IT?

E.B. Titchener invented the word in 1909 in an attempt to translate the German word "Einfühlungsvermögen".

WHY USE THIS METHOD?

1. Empathy is a core skill for designers to design successfully for other people.
2. Empathy is needed for business success.
3. Empathy is needed for products and services to be adopted by the people we design for.
4. Empathy builds trust.

CHALLENGES

1. Increasing use of teams
2. Rapid pace of globalization
3. Global need to retain talent

WHEN TO USE THIS METHOD

1. Define intent
2. Know Context
3. Know User
4. Frame insights
5. Explore Concepts
6. Make Plans
7. Deliver Offering

HOW TO USE THIS METHOD

1. Put yourself in contact and the context of people who you are designing for.
2. Ask questions and listen to the answers.
3. Read between the lines
4. Observe.
5. Listen
6. Ask questions.
7. Restating what you think you heard.
8. Recognize that people are individuals.
9. Notice body language. Most communication is non verbal
10. Withhold judgement when you hear views different to your own.
11. Take a personal interest in people

REFERENCES

1. Miyashiro, Marie R. (2011). The Empathy Factor: Your Competitive Advantage for Personal, Team, and Business Success. Puddledancer Press. p. 256. ISBN 1-892005-25-5.ment and Psychopathology 20: 1053–1080.

case studies: clinical

WHAT IS IT?

A clinical case study is type of case study which focuses on an individual person in depth. It often involves detailed interviews and observation.

WHO INVENTED IT?

Frederic Le Play is credited with creating the first case study in 1829

WHY USE THIS METHOD?

1. It is possible to uncover in-depth information.
2. It is flexible.
3. It can be undertaken in many different contexts.
4. It may be inexpensive.

CHALLENGES

1. You cannot generalize on the basis of an individual case
2. It is difficult to develop general theories on the basis of specific cases.
3. The case study has a bias toward confirming the researcher's preconceived notions.
4. Subjectivity
5. Time consuming

REFERENCES

1. Robert E. Stake, The Art of Case Study Research (Thousand Oaks: Sage, 1995). ISBN 0-8039-5767-X

WHEN TO USE THIS METHOD

1. Know Context
2. Know User
3. Frame insights

HOW TO USE THIS METHOD

1. Select the best type of case study for your audience.
2. Review similar case studies
3. Select your participants.
4. Determine whether you will study an individual or a group.
5. Draft a list of questions.
6. Arrange interviews
7. Obtain consent
8. Conduct interviews
9. Analyze the data
10. Create insights
11. Create recommendations.

RESOURCES

1. Note pad
2. Pens
3. Camera
4. Video camera
5. Digital audio recorder
6. Post-it notes

case studies: historical

WHAT IS IT?

Historical case studies follow the development of an individual, an institution, a system, a community, an organization, an event, or a culture over time.

WHO INVENTED IT?

Frederic Le Play is credited with creating the first case study in 1829

WHY USE THIS METHOD?

1. It is possible to uncover in-depth information.
2. It is flexible.
3. It can be undertaken in many different contexts.
4. It may be inexpensive.

CHALLENGES

1. You cannot generalize on the basis of an individual case
2. It is difficult to develop general theories on the basis of specific cases.
3. The case study has a bias toward confirming the researcher's preconceived notions.
4. Subjectivity
5. Time consuming

REFERENCES

1. Robert E. Stake, The Art of Case Study Research (Thousand Oaks: Sage, 1995). ISBN 0-8039-5767-X

WHEN TO USE THIS METHOD

1. Know Context
2. Know User
3. Frame insights

HOW TO USE THIS METHOD

1. Select the best type of case study for your audience.
2. Review similar case studies
3. Select your participants.
4. Determine whether you will study an individual or a group.
5. Draft a list of questions.
6. Arrange interviews
7. Obtain consent
8. Conduct interviews
9. Analyze the data
10. Create insights
11. Create recommendations.

RESOURCES

1. Note pad
2. Pens
3. Camera
4. Video camera
5. Digital audio recorder
6. Post-it notes

case studies: multi case

WHAT IS IT?

A multi-case study is a collection of case studies of an individual, an institution, a system, a community, an organization, an event, or a culture.

WHO INVENTED IT?

Frederic Le Play is credited with creating the first case study in 1829

WHY USE THIS METHOD?

1. It is possible to uncover in-depth information.
2. It is flexible.
3. It can be undertaken in many different contexts.
4. It may be inexpensive.

CHALLENGES

1. You cannot generalize on the basis of an individual case
2. It is difficult to develop general theories on the basis of specific cases.
3. The case study has a bias toward confirming the researcher's preconceived notions.
4. Subjectivity
5. Time consuming

WHEN TO USE THIS METHOD

1. Know Context
2. Know User
3. Frame insights

HOW TO USE THIS METHOD

1. Select the best type of case study for your audience.
2. Review similar case studies
3. Select your participants.
4. Determine whether you will study an individual or a group.
5. Draft a list of questions.
6. Arrange interviews
7. Obtain consent
8. Conduct interviews
9. Analyze the data
10. Create insights
11. Create recommendations.

RESOURCES

1. Note pad
2. Pens
3. Camera
4. Video camera
5. Digital audio recorder
6. Post-it notes

REFERENCES

1. Robert E. Stake, The Art of Case Study Research (Thousand Oaks: Sage, 1995). ISBN 0-8039-5767-X
2. "Case Study," in Norman K. Denzin and Yvonna S. Lincoln, eds., The Sage Handbook of Qualitative Research, 4th Edition (Thousand Oaks, CA: Sage),

case studies: observational

WHAT IS IT?

Observational case studies focus on observing an individual, an institution, a system, a community, an organization, an event, or a culture.

WHO INVENTED IT?

Frederic Le Play is credited with creating the first case study in 1829

WHY USE THIS METHOD?

1. It is possible to uncover in-depth information.
2. It is flexible.
3. It can be undertaken in many different contexts.
4. It may be inexpensive.

CHALLENGES

1. You cannot generalize on the basis of an individual case
2. It is difficult to develop general theories on the basis of specific cases.
3. The case study has a bias toward confirming the researcher's preconceived notions.
4. Subjectivity
5. Time consuming

WHEN TO USE THIS METHOD

1. Know Context
2. Know User
3. Frame insights

HOW TO USE THIS METHOD

1. Select the best type of case study for your audience.
2. Review similar case studies
3. Select your participants.
4. Determine whether you will study an individual or a group.
5. Obtain consent
6. Conduct observations
7. Analyze the data
8. Create insights
9. Create recommendations.

RESOURCES

1. Note pad
2. Pens
3. Camera
4. Video camera
5. Digital audio recorder
6. Post-it notes

REFERENCES

1. Robert E. Stake, The Art of Case Study Research (Thousand Oaks: Sage, 1995). ISBN 0-8039-5767-X
2. "Case Study," in Norman K. Denzin and Yvonna S. Lincoln, eds., The Sage Handbook of Qualitative Research, 4th Edition (Thousand Oaks, CA: Sage),

case studies:
oral history

WHAT IS IT?

Oral case studies are case studies narrated by one person speaking for and about themselves.

This allows communication of their point of view. The narrator may or may not be aware of the full context of their experiences.

WHO INVENTED IT?

Frederic Le Play is credited with creating the first case study in 1829

WHY USE THIS METHOD?

1. It is possible to uncover in-depth information.
2. It is flexible.
3. It can be undertaken in many different contexts.
4. It may be inexpensive.

CHALLENGES

1. You cannot generalize on the basis of an individual case
2. It is difficult to develop general theories on the basis of specific cases.
3. The case study has a bias toward confirming the researcher's preconceived notions.
4. Subjectivity
5. Time consuming

WHEN TO USE THIS METHOD

1. Know Context
2. Know User
3. Frame insights

HOW TO USE THIS METHOD

1. Select the best type of case study for your audience.
2. Review similar case studies
3. Select your participants.
4. Determine whether you will study an individual or a group.
5. Draft a list of questions.
6. Arrange interviews
7. Conduct interviews
8. Analyze the data
9. Create insights
10. Create recommendations.

RESOURCES

1. Note pad
2. Pens
3. Camera
4. Video camera
5. Digital audio recorder
6. Post-it notes

REFERENCES

1. Robert E. Stake, The Art of Case Study Research (Thousand Oaks: Sage, 1995). ISBN 0-8039-5767-X
2. "Case Study," in Norman K. Denzin and Yvonna S. Lincoln, eds., The Sage Handbook of Qualitative Research, 4th Edition (Thousand Oaks, CA: Sage),

case studies: situational

WHAT IS IT?
This form studies particular events. The view of all participants in the event are sought

WHO INVENTED IT?
Frederic Le Play is credited with creating the first case study in 1829

WHY USE THIS METHOD?
1. It is possible to uncover in-depth information.
2. It is flexible.
3. It can be undertaken in many different contexts.
4. It may be inexpensive.

CHALLENGES
1. You cannot generalize on the basis of an individual case
2. It is difficult to develop general theories on the basis of specific cases.
3. The case study has a bias toward confirming the researcher's preconceived notions.
4. Subjectivity
5. Time consuming

REFERENCES
1. Robert E. Stake, The Art of Case Study Research (Thousand Oaks: Sage, 1995). ISBN 0-8039-5767-X
2. "Case Study," in Norman K. Denzin and Yvonna S. Lincoln, eds., The Sage Handbook of Qualitative Research, 4th Edition (Thousand Oaks, CA: Sage),

WHEN TO USE THIS METHOD
1. Know Context
2. Know User
3. Frame insights

HOW TO USE THIS METHOD
1. Select the best type of case study for your audience.
2. Review similar case studies
3. Select your participants.
4. Determine whether you will study an individual or a group.
5. Draft a list of questions.
6. Arrange interviews
7. Obtain consent
8. Conduct interviews
9. Analyze the data
10. Create insights
11. Create recommendations.

RESOURCES
1. Note pad
2. Pens
3. Camera
4. Video camera
5. Digital audio recorder
6. Post-it notes

open card sort

WHAT IS IT?

This is a method for discovering the relationships of a list of items. Participants asked to arrange individual, unsorted items into groups. For an open card sort the user defines the groups rather than the researcher.

Card sorting is applied when:
1. When there is a large number of items.
2. The items are similar and difficult to organize into categories.
3. Users may have different perceptions related to organizing the items.

WHO INVENTED IT?

Jastrow 1886

Nielsen & Sano 1995

WHY USE THIS METHOD?
1. It is a simple method using index cards,
2. Used to provide insights for interface design.

CHALLENGES
1. Ask participants to fill ot a second card if they feel it belongs in two groups.
2. There are a number of online card sorting tools available.

RESOURCES
1. Post cards
2. Pens
3. Post-it-notes
4. Laptop computer
5. A table

WHEN TO USE THIS METHOD
1. Know Context
2. Know User
3. Frame insights
4. Explore Concepts

HOW TO USE THIS METHOD
1. Recruit between 5 and 15 participants representative of your user group.
2. Provide a small deck of cards.
3. Provide clear instructions. Ask your participants to arrange the cards in ways that make sense to them. 100 cards takes about 1 hour to sort.
4. The user sorts labelled cards into groups by that they define themselves.
5. The user can generate more card labels.
6. If users do not understand a card ask them to exclude it. Ask participants for their rationale for any dual placements of cards.
7. Analyze the piles of cards and create a list of insights derived from the card sort.
8. Analyze the data. Proximity or similarity matrixes, dendrograms, and tree diagrams help create a taxonomical hierarchy for the items being grouped

REFERENCES
1. Jakob Nielsen (May 1995). "Card Sorting to Discover the Users' Model of the Information Space".
2. Jakob Nielsen (July 19, 2004). "Card Sorting: How Many Users to Test"

107

closed card sort

WHAT IS IT?

This is a method for understanding the relationships of a number of pieces of data. Participants asked to arrange individual, unsorted items into groups. A closed sort involves the cards being sorted into groups where the group headings may be defined by the researcher. There are a number of tools available to perform card sorting activities with survey participants via the internet.

Card sorting is applied when:
1. When there is a large number pieces of data.
2. The individual pieces of data are similar.
3. Participants have different perceptions of the data.

WHO INVENTED IT?

Jastrow 1886

Nielsen & Sano 1995

WHY USE THIS METHOD?

1. It is a simple method using index cards,
2. Used to provide insights for interface design.

CHALLENGES

1. Ask participants to fill out a second card if they feel it belongs in two groups.

REFERENCES

1. Jakob Nielsen (May 1995). "Card Sorting to Discover the Users' Model of the Information Space".
2. Jakob Nielsen (July 19, 2004). "Card Sorting: How Many Users to Test".

WHEN TO USE THIS METHOD

1. Know Context
2. Know User
3. Frame insights
4. Explore Concepts

HOW TO USE THIS METHOD

1. Recruit 15 to 20 participants representative of your user group.
2. Provide a deck of cards using words and or images relevant to your concept.
3. Provide clear instructions. Ask your participants to arrange the cards in ways that make sense to them. 100 cards takes about 1 hour to sort.
4. The user sorts labelled cards into groups by under header cards defined by the researcher.
5. The user can generate more card labels.
6. If users do not understand a card ask them to exclude it. Ask participants for their rationale for any dual placements of cards.
7. Discuss why the cards are placed in a particular pile yields insight into user perceptions.
8. Analyze the data. Create a hierarchy for the information
9. Use post cards or post-it notes.

RESOURCES

1. Post cards
2. Pens
3. Post-it-notes
4. Laptop computer
5. A table

cognitive task analysis

WHAT IS IT?

The purpose of a cognitive task analysis is to define the decision requirements and psychological processes used by expert individuals. Task analysis makes it possible to design and develop strategy for tasks related to a system or service being designed.

Factors analyzed could include:
1. Task duration and variability
2. Task frequency
3. Task sequence
4. Task allocation
5. Task complexity
6. Environmental conditions
7. Data and information dependencies
8. Tools needed for the activity
9. User knowledge and skills.

WHO INVENTED IT?

IBM circa 1985

WHY USE THIS METHOD?
1. Generates detailed data
2. Analyze the participant's perceptions and motivations related to tasks.

CHALLENGES
1. Can be time intensive and costly.

WHEN TO USE THIS METHOD
1. Define intent
2. Know Context
3. Know User
4. Frame insights
5. Explore Concepts

HOW TO USE THIS METHOD
1. Develop some general understanding of the domain area in which the cognitive task analysis will be conducted,
2. Identify experts
3. Identify the activity's knowledge structures with observations and interviews
4. Develop a strategy for each of the tasks.
5. Analyze and verify data

RESOURCES
1. Computers
2. Workstations
3. Video Cameras
4. White board
5. Notebook
6. Pens

REFERENCES
1. Crandall, B., Klein, G., and Hoffman, R. (2006). Working minds: A practitioner's guide to cognitive task analysis. MIT Press.

collage

WHAT IS IT?

A collage involves gluing images or words onto paper. Research participants are given a large and diverse supply of images and words. The images and words chosen should be abstract so as not to influence the participants too much but may include images of objects and people and interactions. The moderator provides the participants with guidelines for the activity. They are a useful medium for communicating emotions and ideas and starting a conversation.

WHO INVENTED IT?

Invented in China, around 200 BC
Pablo Picasso and Georges Braque 1912
The word cllages comes from the French word "coller" which means to glue.

WHY USE THIS METHOD?

1. The creation of a collage is a process that is both creative and analytical.
2. Collages can provide clues to the researcher about the participants lifestyle, aesthetic likes and dislikes.
3. A collage can give direction in selecting colors for a manufactured product
4. Collages are very suitable to present a particular atmosphere or context that you want to capture in the form of the new product ideas and concepts.

WHEN TO USE THIS METHOD

1. Know Context
2. Know User
3. Frame insights
4. Explore Concepts

HOW TO USE THIS METHOD

1. Define the theme.
2. Define the scope of the study such as number of words or images.
3. Print words and images onto sticker sheets.
4. Distribute scissors.
5. Group creates collages.
6. Subjects tell own stories through the collages.
7. Collect the stories.
8. Analyze the stories.

RESOURCES

1. Scissors
2. Magazines or preprinted stickers
3. Paper
4. Glue

REFERENCES

1. Brandon Taylor. Urban walls : a generation of collage in Europe & America : Burhan Dogançay with François Dufrêne, Raymond Hains, Robert Rauschenberg, Mimmo Rotella, Jacques Villeglé, Wolf Vostell ISBN 978-1-55595-288-4; ISBN 1-55595-288-7New York : Hudson Hills Press ; [Lanham, MD] : Distributed in the United States by National Book Network, 2008

111

COMMUNICATIONS MAP

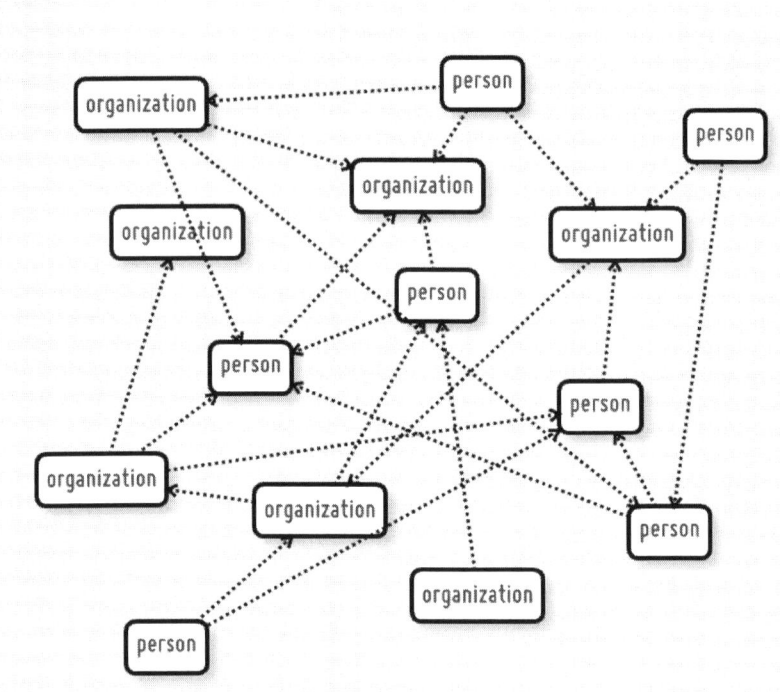

It is possible to show existing and planned relationships on your communications map

communications map

WHAT IS IT?

A communications map is a tool to study and create strategy for communications. It may be used in a project to understand where there are gaps which could affect the project outcomes. The project communication map processes documents the critical links among people and information that are necessary for successful project outcomes.

WHY USE THIS METHOD?

1. It may show where there are gaps in communications which need to be addressed.
2. Assists the project team to provide timely and accurate information to all stakeholders.

WHEN TO USE THIS METHOD

1. Know Context
2. Know User
3. Frame insights

RESOURCES

1. Pens
2. Paper
3. White board
4. Dry-erase markers

HOW TO USE THIS METHOD

1. Identify stakeholders.
2. Identify those with whom
3. Your organization needs the strongest communications linkages.
4. Identify Internal audiences.
5. Identify Peer groups or sub groups.
6. Identify Strong and frequent communications
7. Connectivity needed to a primary audience.
8. Identify less frequent communications connectivity needed to a secondary audience.
9. Determine stakeholder needs.
10. Identify communication methods and resources.
11. Prepare communication map showing existing and desired communications.
12. Distribute to stakeholders for feedback.
13. Incorporate Changes
14. Implement.

CONJOINT ANALYSIS

Please rate how you like these types of cheese

	I really dislike it	I do not like it	Neutral	I like it	I like it a lot
Cheddar	☐	☐	☐	☐	☐
Stilton	☐	☐	☐	☐	☐
Danish Blue	☐	☐	☐	☐	☐
Gorgonzola	☐	☐	☐	☐	☐

conjoint analysis

WHAT IS IT?

Conjoint analysis is a method to gain insight into how people value features or components of a product, service or experience. It can be used to decide features a new product should have and how a new product should be priced.

WHO INVENTED IT?

Paul Green University of Pennsylvania.
V. "Seenu" Srinivasan Stanford University

WHY USE THIS METHOD?

1. Uncovers perceptions that the respondent may not be consciously aware of.
2. Can use physical objects.
3. Attempts to measure psychological trade-offs when evaluating several attributes together
4. Can be carried out telephone or face-to-face.

CHALLENGES

1. Studies can be complex

RESOURCES

1. Paper
2. Pens
3. Phone
4. Questionnaires
5. Software

WHEN TO USE THIS METHOD

1. Define intent
2. Know Context
3. Know User
4. Frame insights

HOW TO USE THIS METHOD

1. The respondent is shown a number of features sometimes in pairs
2. The respondent rates or chooses combinations of features.
3. The data is analyzed and the features ranked.
4. Mathematical models are used to determine the respondent's product or service of choice.

REFERENCES

1. Green, P. and Srinivasan, V. (1978) Conjoint analysis in consumer research: Issues and outlook, Journal of Consumer Research, vol 5, September 1978, pp 103-123.
2. Orme, B. (2005) Getting Started with Conjoint Analysis Madison, WI: Research Publishers LLC. ISBN 0-9727297-4-7
3. Louviere, Jordan J. "Conjoint Analysis Modelling of Stated Preferences: A Review of Theory, Methods, Recent Developments and External Validity." Journal of Transport Economics and Policy, Vol. 22, No. 1, Stated Preference Methods in Transport Research (Jan., 1988), pp. 93-119.

cultural inventory

WHAT IS IT?
It is a survey focused on the cultural assets of a location or organization.

WHO INVENTED IT?
Julian Haynes Steward may have been the first to use the term in 1947.

WHY USE THIS METHOD?
1. Can be used in strategic planning
2. Can be used to solve problems.

CHALLENGES
1. Requires time and resources

WHEN TO USE THIS METHOD
1. Know Context
2. Know User
3. Frame insights
4. Explore Concepts

HOW TO USE THIS METHOD
1. Create your team
2. Collect existing research
3. Review existing research and identify gaps
4. Host a meeting of stakeholders
5. Promote the meeting
6. Ask open-ended questions about the culture and heritage
7. Set a time limit of 2 hours for the meeting.
8. Plan the collection phase
9. Compile inventory. This can be in the form of a web site
10. Distribute the inventory and obtain feedback.

RESOURCES
1. Diary
2. Notebooks
3. Pens
4. Post-it notes
5. Voice recorder
6. Post cards
7. Digital Camera

REFERENCES
1. Spradley, James P. Participant Observation. Holt, Rinehart and Winston, 1980.

cultural probes

WHAT IS IT?

A cultural probe is a method of collecting information about people, their context and their culture. The aim of this method is to record events, behaviors and interactions in their context. This method involves the participants to record and collect the data themselves.

WHO INVENTED IT?

Bill Gaver Royal College of Art London 1969

WHY USE THIS METHOD?

1. This is a useful method when the participants that are being studied are hard to reach for example if they are travelling.
2. It is a useful technique if the activities being studied take place over an extended period or at irregular intervals.
3. The information collected can be used to build personas.

CHALLENGES

4. It is important with this method to select the participants carefully and give them support during the study.

SEE ALSO

1. Diary study

WHEN TO USE THIS METHOD

1. Define intent
2. Know Context
3. Know User
4. Frame insights

HOW TO USE THIS METHOD

1. Define the objective of your study.
2. Recruit your participants.
3. Brief the participants
4. Supply participants with kit. The items in the kit are selected to collect the type of information you want to gather and can include items such as notebooks, diary, camera, voice recorder or post cards.
5. You can use an affinity diagram to analyze the data collected

RESOURCES

1. Diary
2. Notebooks
3. Pens
4. Post-it notes
5. Voice recorder
6. Post cards
7. Digital Camera

REFERENCES

1. Bailey, Kathleen M. (1990) The use of diary studies in teacher education programs In Richards, J. C. & Nunan, D. (org.). Second Language Teacher Education (pp. 215-226). Cambridge: Cambridge University Press.

	ANTICIPATE	ENTER	ENGAGE	EXIT	REVIEW
CUSTOMER MORE POSITIVE EXPERIENCES					
CUSTOMER POSITIVE EXPERIENCES					
BASELINE					
CUSTOMER NEGA-TIVE EXPERIENCES					
CUSTOMER MORE NEGATIVE EXPERIENCES					
EMOTIONAL EXPERIENCE					

customer experience map

WHAT IS IT?

Customer experience also called customer journey mapping is a method of documenting and visualizing the experiences that customers have as they use a product or service and their responses to their experiences.

It allows your team to access and analyze the interacting factors that form a customer experience.

WHY USE THIS METHOD?

1. Helps develop a consistent, predictable customer experience,
2. Presents an overview of your customer's experience from their point of view.
3. Helps reduce the number of dissatisfied customers
4. Can be used with different personas.

WHEN TO USE THIS METHOD

1. Know Context
2. Know User
3. Frame insights

HOW TO USE THIS METHOD

1. Identify your team.
2. Identify the customer experience to be analyzed. Identify the context. Identify personas.
3. Define the experience as a time line with stages such as anticipation, entry, engagement, exit, and reflection.
4. Use post-it notes to add positive and negative experiences to the relevant parts of the time line.
5. Order the experiences around a baseline by how positive or negative the experience were.
6. Analyze the parts of the time line and activities that have the most negative experiences. These are opportunities for design.

RESOURCES

1. Post-it-notes
2. Printed or projected template
3. White board
4. Markers

REFERENCES

1. Joshi, Hetal. "Customer Journey Mapping: The Road to Success." Cognizant. (2009) Web. 26 Jul. 2013.
2. World Class Skills Programme. "Customer Journey Mapping." Developing Responsive Provision. (2006): n. page. Web. 27 Jul. 2013.

customer experience audit

WHAT IS IT?

A customer experience audit is a method of systematically analyzing an organization's with their customers. It is a systematic way of understanding how your customers see your organization.

WHY USE THIS METHOD?

1. Increase employee engagement
2. Establish a baseline of Customer Experience
3. Provide insights into opportunities
4. Prepare a team for Customer Journey Mapping
5. Reveal customer perspective to employees
6. A customer perspective allows your organization to shift its culture from opinion to
7. Fact based thinking.
8. Audit findings get people on the same page.

CHALLENGES

1. When your customer experience has evolved over time, rather than being intentionally designed, product and company performance suffer.
2. Which customers are your most valuable
3. Which interactions these key customers most value

WHEN TO USE THIS METHOD

1. Know Context
2. Know User
3. Frame insights

HOW TO USE THIS METHOD

Will depend on your organization anf customer base, but could typically include;

1. Customer surveys and interviews with; existing and past customers as well as potential customers
2. Mystery shopping
3. Focus groups
4. Interviews with staff who interact with your customers.
5. Review of customer interactions and literature including face-to-face interviews, telephone and online surveys
6. Prospective, current, and lost customers.
7. Signs
8. Advertisements
9. Website
10. E-mail or Newsletters
11. Facebook or other social pages
12. Retail Space
13. Marketing Materials
14. Information Forms

REFERENCES

1. Rubin, Herbert and Irene Rubin. Qualitative Interviewing: The Art of Hearing Data. 2nd edition. Thousand Oaks, CA: Sage Publications, 2004. Print.

customer first questions

WHAT IS IT?

Customer first questions predict the reaction of customers to a new product or service.

WHO INVENTED IT?

Edith Wilson, Hewlett-Packard,

WHY USE THIS METHOD?

1. To identify customer needs and desires.
2. To reduce the risk of product development
3. To reduce the number of product design changes during the development process.
4. The Customer first questions method has been used by many large organizations

WHEN TO USE THIS METHOD

1. Define intent
2. Know Context
3. Know User
4. Frame insights

HOW TO USE THIS METHOD

1. Brainstorm the most appropriate research methods.
   - What customer problems does our product/service solve that our competitors do not?
   - What benefits does our product/service offer that our competitors do not?
   - What motivates the customer to purchase our product/service over that of our competitors?
2. Identify using research the needs and desires of customers.
3. Analyze how the product satisfies these needs and desired and how this compares to competitor's products.
4. Analyze whether customers will prefer the product to competitor's products.

RESOURCES

1. Paper
2. Pens
3. White board
4. Dry erase markers

CUSTOMER NEEDS MATRIX

	CUSTOMER DEMOGRAPHICS	CUSTOMER NEEDS	USAGE				
			WHO	WHAT	WHEN	WHERE	HOW
1							
2							
3							
4							
5							
6							
7							
8							
9							
10							
11							
12							

customer needs matrix

WHAT IS IT?

The customer needs table helps integrated product development teams (IPDT) translate customer needs and wants into required designs that may meet customer expectations prior to the potential development of new products or service development.

WHY USE THIS METHOD?

1. To uncover customer needs and desires
2. To translate customer needs and desires into product features.
3. To reduce changes necessary during product development.

RESOURCES

1. Paper
2. Pens
3. White board
4. Dry erase markers

WHEN TO USE THIS METHOD

1. Define intent
2. Know Context
3. Know User
4. Frame insights

HOW TO USE THIS METHOD

1. The design team selects methods for collecting data.
2. Data collection methods : Customer surveys, interviews, focus groups, benchmarks, similar product data, summarized studies, product demos, and others.
3. A sample of customers is selected and interviewed in relation to the factors listed on the customer needs matrix.
4. The responses are entered into the table.
5. The table is reviewed by the team.
6. The team creates a list of insights.

diary study

WHAT IS IT?

This method involves participants recording specific events, feelings or interactions, in a diary supplied by the researcher. User Diaries help provide insight into behavior. Participants record their behavior and thoughts. Diaries can uncover behavior that may not be articulated in an interview or easily visible to outsiders.

WHO INVENTED IT?

Gordon Allport, may have been the first to describe diary studies in 1942.

WHY USE THIS METHOD?

1. Can capture data that is difficult to capture using other methods.
2. Useful when you wish to gather information and minimize your influence on research subjects.
3. When the process or event you're exploring takes place intermittently or
4. When the process or event you're exploring takes place over a long period.

CHALLENGES

1. Process can be expensive and time consuming.
2. Needs participant monitoring.
3. Diary can fit into users' pocket.
4. It is difficult to get materials back.

WHEN TO USE THIS METHOD

1. Know Context
2. Know User
3. Frame insights

HOW TO USE THIS METHOD

1. A diary can be kept over a period of one week or longer.
2. Define focus for the study.
3. Recruit participants carefully.
4. Decide method: preprinted, diary notebook or online.
5. Prepare diary packs. Can be preprinted sheets or blank 20 page notebooks with prepared questions or online web based diary.
6. Brief participants.
7. Distribute diaries directly or by mail.
8. Conduct study. Keep in touch with participants.
9. Conduct debrief interview.
10. Look for insights.

RESOURCES

1. Diary
2. Preprinted diary sheets
3. Online diary
4. Pens
5. Disposable cameras
6. Digital camera
7. Self addressed envelopes

REFERENCES

1. Bailey, Kathleen M. (1990) The use of diary studies in teacher education programs In Richards, J. C. & Nunan, D. (org.). Second Language Teacher Education (pp. 215-226). Cambridge: Cambridge University Press.

SEE ALSO

Empathy probe

day experience method

WHAT IS IT?

The method requires participants to record answers to questions during a day. The person's mobile phone is used to prompt them The participants use a notebook, a camera or a voice recorder to answer your questions. The interviews are followed by a focus group.

WHO INVENTED IT?

Intille 2003

WHY USE THIS METHOD?

1. The participants are co-researchers.
2. Reduces the influence of the researcher on the participant when compared to methods such as interviews or direct observation.

CHALLENGES

1. Cost of devices.
2. This method should be used with other methods.

WHEN TO USE THIS METHOD

1. Know Context
2. Know User
3. Frame insights

HOW TO USE THIS METHOD

1. Conduct a preliminary survey to focus the method on preferred questions.
2. Recruit participants.
3. The experience sampling takes place over one day.
4. The participants are asked to provide answers to questions at irregular intervals when promoted by a SMS message via the participant's mobile phone.
5. The interval can be 60 to 90 minutes.
6. The participant can record the activity with a camera, notebook or voice recorder.
7. Soon after the day organize a focus group with the participants.
8. The participants describe their day using the recorded material.

RESOURCES

1. Mobile phone
2. Automated SMS messaging
3. Notebook
4. Camera
5. Software

REFERENCES

1. Kahneman, D., Krueger, A. B., Schkade, D. A., Schwarz, N., & Stone, A. A. (2004). 'A Survey Method for Characterizing Daily Life Experience: The Day Reconstruction Method'. Science, 306(5702), 1776-1780.

125

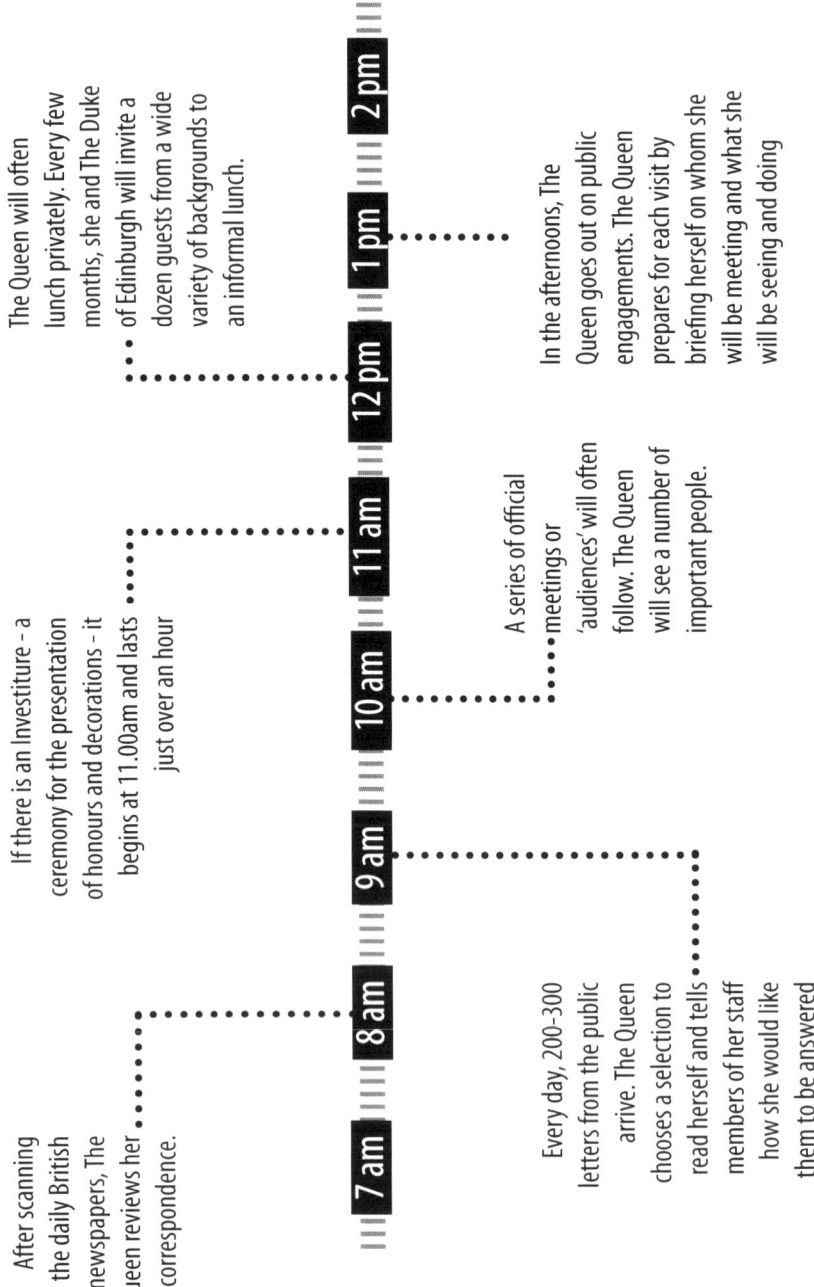

7 am — After scanning the daily British newspapers, The Queen reviews her correspondence.

Every day, 200-300 letters from the public arrive. The Queen chooses a selection to read herself and tells members of her staff how she would like them to be answered

8 am

9 am

10 am — A series of official meetings or 'audiences' will often follow. The Queen will see a number of important people.

11 am — If there is an Investiture - a ceremony for the presentation of honours and decorations - it begins at 11.00am and lasts just over an hour

12 pm — The Queen will often lunch privately. Every few months, she and The Duke of Edinburgh will invite a dozen guests from a wide variety of backgrounds to an informal lunch.

1 pm — In the afternoons, The Queen goes out on public engagements. The Queen prepares for each visit by briefing herself on whom she will be meeting and what she will be seeing and doing

2 pm

day in the life

WHAT IS IT?
A study in which the designer observes the participant in the location and context of their usual activities, observing and recording events to understand the activities from the participant's point of view. This is sometimes repeated. Mapping a 'Day in the Life' as a storyboard can provide a focus for discussion.

WHO INVENTED IT?
ALex Bavelas 1944

WHY USE THIS METHOD?
1. This method informs the design process by observation of real activities and behaviors.
2. This method provides insights with relatively little cost and time.

CHALLENGES
1. Choose the participants carefully
2. Document everything. Something that seems insignificant may become significant later.

WHEN TO USE THIS METHOD
1. Know Context
2. Know User
3. Frame insights

HOW TO USE THIS METHOD
1. Define activities to study
2. Recruit participants
3. Prepare
4. Observe subjects in context.
5. Capture data,
6. Create storyboard with text and timeline.
7. Analyze data
8. Create insights.
9. Identify issues
10. Identify needs
11. Add new/more requirements to concept development

RESOURCES
1. Camera
2. Notebook
3. Video camera
4. Voice recorder
5. Pens

REFERENCES
1. Shadowing: And Other Techniques for Doing Fieldwork in Modern Societies [Paperback] Barbara Czarniawska. Publisher: Copenhagen Business School Pr (December 2007) ISBN-10: 8763002159 ISBN-13: 978-8763002158

desirability testing

WHAT IS IT?

Desirability testing are a number of qualitative and quantitative attitudinal methods that assess people's attitudes to a product or service.

WHY USE THIS METHOD?

1. A manager often feels his or her perception of a design is just as valid as the designer's
2. These methods help the design team understand the response of customers to a proposed design.
3. Reduces the subjectivity of design decisions.

CHALLENGES

1. This method measures attitude rather than behavior.

WHEN TO USE THIS METHOD

1. Define intent
2. KNOW PEOPLE AND CONTEXT
3. Frame insights
4. Explore Concepts

HOW TO USE THIS METHOD

1. Participants are given cards that have words on each card such as desirable, high quality, valuable, useful, reliable, fun confusing, complex, familiar.
2. The participants select the cards that go with each design.
3. The researcher asks the participants why they made the selections.

RESOURCES

1. Word cards
2. Table
3. Prototype products or services

digital ethnography

WHAT IS IT?

Digital Ethnography is research that is undertaken in online, virtual or digitally enabled environments. It uses digital tools to gather, analyze, and present ethnographic data.

WHY USE THIS METHOD?

1. Can be faster and less expensive than non-digital methods.
2. Data collected real time
3. Access to people may be easier
4. People carry digital devices such as smart phones, cameras, laptops and tablets
5. Data can be gathered in context

CHALLENGES

1. Can miss non verbal feedback.
2. Technology may be unreliable

WHEN TO USE THIS METHOD

1. Define intent
2. Know Context
3. Know User
4. Frame insights
5. Explore Concepts
6. Make Plans
7. Deliver Offering

HOW TO USE THIS METHOD

There are many different methods which use or access:

1. Audio conferences
2. Web conferences
3. Virtual in depth interviews
4. Focus groups
5. Mobile diaries
6. Online forums
7. Private online communities

RESOURCES

1. Smart phones,
2. Cameras,
3. Laptops and
4. Tablets

REFERENCES

1. Coover, R. (2004) 'Using Digital Media Tools and Cross-Cultural Research,Analysis and Representation', Visual Studies19(1): 6–25.
2. Dicks, B., B. Mason, A. Coffey and P. Atkinson (2005) Qualitative Research and Hypermedia: Ethnography for the Digital Age. London: SAGE.
3. Kozinets R.V. (2010a), Netnography. Doing Ethnographic Research Online, Sage, London.

dramaturgy

WHAT IS IT?

Dramaturgy is a method that uses drama techniques to help understand user behaviors and needs. It a form of prototyping.

WHO INVENTED IT?

Robert, Benford D., and Scott A. Hunt

WHY USE THIS METHOD?

1. Created to make personas more dynamic.

CHALLENGES

1. Some team members may be uncomfortable with drama based activity.
2. The method is not in context
3. The method may be subjective as it does not involve the people being designed for,

WHEN TO USE THIS METHOD

4. Know Context
5. Know User
6. Frame insights
7. Explore Concepts

HOW TO USE THIS METHOD

1. Choose a character
2. Create groups of 2 or 3 members of your design team
3. Ask your teams to write monologues for the characters based on public, private and intimate levels.
4. Ask your team to discuss the rituals of the character's lives
5. Ask your team to create maps of the stakeholders
6. Create scenes exploring crucial moments in your character's experiences or interactions.
7. Present these scenarios with groups of actors.
8. Explore the problems and challenges of the character's experiences and interactions.

REFERENCES

1. Robert, Benford D., and Scott A. Hunt. "Dramaturgy and Social Movements: The Social Construction and Communication of Power." Social Inquiry 62.1 (2007): 36-55. Wiley Online Library.

field experiment

WHAT IS IT?

A field experiment is an experiment conducted outside the laboratory, in a 'natural' context This method often involves changing one or more variables in a context to understand their effect and randomizing participants into treatment and control groups.

WHO INVENTED IT?

Abu Rayman al-Biruni 1030 AD

WHY USE THIS METHOD?

1. Because the settings are more natural it is assumed that people will behave more naturally
2. Less sample bias.
3. Fewer demand characteristics if participants are unaware.
4. Designers conduct field experiments with prototypes to obtain feedback and refine designs.

CHALLENGES

1. Difficult to replicate
2. Informed consent may be difficult to obtain.
3. Less control of variables
4. Difficult to replicate.
5. Difficult to record data accurately.
6. If participants are unaware of the study how can the consent to take part or withdraw from the experiment?
7. Many participants are required to make reliable claims

WHEN TO USE THIS METHOD

1. Know Context
2. Know User
3. Frame insights

HOW TO USE THIS METHOD

Various methods are possible
Consider:
1. What resources are available
2. What will you test and compare?
3. What will be your methods?
4. How will you gain access and participation?

RESOURCES

1. Note pad
2. Pens
3. Camera
4. Video camera
5. Digital voice recorder

REFERENCES

1. Reichardt, C. S. & Mark, M. M. (2004). Quasi-Experimentation. In J. S. Wholey, H. P. Hatry, & K. E. Newcomber (Eds.) Handbook of Practical Program Evaluation, Second Edition, San Franciso: Jossey-Bass.

drawing experiences

WHAT IS IT?

This method involves asking respondents to create drawings to illustrate their experiences.

WHO INVENTED IT?

Used by design consultants IDEO

WHY USE THIS METHOD?

1. Drawing can elicit information difficult for respondents to describe in words.

CHALLENGES

1. A drawing of an experience is different to an experience which involves all senses.
2. Some people are not confident expressing themselves through drawing.

WHEN TO USE THIS METHOD

1. Know Context
2. Know User
3. Frame insights

HOW TO USE THIS METHOD

1. Select a moderator
2. Select a group of 4 to 12 users
3. Ask users to create an image of an experience through a drawing.

RESOURCES

1. Pens
2. Paper

REFERENCES

1. IDEO method cards. Publication Date: November 2003 ISBN-10: 0954413210 ISBN-13: 978-0954413217

EMOTIONAL JOURNEY MAP

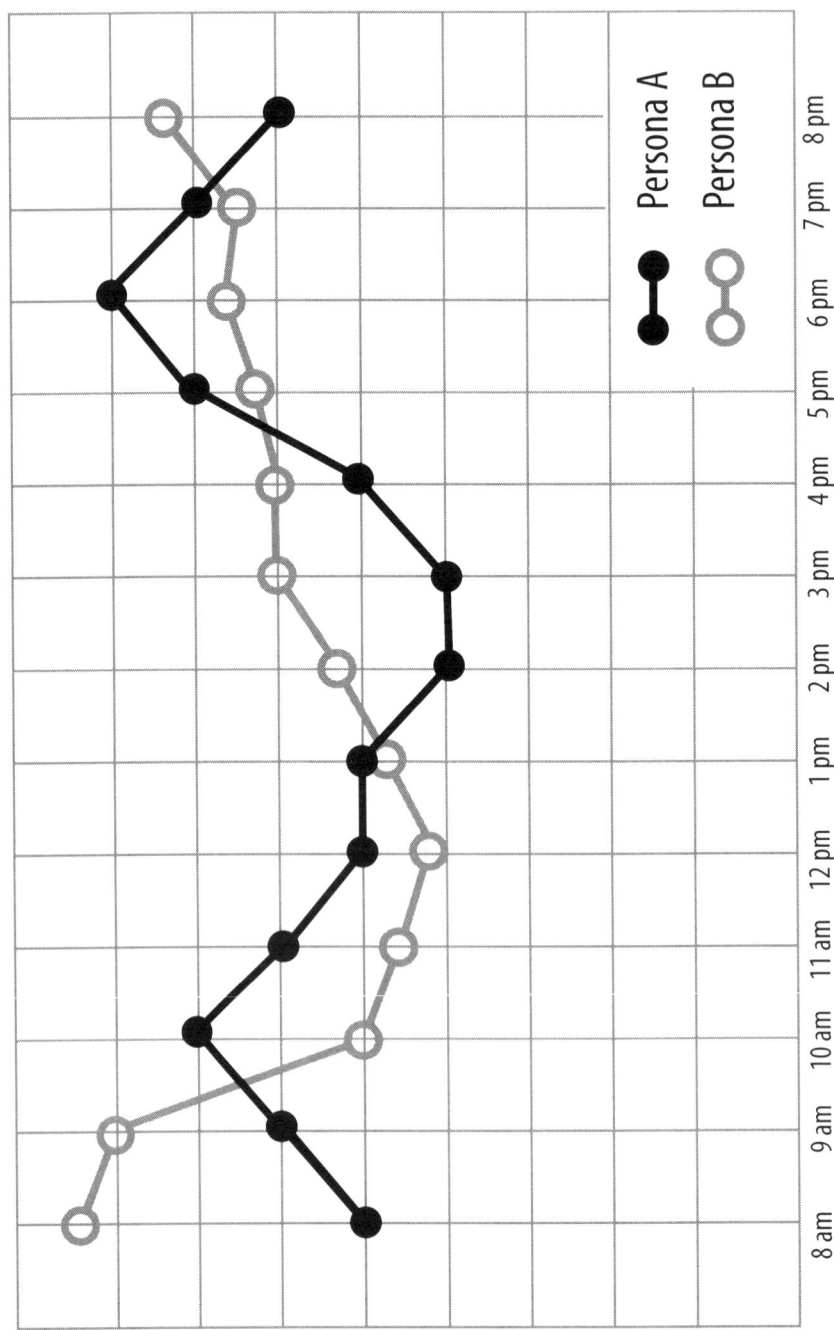

Persona A

Persona B

8 am · 9 am · 10 am · 11 am · 12 pm · 1 pm · 2 pm · 3 pm · 4 pm · 5 pm · 6 pm · 7 pm · 8 pm

emotional journey map

WHAT IS IT?

An emotional journey map is a map that visually illustrates people's emotional experience throughout an interaction with an organization or brand.

WHY USE THIS METHOD?

1. It provides a focus for discussion
2. It focusses on what may make your customers unhappy
3. Provides a visually compelling story of customer experience.
4. Customer experience is more than interaction with a product.
5. By understanding the journey that your customers are making, you will be in a position to make informed improvements.

CHALLENGES

1. Customers often do not take the route in an interaction that the designer expects.
2. Failure to manage experiences can lead to lost customers.

WHEN TO USE THIS METHOD

1. Know Context
2. Know User
3. Frame insights
4. Explore Concepts
5. Make Plans

HOW TO USE THIS METHOD

1. Define the activity of your map. For example it could be a ride on the underground train.
2. Collect internal insights
3. Research customer perceptions
4. Analyze research
5. Map journey.
6. Across the top of the page do a time line Break the journey into stages using your customer's point of view
7. Capture each persona's unique experience
8. Use a scale from 0 to 10. The higher the number, the better the experience.
9. Plot the emotional journey.
10. Analyze the lease pleasant emotional periods and create ideas for improving the experience during those periods.
11. Create a map for each persona.

RESOURCES

1. Paper
2. Pens
3. White board
4. Post-it-notes

REFERENCES

1. Joshi, Hetal. "Customer Journey Mapping: The Road to Success." Cognizant. (2009) Web. 26 Jul. 2013.
2. World Class Skills Programme. "Customer Journey Mapping." Developing Responsive Provision. (2006): n. page. Web. 27 Jul. 2013.

EMPATHY MAP

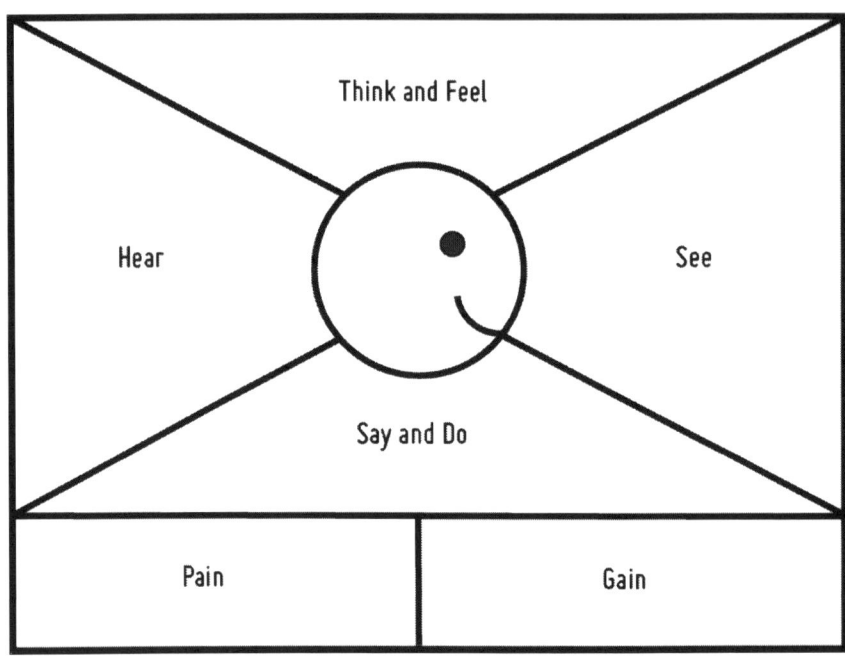

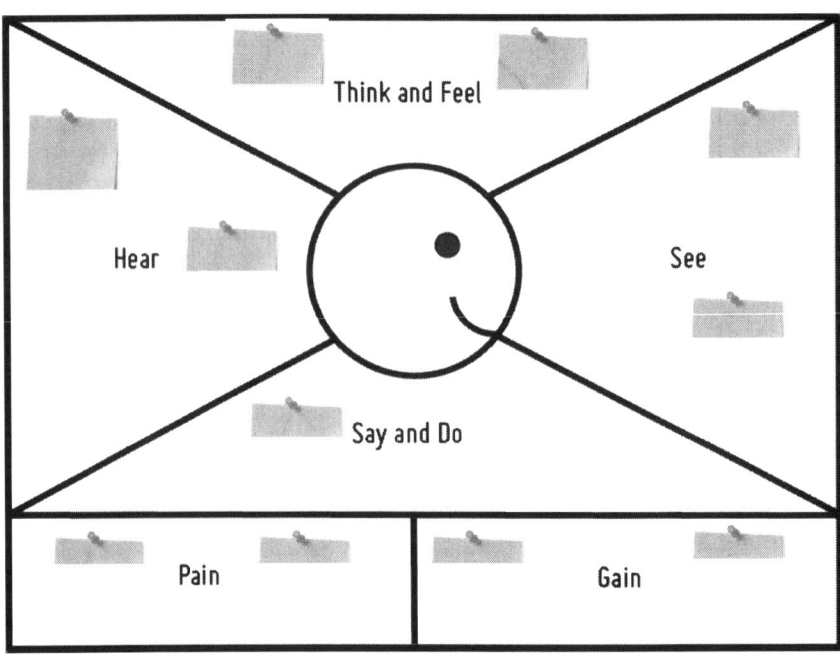

empathy map

WHAT IS IT?

Empathy Map is a tool that helps the design team empathize with people they are designing for, You can create an empathy map for a group of customers or a persona.

WHO INVENTED IT?

Scott Matthews and Dave Gray at PLANE now Dachis Group.

WHY USE THIS METHOD?

This tool helps a design team understand the customers and their context.

CHALLENGES

1. Emotions must be inferred by observing clues.
2. This method does not provide the same level of rigor as traditional personas but requires less investment.

WHEN TO USE THIS METHOD

1. Know Context
2. Know User
3. Frame insights

RESOURCES

1. Empathy map template
2. White board
3. Dry-erase markers
4. Post-it-notes
5. Pens
6. Video Camera

HOW TO USE THIS METHOD

1. A team of 3 to 10 people is a good number for this method.
2. This method can be used with personas.
3. Draw a cirle to represent your target persona.
4. Divide the circle into sections that represent aspects of that person's sensory experience.
5. Ask your team to describe from the persona's point of view their experience.
6. What are the persona's needs and desires?
7. Populate the map by taking note of the following traits of your user as you review your notes, audio, and video from your fieldwork: What are they thinking, feeling, saying, doing, hearing, seeing?
8. Fill in the diagram with real, tangible, sensory experiences.
9. 20 minutes to one hour is a good duration for this exercise.
10. Ask another group of people to look at your map and suggest improvements or refinements.

REFERENCES

1. Gray, Dave; Brown, Sunni; Macanufo, James (2010). Gamestorming: A Playbook for Innovators, Rulebreakers, and Changemakers. O'Reilly Media, Inc

empathy probes

WHAT IS IT?

This method involves participants recording specific events, feelings or interactions, in a diary supplied by the researcher. User Diaries help provide insight into behavior. Participants record their behavior and thoughts. Diaries can uncover behavior that may not be articulated in an interview or easily visible to outsiders.

WHO INVENTED IT?

Gordon Allport, may have been the first to describe diary studies in 1942.

WHY USE THIS METHOD?

1. Can capture data that is difficult to capture using other methods.
2. Cultural probes are appropriate when you need to gather information from users with minimal influence on their actions,

CHALLENGES

1. Process can be expensive and time consuming.
2. Needs participant monitoring.
3. Diary can fit into users' pocket.
4. It is difficult to get materials back.

WHEN TO USE THIS METHOD

1. Know Context
2. Know User
3. Frame insights

HOW TO USE THIS METHOD

1. A diary can be kept over a period of one week or longer.
2. Define focus for the study.
3. Recruit participants carefully.
4. Decide method: preprinted, diary notebook or online.
5. Prepare diary packs. Can be preprinted sheets or blank 20 page notebooks with prepared questions or online web based diary.
6. Brief participants.
7. Distribute diaries directly or by mail.
8. Conduct study. Keep in touch with participants.
9. Conduct debrief interview.
10. Look for insights.

RESOURCES

1. Diary
2. Preprinted diary sheets
3. Online diary
4. Pens
5. Disposable cameras
6. Digital camera
7. Self addressed envelopes

REFERENCES

1. Bailey, Kathleen M. (1990) The use of diary studies in teacher education programs In Richards, J. C. & Nunan, D. (org.). Second Language Teacher Education (pp. 215-226). Cambridge: Cambridge University Press.

SEE ALSO

Diary study

empathy tools

WHAT IS IT?

Empathy tools are aids or tools that help designers empathize with the people they are designing for. They can be used to test a prototype design or in activities such as role playing or body storming.

WHO INVENTED IT?

Brandt, E. and Grunnet, C 2000

WHY USE THIS METHOD?

1. To help a designer understand the experiences of people that they are designing for.

CHALLENGES

1. Empathy tools are imperfect approximations of user experiences.

WHEN TO USE THIS METHOD

1. Know Context
2. Know User
3. Frame insights
4. Explore Concept

HOW TO USE THIS METHOD

1. Wear heavy gloves to experience less sensitivity in your hands
2. Wear fogged glasses to experience less acute vision
3. Wear black glasses to eat to experience issues locating food and utensils.
4. Spend a day in a wheelchair.
5. Wear earplugs to experience diminished hearing

RESOURCES

1. Wheelchair
2. Fogged glasses
3. Blackened glasses
4. Gloves
5. Earplugs
6. Crutches
7. Walking stick

REFERENCES

1. Brandt, E. and Grunnet, C., "Evoking the Future: Drama and Props in User-centered Design", PDC 2000

EVALUATION MATRIX

CRITERIA	WEIGHT	DESIGN A		DESIGN B		DESIGN C		DESIGN D	
		SCORE	WEIGHTED	SCORE	WEIGHTED	SCORE	WEIGHTED	SCORE	WEIGHTED
TOTAL									

evaluation matrix

WHAT IS IT?

A simple tool used for planning and conducting an evaluation that aids the team in making informed decisions by comparing many options. The use of an evaluation matrix is a method of evaluating a number of options against a number of criteria. A Weighted Alternatives Evaluation Matrix, or Weighted Matrix, assigns weighting factors to criteria when comparing alternatives

WHY USE THIS METHOD?

1. Control costs by focusing resources
2. Answer/discover critical questions.
3. Fast and cost effective method.
4. Allows you to identify strengths and weaknesses.
5. An efficient way of conveying information.

CHALLENGES

1. Can emphasize data which is not most important.
2. Assignment of weights and scores is subjective

WHEN TO USE THIS METHOD

1. Know Context
2. Know User
3. Frame insights
4. Explore Concepts
5. Make Plans

HOW TO USE THIS METHOD

1. Establishing Evaluation Criteria.
2. Prioritizing criteria
3. List mandatory criteria
4. List desirable criteria
5. The simplest Alternatives Evaluation Matrix indicates with a yes or no whether each criterion was met.
6. Weighting factors are used to define the level of importance of criteria. Assigning meaning to weighting factors is subjective. Keep the number of weighting factors small
7. You can have the members of a group do their own ranking and then combine the results onto one summary report.
8. Analyze the criteria rankings

RESOURCES

1. Paper
2. Pens
3. White board
4. Dry-erase markers

eyetracking

WHAT IS IT?

Eye tracking is a group of methods of studying and recording a person's eye movements over time. The most widely used current designs are video-based eye trackers. One of the most prominent fields of commercial eye tracking research is web usability but this method is also used widely for evaluating retail interiors and products.

WHO INVENTED IT?

Louis Émile Javal 1879
Alfred L. Yarbus 1950s

WHY USE THIS METHOD?

1. Examine which details attract attention.
2. To record where a participant's attention is focussed for example on a supermarket shelf which products and parts of products attract the most attention from shoppers.

CHALLENGES

1. Each method of eye tracking has advantages and disadvantages, and the choice of an eye tracking system depends on considerations of cost and application.
2. A poorly adjusted system can produce unreliable information.

WHEN TO USE THIS METHOD

1. Know Context
2. Know User
3. Frame insights
4. Explore Concepts

TYPES OF SYSTEMS

1. Measures eye movement with a device attached to the eye. For example a contact lens with a magnetic field sensor.
2. Non contact measurement of eye movement. For example infrared, is reflected from the eye and sensed by a video camera.
3. Measures eye movement with electrodes placed around the eyes.

TYPES OF OUTPUTS

1. Heat maps
2. Gaze plots
3. Gaze replays

RESOURCES

1. Eye tracking device
2. Software
3. Laptop computer

REFERENCES

1. Bojko, A. (2006). Using Eye Tracking to Compare Web Page Designs: A Case Study. Journal of Usability Studies, Vol.1, No. 3.
2. Chandon, Pierre, J. Wesley Hutchinson, and Scott H. Young (2001), Measuring Value of Point-of-Purchase Marketing with Commercial Eye-Tracking Data.
3. Wedel, M. & Pieters, R. (2000). Eye fixations on advertisements and memory for brands: a model and findings. Marketing Science, 19 (4), 2000, 297–312.

field study

WHAT IS IT?

A field study is a study carried on in the context of people rather than in design studio or a laboratory. A field study is primary research It involves observing or interviewing people in their natural environments.

WHO INVENTED IT?

James Cowles Prichard 1841
Margaret Mead, 1928
Bronisław Malinowski, 1929
Pierre Bourdieu 1958-1962

WHY USE THIS METHOD?

1. A field study can be used to inform design and to create more successful outcomes for design by better informing the designer of the behaviors, desires and needs of the people being designed for.

CHALLENGES

1. May be more expensive than secondary research.
2. Information may become obsolete

WHEN TO USE THIS METHOD

1. Define intent
2. Know Context
3. Know User
4. Frame insights
5. Explore Concepts
6. Make Plans
7. Deliver Offering

HOW TO USE THIS METHOD

1. Define goals.
2. Develop plan
3. Create study materials such as question guides, release forms,
4. Prepare for site visits
5. Perform observations and interviews.
6. Analyze data
7. Develop insights
8. Make recommendations.

RESOURCES

1. Note pads
2. Pens
3. Digital camera
4. Video camera
5. Post-it notes

REFERENCES

1. Jarvie, I. C. (1967) On Theories of Fieldwork and the Scientific Character of Social Anthropology, Philosophy of Science, Vol. 34, No. 3 (Sep., 1967), pp. 223-242.
2. Marek M. Kaminski. 2004. Games Prisoners Play. Princeton University Press. ISBN 0-691-11721-7

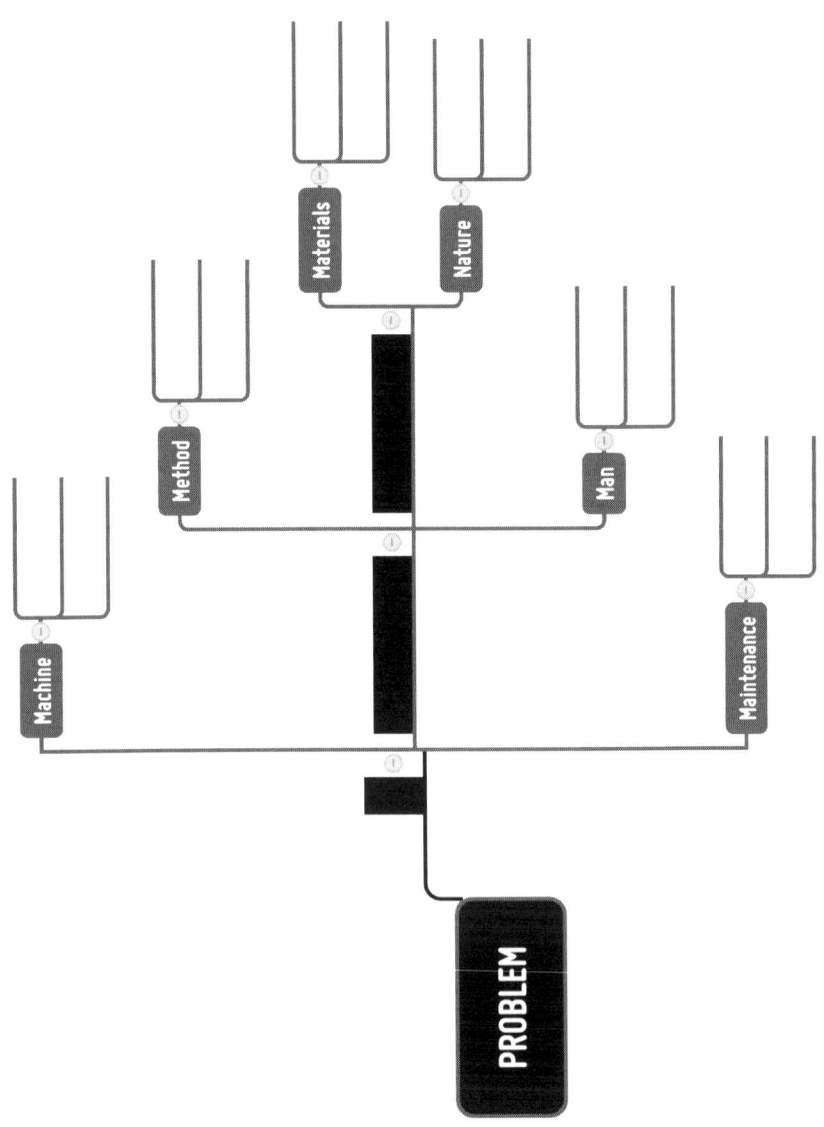

144

fishbone diagram

WHAT IS IT?

Fishbone diagrams also called Ishikawa diagrams, are diagrams that show the causes of a specific event.

Mazda Motors used an Ishikawa diagram to design the Miata sports car, The goal was was "Jinba Ittai" Horse and Rider as One. Every factor identified in the diagram was included in the final design. Ishikawa described the process as fishboning your problem and letting it cook overnight.

WHO INVENTED IT?

Kaoru Ishikawa University of Tokyo 1968

WHY USE THIS METHOD?

1. People tend to fix a problem by responding to an immediately visible cause while ignoring the deeper issues. This approach may lead to a problem reoccurring.
2. Use in the predesign phase to understand the root causes of a problem to serve as the basis for design.
3. Identifies the relationship between cause and effect.

WHEN TO USE THIS METHOD

1. Define intent
2. Know Context
3. Know User
4. Frame insights

HOW TO USE THIS METHOD

1. Prepare the six arms of the Ishikawa Diagram on a white board.
2. Define the problem clearly as a short statement in the head of the diagram.
3. Describe the causes of each bone and write them at the end of each branch. Use the 4 M's as categories; Machine, Man Methods, Materials.
4. Conduct the brainstorming session using brainstorming guidelines Ask each team member to define the cause of the problem. You may list as many causes as necessary. Typically 3 to 6 are listed.
5. Minor causes are then listed around the major causes.
6. Interpret the Ishikawa Diagram once it's finished.

RESOURCES

1. White board
2. Dry-erase markers
3. Room with privacy
4. Paper
5. Pens

REFERENCES

1. Ishikawa, Kaoru, Guide to Quality Control, Asian Productivity Organization, UNIPUB, 1976, ISBN 92-833-1036-5
2. Ishikawa, Kaoru (1990); (Translator: J. H. Loftus); Introduction to Quality Control; 448 p; ISBN 4-906224-61-X OCLC 41428

145

FORCE FIELD DIAGRAM

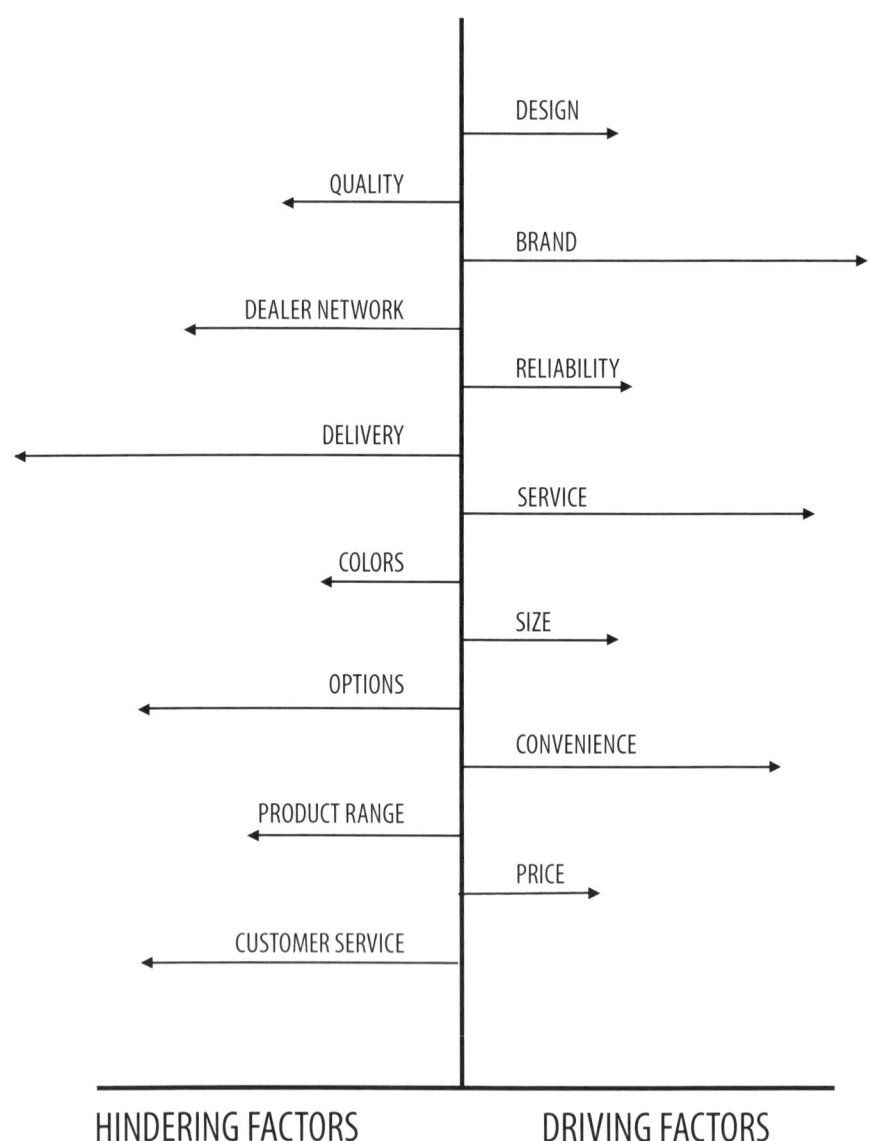

HINDERING FACTORS   DRIVING FACTORS

force field analysis

WHAT IS IT?

Force field analysis is a method of mapping and analyzing factors which assist or work against desired goals.

WHO INVENTED IT?

Kurt Lewin 1940s
John R. P. French 1947

WHY USE THIS METHOD?

1. Allows visual comparison of factors affecting the success of a project for discussion of solutions.

CHALLENGES

1. It is best to focus on barriers.
2. Assign a strategy to each barrier

RESOURCES

1. Pen
2. Paper
3. White board
4. Dry erase markers
5. Post-it notes.

REFERENCES

1. Cartwright, D. (1951). Foreword to the 1951 Edition. Field Theory in Social Science and Selected Theoretical Papers-Kurt Lewin. Washington, D.C.: American Psychological Association, 1997. Originally published by Harper & Row.

HOW TO USE THIS METHOD

1. Select a moderator and a team of stakeholders.
2. The moderator describes the problem being focused on to the team
3. The moderator draws the letter T on a white board
4. The moderator writes the problem above the cross stroke on the T
5. The team brainstorms a list of forces working against the goal and the moderator lists them on the right hand of the upstroke on the letter T.
6. The team brainstorms a list or forces working towards the goal and the moderator writes them on the right hand of the upstroke on the letter T.
7. Forces listed can be internal and external.
8. They can be associated with the environment, the organization, people strategy, culture, values, competitors, conflicts or other factors.
9. Prioritize and quantify both lists of forces
10. The moderator draws a horizontal letter T and above the horizontal line draws arrows for each factor indicating their relative significance in the opinion of the team.
11. The moderator draws arrows for each negative factor below the line showing their relative significance.

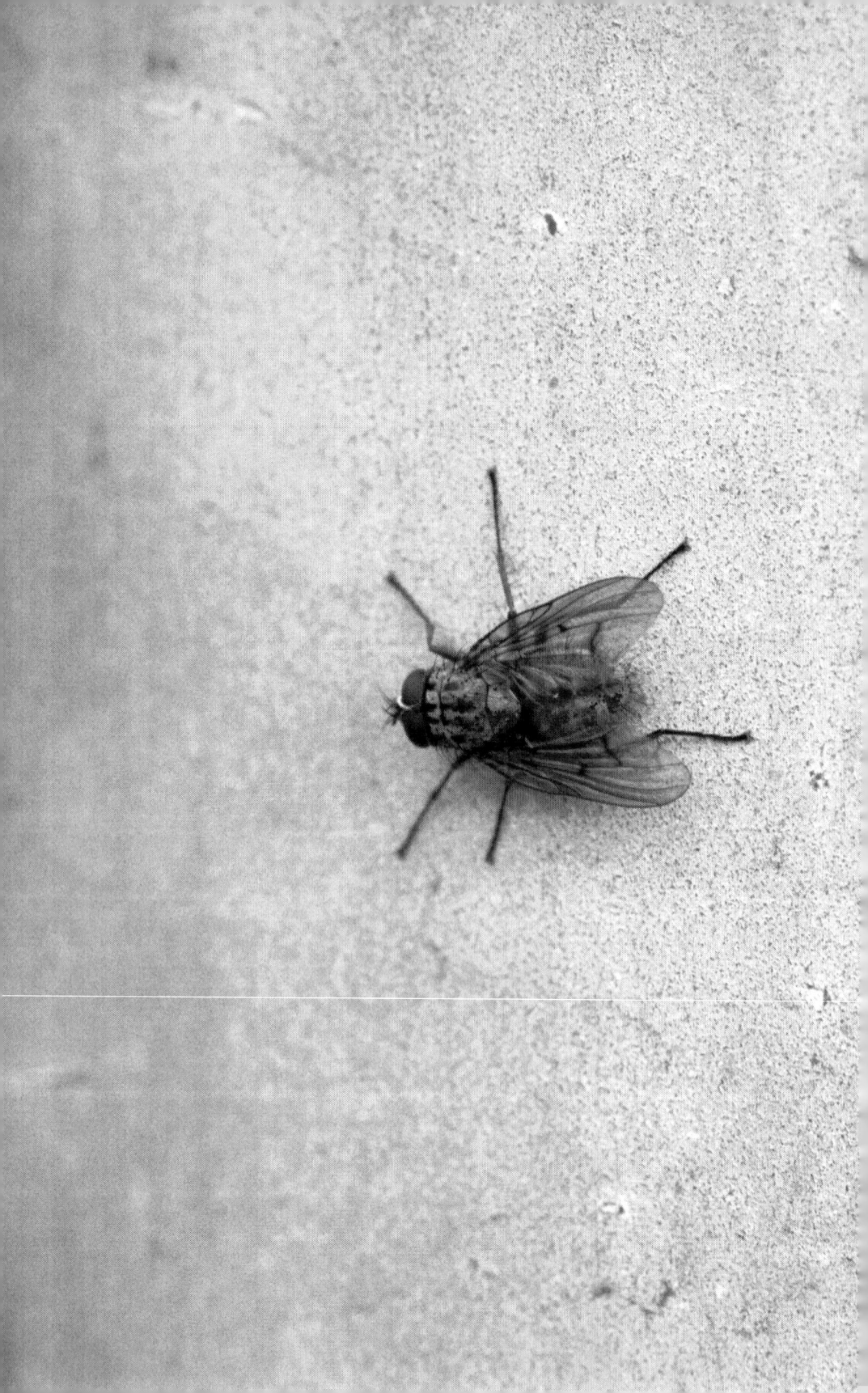

fly-on-the-wall

WHAT IS IT?

Observation method where the observer remains as unobtrusive as possible and observes and collects data relevant to a research study in context with no interaction with the participants being observed. The name derived from the documentary film technique of the same name.

WHO INVENTED IT?

ALex Bavelas 1944
Lucy Vernile, Robert A. Monteiro 1991

WHY USE THIS METHOD?

1. Low cost
2. No setup necessary
3. Can observe a large number of participants.
4. Objective observations
5. Compared to other methods such as focus groups, setup, data collection, and processing are much faster.

CHALLENGES

1. No interaction by the observer.
2. Requires that the observer be silent during the presentation without asking questions or making suggestions.
3. Observer cannot delve deeper during a session.
4. No interruption allowed
5. Observer cannot obtain details on customer comments during a session

Photo: photocase.com - FreyaSapphire

WHEN TO USE THIS METHOD

1. Know Context
2. Know User
3. Frame insights

HOW TO USE THIS METHOD

1. Define activity to study
2. Select participants thoughtfully
3. Choose a context for the observation
4. Carefully observe the interaction or experience. This is best done by members of your design team.
5. It is important to influence the participants as little as possible by your presence.
6. Observe but do not interact with participants while observing them in context.
7. Capture Data
8. Identify issues
9. Identify needs
10. Create design solutions based on observed and experienced human needs.

RESOURCES

1. Digital camera
2. Video camera
3. Voice recorder

REFERENCES

1. McDonald, Seonaidh. "Studying Actions in Context: A Qualitative Shadowing Method for Organizational Research." Qualitative Research. The Robert Gordon University. SAGE Publications. London. 2005.
   p455-473.

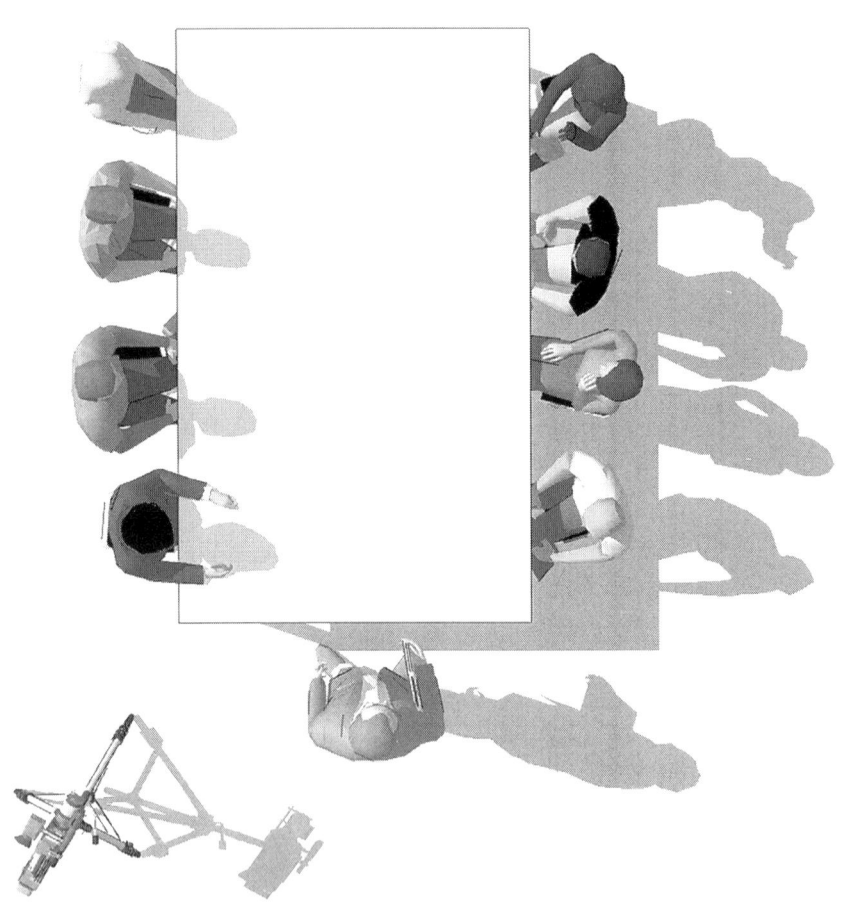

focus groups

WHAT IS IT?

Focus groups are discussions usually with 6 to 12 participants led by a moderator. Focus groups are used during the the design of products, services and experiences to get feedback from people

Powell defined a focus group as "A group of individuals selected and assembled by researchers to discuss and comment on, from personal experience, the topic that is the subject of the research."

WHO INVENTED IT?

Robert K. Merton 1940 Bureau of Applied Social Research.

WHY USE THIS METHOD?

1. To identify the expectations, needs and desires of customers.
2. It is useful to gain several different perspectives about a design problem.
3. A disadvantage of this method is that it removes the subjects from their context.

CHALLENGES

1. Focus group study results may not be not be generalizable.
2. Focus group participants can influence each other.

WHEN TO USE THIS METHOD

1. Know Context
2. Know User
3. Frame insights
4. Explore Concepts

HOW TO USE THIS METHOD

1. Select a good moderator.
2. Prepare a screening questionnaire.
3. Decide incentives for participants.
4. Select facility.
5. Recruit participants. Invite participants to your session well in advance and get firm commitments to attend. Remind participants the date of the event.
6. Participants should sit around a large table. Follow discussion guide.
7. Describe rules. Provide refreshments.
8. First question should encourage talking and participation.
9. The moderator manages responses and asks important questions
10. Moderator collects forms and debriefs focus group.
11. Analyze results while still fresh.
12. Summarize key points.
13. Run additional focus groups to deepen analysis.

RESOURCES

1. Focus group space.
2. Sound and video recording equipment
3. White board
4. Pens
5. Post-it-notes

REFERENCES

1. Nachmais, Chava Frankfort; Nachmais, David. 2008. Research methods in the Social Sciences: Seventh Edition New York, NY: Worth Publishers

focus groups
client participant

WHAT IS IT?

A client participant focus group allows the client to participate either visibly or invisibly through a one way mirror. This method allows the client to interpret the answers and the a participant's body language and to ensure that the discussion covers what the client would like to be covered.

WHO INVENTED IT?

Robert K. Merton 1940 Bureau of Applied Social Research.

WHY USE THIS METHOD?

1. A focus group allows an in depth probe.
2. Interaction between participants can uncover broader insights.
3. They are cost effective for the volume and quality of data
4. Are less expensive than conducting 8 to 12 in depth interviews
5. Are time efficient
6. Clients can gain insights by observing the group interaction through a one way mirror.

CHALLENGES

1. Participants can influence each other.
2. Data is not quantifiable.
3. Responses are limited.
4. Data may be difficult to analyze
5. The participants are out of the context of their usual environments.

WHEN TO USE THIS METHOD

1. Know Context
2. Know User
3. Frame insights
4. Explore Concepts

HOW TO USE THIS METHOD

1. Focus groups often take one and a half to two hours.
2. Ask 5 to 10 questions.
3. Define purpose
4. Ask:
- Why a focus group?
- Who are the stakeholders?
- Who is the target population?
- What problems will be explored?
5. Define resources
6. Write question guide.
7. Recruit participants.
8. Conduct focus group.
9. Analyze data.
10. Create insights.
11. Take actions.

RESOURCES

1. Focus group space.
2. Sound and video recording equipment
3. White board
4. Pens
5. Post-it-notes

REFERENCES

1. Nachmais, Chava Frankfort; Nachmais, David. 2008. Research methods in the Social Sciences: Seventh Edition New York, NY: Worth Publishers

focus groups
devil's advocate

WHAT IS IT?
This with method two moderators present contrary viewpoints. The different ways of thinking provide new insights.

WHO INVENTED IT?
Robert K. Merton 1940 Bureau of Applied Social Research.

WHY USE THIS METHOD?
1. A focus group allows an in depth probe.
2. Interaction between participants can uncover broader insights.
3. They are cost effective for the volume and quality of data
4. Are less expensive than conducting 8 to 12 in depth interviews
5. Are time efficient
6. Clients can gain insights by observing the group interaction through a one way mirror.

CHALLENGES
1. Participants can influence each other.
2. Data is not quantifiable.
3. Responses are limited.
4. Data may be difficult to analyze
5. The participants are out of the context of their usual environments.

WHEN TO USE THIS METHOD
1. Know Context
2. Know User
3. Frame insights
4. Explore Concepts

HOW TO USE THIS METHOD
1. Focus groups often take one and a half to two hours.
2. Ask 5 to 10 questions.
3. Define purpose
4. Ask:
- Why a focus group?
- Who are the stakeholders?
- Who is the target population?
- What problems will be explored?
5. Define resources
6. Write question guide.
7. Recruit participants.
8. Conduct focus group.
9. Analyze data.
10. Create insights.
11. Take actions.

RESOURCES
1. Focus group space.
2. Sound and video recording equipment
3. White board
4. Pens
5. Post-it-notes

REFERENCES
1. Nachmais, Chava Frankfort; Nachmais, David. 2008. Research methods in the Social Sciences: Seventh Edition New York, NY: Worth Publishers

focus groups
dual moderator

WHAT IS IT?

The dual moderator focus group involves two moderators. One moderator manages the time progression. The second moderator ensures that the discussion remains on the focus topics.

WHO INVENTED IT?

Robert K. Merton 1940 Bureau of Applied Social Research.

WHY USE THIS METHOD?

1. A focus group allows an in depth probe.
2. Interaction between participants can uncover broader insights.
3. They are cost effective for the volume and quality of data
4. Are less expensive than conducting 8 to 12 in depth interviews
5. Are time efficient
6. Clients can gain insights by observing the group interaction through a one way mirror.

CHALLENGES

1. Participants can influence each other.
2. Data is not quantifiable.
3. Responses are limited.
4. Data may be difficult to analyze
5. The participants are out of the context of their usual environments.

WHEN TO USE THIS METHOD

1. Know Context
2. Know User
3. Frame insights
4. Explore Concepts

HOW TO USE THIS METHOD

1. Focus groups often take one and a half to two hours.
2. Ask 5 to 10 questions.
3. Define purpose
4. Ask:
- Why a focus group?
- Who are the stakeholders?
- Who is the target population?
- What problems will be explored?
5. Define resources
6. Write question guide.
7. Recruit participants.
8. Conduct focus group.
9. Analyze data.
10. Create insights.
11. Take actions.

RESOURCES

1. Focus group space.
2. Sound and video recording equipment
3. White board
4. Pens
5. Post-it-notes

REFERENCES

1. Nachmais, Chava Frankfort; Nachmais, David. 2008. Research methods in the Social Sciences: Seventh Edition New York, NY: Worth Publishers

focus groups
mini focus group

WHAT IS IT?

A mini focus group has four or five participants. Other methods commonly involve eight to twelve participants. This method may be appropriate for exploring more intimate or sensitive subjects.

WHO INVENTED IT?

Robert K. Merton 1940 Bureau of Applied Social Research.

WHY USE THIS METHOD?

1. A focus group allows an in depth probe.
2. Interaction between participants can uncover broader insights.
3. They are cost effective for the volume and quality of data
4. Are less expensive than conducting 8 to 12 in depth interviews
5. Are time efficient
6. Clients can gain insights by observing the group interaction through a one way mirror.

CHALLENGES

1. Participants can influence each other.
2. Data is not quantifiable.
3. Responses are limited.
4. Data may be difficult to analyze
5. The participants are out of the context of their usual environments.

WHEN TO USE THIS METHOD

1. Know Context
2. Know User
3. Frame insights
4. Explore Concepts

HOW TO USE THIS METHOD

1. Focus groups often take one and a half to two hours.
2. Ask 5 to 10 questions.
3. Define purpose
4. Ask:
- Why a focus group?
- Who are the stakeholders?
- Who is the target population?
- What problems will be explored?
5. Define resources
6. Write question guide.
7. Recruit participants.
8. Conduct focus group.
9. Analyze data.
10. Create insights.
11. Take actions.

RESOURCES

1. Focus group space.
2. Sound and video recording equipment
3. White board
4. Pens
5. Post-it-notes

REFERENCES

1. Nachmais, Chava Frankfort; Nachmais, David. 2008. Research methods in the Social Sciences: Seventh Edition New York, NY: Worth Publishers

focus groups online

WHAT IS IT?
This is a focus group where the participants are involved from different locations via their computers.

WHO INVENTED IT?
Robert K. Merton 1940 Bureau of Applied Social Research.

WHY USE THIS METHOD?
1. A focus group allows an in depth probe.
2. Interaction between participants can uncover broader insights.
3. They are cost effective for the volume and quality of data
4. Are less expensive than conducting 8 to 12 in depth interviews
5. Are time efficient
6. Clients can gain insights by observing the group interaction through a one way mirror.

CHALLENGES
1. Participants can influence each other.
2. Data is not quantifiable.
3. Responses are limited.
4. Data may be difficult to analyze
5. The participants are out of the context of their usual environments.

WHEN TO USE THIS METHOD
1. Know Context
2. Know User
3. Frame insights
4. Explore Concepts

HOW TO USE THIS METHOD
1. Define purpose
2. Ask:
- Why a focus group?
- Who are the stakeholders?
- Who is the target population?
- What problems will be explored?
3. Define resources
4. Write question guide.
5. Recruit participants.
6. Conduct focus group.
7. Analyze data.
8. Create insights.
9. Take actions.

RESOURCES
1. Focus group space.
2. Sound and video recording equipment
3. White board
4. Pens
5. Post-it-notes

REFERENCES
1. Nachmais, Chava Frankfort; Nachmais, David. 2008. Research methods in the Social Sciences: Seventh Edition New York, NY: Worth Publishers

focus groups
other participant

WHAT IS IT?

One or more selected people participate as a group member or moderator in the discussion temporarily or for the full duration. This may be an expert such as the designer, writer, or some other specialist.

WHO INVENTED IT?

Robert K. Merton 1940 Bureau of Applied Social Research.

WHY USE THIS METHOD?

1. A focus group allows an in depth probe.
2. Interaction between participants can uncover broader insights.
3. They are cost effective for the volume and quality of data
4. Are less expensive than conducting 8 to 12 in depth interviews
5. Are time efficient
6. Clients can gain insights by observing the group interaction through a one way mirror.

CHALLENGES

1. Participants can influence each other.
2. Data is not quantifiable.
3. Responses are limited.
4. Data may be difficult to analyze
5. The participants are out of the context of their usual environments.

WHEN TO USE THIS METHOD

1. Know Context
2. Know User
3. Frame insights
4. Explore Concepts

HOW TO USE THIS METHOD

1. Focus groups often take one and a half to two hours.
2. Ask:
- Why a focus group?
- Who are the stakeholders?
- Who is the target population?
- What problems will be explored?
3. Define resources
4. Write question guide.
5. Recruit participants.
6. Conduct focus group.
7. Analyze data.
8. Create insights.
9. Take actions.

RESOURCES

1. Focus group space.
2. Sound and video recording equipment
3. White board
4. Pens
5. Post-it-notes

REFERENCES

1. Nachmais, Chava Frankfort; Nachmais, David. 2008. Research methods in the Social Sciences: Seventh Edition New York, NY: Worth Publishers

focus groups
respondent moderator

WHAT IS IT?

A respondent moderator focus group involves the participants and moderator exchanging roles. A diversity of viewpoints from a number of different moderators results in more honest diverse responses

WHO INVENTED IT?

Robert K. Merton 1940 Bureau of Applied Social Research.

WHY USE THIS METHOD?

1. A focus group allows an in depth probe.
2. Interaction between participants can uncover broader insights.
3. They are cost effective for the volume and quality of data
4. Are less expensive than conducting 8 to 12 in depth interviews
5. Are time efficient
6. Clients can gain insights by observing the group interaction through a one way mirror.

CHALLENGES

1. Participants can influence each other.
2. Data is not quantifiable.
3. Responses are limited.
4. Data may be difficult to analyze
5. The participants are out of the context of their usual environments.

WHEN TO USE THIS METHOD

1. Know Context
2. Know User
3. Frame insights
4. Explore Concepts

HOW TO USE THIS METHOD

1. Focus groups often take one and a half to two hours.
2. Ask 5 to 10 questions.
3. Define purpose
4. Ask:
- Why a focus group?
- Who are the stakeholders?
- Who is the target population?
- What problems will be explored?
5. Define resources
6. Write question guide.
7. Recruit participants.
8. Conduct focus group.
9. Analyze data.
10. Create insights.
11. Take actions.

RESOURCES

1. Focus group space.
2. Sound and video recording equipment
3. White board
4. Pens
5. Post-it-notes

REFERENCES

1. Nachmais, Chava Frankfort; Nachmais, David. 2008. Research methods in the Social Sciences: Seventh Edition New York, NY: Worth Publishers

focus groups
structured

WHAT IS IT?
With a structured focus group each question has a pre determined time for discussion and when this time is reached the moderator moves the group onto the next question for discussion.

WHO INVENTED IT?
Robert K. Merton 1940 Bureau of Applied Social Research.

WHY USE THIS METHOD?
1. A focus group allows an in depth probe.
2. Interaction between participants can uncover broader insights.
3. They are cost effective for the volume and quality of data
4. Are less expensive than conducting 8 to 12 in depth interviews
5. Are time efficient
6. Clients can gain insights by observing the group interaction through a one way mirror.

CHALLENGES
1. Participants can influence each other.
2. Data is not quantifiable.
3. Responses are limited.
4. Data may be difficult to analyze
5. The participants are out of the context of their usual environments.

WHEN TO USE THIS METHOD
1. Know Context
2. Know User
3. Frame insights
4. Explore Concepts

HOW TO USE THIS METHOD
1. Focus groups often take one and a half to two hours.
2. Ask:
- Why a focus group?
- Who are the stakeholders?
- Who is the target population?
- What problems will be explored?
3. Define resources
4. Write question guide.
5. Recruit participants.
6. Conduct focus group.
7. Analyze data.
8. Create insights.
9. Take actions.

RESOURCES
1. Focus group space.
2. Sound and video recording equipment
3. White board
4. Pens
5. Post-it-notes

REFERENCES
1. Nachmais, Chava Frankfort; Nachmais, David. 2008. Research methods in the Social Sciences: Seventh Edition New York, NY: Worth Publishers

focus groups
teleconference

WHAT IS IT?

This method involves conducting a focus group via teleconference. It allows participation at lower cost from diverse geographical locations.

WHY USE THIS METHOD?

1. A focus group allows an in depth probe.
2. Interaction between participants can uncover broader insights.
3. They are cost effective for the volume and quality of data
4. Are less expensive than conducting 8 to 12 in depth interviews
5. Are time efficient
6. Clients can gain insights by observing the group interaction through a one way mirror.

CHALLENGES

1. Participants cannot read each other's body language.
2. Participants can influence each other.
3. Data is not quantifiable.
4. Responses are limited.
5. Data may be difficult to analyze
6. The participants are out of the context of their usual environments.

WHEN TO USE THIS METHOD

1. Know Context
2. Know User
3. Frame insights
4. Explore Concepts

HOW TO USE THIS METHOD

1. Define purpose
2. Ask:
- Why a focus group?
- Who are the stakeholders?
- Who is the target population?
- What problems will be explored?
3. Define resources
4. Write question guide.
5. Recruit participants.
6. Conduct focus group.
7. Analyze data.
8. Create insights.
9. Take actions.

RESOURCES

1. Focus group space.
2. Sound and video recording equipment
3. White board
4. Pens
5. Post-it-notes

REFERENCES

1. Nachmais, Chava Frankfort; Nachmais, David. 2008. Research methods in the Social Sciences: Seventh Edition New York, NY: Worth Publishers

focus groups
two way

WHAT IS IT?

With this method there are two groups of participants. One group watches the other group's responses. The second group will have different discussions and conclusions based on the first group's responses.

WHO INVENTED IT?

Robert K. Merton 1940 Bureau of Applied Social Research.

WHY USE THIS METHOD?

1. A focus group allows an in depth probe.
2. Interaction between participants can uncover broader insights.
3. They are cost effective for the volume and quality of data
4. Are less expensive than conducting 8 to 12 in depth interviews
5. Are time efficient
6. Clients can gain insights by observing the group interaction through a one way mirror.

CHALLENGES

1. Participants can influence each other.
2. Data is not quantifiable.
3. Responses are limited.
4. Data may be difficult to analyze
5. The participants are out of the context of their usual environments.

WHEN TO USE THIS METHOD

1. Know Context
2. Know User
3. Frame insights
4. Explore Concepts

HOW TO USE THIS METHOD

1. Focus groups often take one and a half to two hours.
2. Ask 5 to 10 questions.
3. Define purpose
4. Ask:
- Why a focus group?
- Who are the stakeholders?
- Who is the target population?
- What problems will be explored?
5. Define resources
6. Write question guide.
7. Recruit participants.
8. Conduct focus group.
9. Analyze data.
10. Create insights.
11. Take actions.

RESOURCES

1. Focus group space.
2. Sound and video recording equipment
3. White board
4. Pens
5. Post-it-notes

REFERENCES

1. Nachmais, Chava Frankfort; Nachmais, David. 2008. Research methods in the Social Sciences: Seventh Edition New York, NY: Worth Publishers

focus groups
unstructured

WHAT IS IT?

An unstructured focus group has flexible moderation. The moderator allows conversations to go in different directions and may allow more time for discussion if required to explore topics.

WHO INVENTED IT?

Robert K. Merton 1940 Bureau of Applied Social Research.

WHY USE THIS METHOD?

1. A focus group allows an in depth probe.
2. Interaction between participants can uncover broader insights.
3. They are cost effective for the volume and quality of data
4. Are less expensive than conducting 8 to 12 in depth interviews
5. Are time efficient
6. Clients can gain insights by observing the group interaction through a one way mirror.

CHALLENGES

1. Participants can influence each other.
2. Data is not quantifiable.
3. Responses are limited.
4. Data may be difficult to analyze
5. The participants are out of the context of their usual environments.

WHEN TO USE THIS METHOD

1. Know Context
2. Know User
3. Frame insights
4. Explore Concepts

HOW TO USE THIS METHOD

1. Focus groups often take one and a half to two hours.
2. Ask:
- Why a focus group?
- Who are the stakeholders?
- Who is the target population?
- What problems will be explored?
3. Define resources
4. Write question guide.
5. Recruit participants.
6. Conduct focus group.
7. Analyze data.
8. Create insights.
9. Take actions.

RESOURCES

1. Focus group space.
2. Sound and video recording equipment
3. White board
4. Pens
5. Post-it-notes

REFERENCES

1. Nachmais, Chava Frankfort; Nachmais, David. 2008. Research methods in the Social Sciences: Seventh Edition New York, NY: Worth Publishers

focus troupe

WHAT IS IT?

The design team and users act out dramatic vignettes following scripts demonstrating a new product, service or experience. The play presents the problems, and expectations of the design. If actors have some experience of the product or service they can use this.

WHO INVENTED IT?

Sato and Salvador 1999

WHY USE THIS METHOD?

1. You are likely to find new possibilities and problems.
2. Generates empathy for users.
3. This method is an experiential design tool. Bodystorming helps design ideation by exploring context.
4. It is fast and inexpensive.
5. It is a form of physical prototyping
6. It is difficult to imagine misuse scenarios

CHALLENGES

1. Works best with a physical prototype of design.
2. Time is required to write scripts.
3. Some team members may find acting a difficult task.

WHEN TO USE THIS METHOD

1. Know Context
2. Know User
3. Frame insights

HOW TO USE THIS METHOD

1. Select team.
2. Define the locations where a design will be used.
3. Go to those locations and observe how people interact. the artifacts in their environment.
4. Develop the prototypes and props that you need to explore an idea. Identify the people, personas and scenarios that may help you with insight into the design directions.
5. Write scripts
6. Bodystorm the scenarios.
7. Record the scenarios with video and analyze them for insights.

RESOURCES

1. Empathy tools
2. A large room
3. White board
4. Video camera

REFERENCES

1. Understanding Your Users: A Practical Guide to User Requirements Methods By Catherine Courage, Kathy Baxter, Catherine Courage

FREE LIST

Name of List ....
Prepared for ....
Date ....

Number	Name	Category	Use	Status	Checklist
1					
2					
3					
4					
5					
6					
7					
8					
9					
10					

Signature ....

free list

WHAT IS IT?

A free list is a list all words and concepts related to a particular area that is created by a participant. Because free lists are used to understand group culture frequency is important.

WHO INVENTED IT?

Trotter & Schensul 1998

WHY USE THIS METHOD?

1. Uncovers common perceptions meanings and classification systems
2. Low- cost
3. Little training required
4. Good source for baseline data
5. Works with individuals and groups
6. It is simple.
7. Can be used to compare different groups.
8. Can be used with brainstorming.
9. Helps researchers from using appropriate terms.
10. This method can be used when you have limited time with a group.

CHALLENGES

1. Not a stand alone method
2. Danger of making false associations
3. No accepted ways to check reliability of the procedure.

WHEN TO USE THIS METHOD

1. Know Context
2. Know User
3. Frame insights

HOW TO USE THIS METHOD

1. Consider what information would be valuable
2. Decide which domains you would like to define.
3. Formulate the question.
4. Test your question on several people to ensure the wording is coherent and appropriate.
5. Develop a short set of instructions.
6. Ask the free listing question.
7. It may be necessary to probe your informant for a more comprehensive list.
8. Ask informants to clarify items.
9. Collect data from multiple participants
10. Tally items to calculate the response frequency.
11. Combine the data collected through free listing with other methods to enrich your understanding.

RESOURCES

1. Pens
2. Laptop
3. Paper
4. Note pad.

REFERENCES

1. Weller, S.C. & Romney, A.K. (1988). Systematic Data Collection, Thousand Oaks, CA: Sage.

generative research

WHAT IS IT?

Generative research is research where participants make things to help express their ideas. Generative research can include methods from workshops where participants articulate their ideas by creating models using construction kits to diary methods.

WHO INVENTED IT?

Liz Sanders has been a pioneer of some generative methods.

WHY USE THIS METHOD?

1. Insights come from creative play.
2. Non designers can express their ideas creatively using generative tools.

CHALLENGES

1. Interpretation can be subjective.

WHEN TO USE THIS METHOD

1. Know Context
2. Know User
3. Frame insights

SEE ALSO

1. Diary studies
2. Creative toolkits
3. Photo diaries

RESOURCES

1. Construction kits
2. Diaries
3. White board
4. Pens
5. Creative space

REFERENCES

1. Sanders, E.B.-N. (2001) Virtuosos of the experience domain. In Proceedings of the 2001 IDSA Education Conference.

guerilla ethnography

WHAT IS IT?

Guerrilla ethnography is a collection of low cost responsive and flexible creative research methods. Examples include man on the street interviews, rapid iterative prototypes. remote usability testing. and empathy maps.

WHO INVENTED IT?

Jay Conrad Levinson 1984

WHY USE THIS METHOD?

1. Guerrilla methods are fast,
2. Guerrilla methods are less expensive.
3. Provide direction and data rather than opinions and speculation.
4. Uncover how people think and behave.
5. Provides sufficient insight to make more informed design decisions and guide design decisions.

CHALLENGES

1. Sometime the information gathered is more like a compass for design decisions rather than a road map.

WHEN TO USE THIS METHOD

1. Know Context
2. Know User
3. Frame insights

HOW TO USE THIS METHOD

1. Start by defining an activity, context, and time frame to focus on.
2. Create a plan.
3. Recruit from online sources like Facebook, Mechanical Turk, Ethnio, Craigslist, Twitter, or friends and family.
4. Observe real people in real-life situations
5. Capture Data
6. Reflection and Analysis
7. Brainstorming for solutions
8. Develop prototypes of possible solutions
9. Evaluate and refine the prototypes. Test several iterative refinements.
10. Ask for them to show and tell
11. Listen for pain points and seek opportunities.
12. Don't lead the user to the "right" path
13. Allow for exploration and discovery
14. Make simple prototypes of your favored designs. Only build what you need. No more.

RESOURCES

1. Digital camera
2. Notebook
3. Pens
4. Video camera

hawthorne effect

WHAT IS IT?

The Hawthorne effect is a psychological theory that the behavior of a person or a group of people will change if they know that they are being observed.

WHO INVENTED IT?

First documented by a research team led by Elton Mayo between 1924 and 1932 at the Western Electric Company Hawthorne plant in Cicero, Illinois. The term was first used by Elton Mayo and Fritz Roethlisberger around 1950.

WHY USE THIS METHOD?

1. Researchers should be aware of the effect to obtain valid results.

CHALLENGES

1. Various writers believe that the original observations and conclusions were overstated including Steven Levitt, John A. List, Adair and H. McIlvaine Parsons

WHEN TO USE THIS METHOD

1. Know Context
2. Know User
3. Frame insights

HOW TO USE THIS METHOD

1. If you conduct a taste test of two beverages and tell the participants who makes the beverages before the test it may influence which beverage that the participants say they prefer.
2. It you tell some participants that they are taking an appetite suppressant then they may eat less even if they are not taking an appetite suppressant.

REFERENCES

1. French, John R. P., "Experiments in Field Settings," in Leon Festinger and Daniel Katz(Eds.), Research Methods in the Behavorial Sciences, Dryden Press, 1953, p. 101.
2. Levitt, Steven D. & List, John A. (2011). "Was There Really a Hawthorne Effect at the Hawthorne Plant? An Analysis of the Original Illumination Experiments". American Economic Journal: Applied Economics 3 (1): 224–238.

historical method

WHAT IS IT?

Compare something today with something in history. Research the development of a product, service or experience.
Some areas of interest for designers are:
1. An understanding of the origin of an idea.
2. Knowledge of the author of an idea.
3. Local differences

WHO INVENTED IT?

Herodotus 5th century BC, was one of the earliest historians.

WHY USE THIS METHOD?

1. A review of history often uncovers insights relevant to a current design project.
2. Good ideas are sometimes forgotten and need to be rediscovered.
3. We want to avoid revisiting old but unsuccessful solutions

CHALLENGES

1. All constructed histories are written with a viewpoint or bias.
2. Choose sources that have no apparent benefit from presenting a biased account of events.

RESOURCES

1. Primary and secondary historical sources
2. Digital voice recorder
3. Post-it-notes

WHEN TO USE THIS METHOD

1. Know Context
2. Know User
3. Frame insights
4. Explore Concepts

HOW TO USE THIS METHOD

1. Define your subject of research.
2. Find out what secondary sources exist.
3. Create a research plan.
4. Create a goal for your research.
5. Make a list of necessary equipment, people, and materials.
6. Define a schedule for the research.
7. Plan tasks deliverable and milestones with dates.
8. Explore primary Sources.
9. Conduct primary source research.
10. Compile a list of citations.
11. Write the history.
12. Archive the data.

REFERENCES

1. Gilbert J. Garraghan, A Guide to Historical Method, Fordham University Press: New York (1946). ISBN 0-8371-7132-6
2. Martha Howell and Walter Prevenier, From Reliable Sources: An Introduction to Historical Methods, Cornell University Press: Ithaca (2001). ISBN 0-8014-8560-6.
3. R. J. Shafer, A Guide to Historical Method, The Dorsey Press: Illinois (1974). ISBN 0-534-10825-3.

heuristic evaluation

WHAT IS IT?

Also known as expert evaluation.
A technique used to identify user problems.
Experts judge whether a user interface follows a list of established usability heuristics

WHO INVENTED IT?

Jacob Nielsen, 1990 Denmark

WHY USE THIS METHOD?

1. Inexpensive and fast.
2. Can be used early in the design process.
3. Fast feedback.
4. Reliable data.
5. Apply this method before testing prototypes with users.

CHALLENGES

1. Focuses on problems
2. Use before research subjects are studied for further testing.
3. This method will not uncover all problems.

WHEN TO USE THIS METHOD

1. Know Context
2. Know User
3. Frame insights
4. Explore Concepts

HOW TO USE THIS METHOD

1. Establish a panel of experts.
2. Establish an agreed set of evaluative criteria.
3. Brief experts and agree on criteria for the evaluation.
4. Each expert inspects the interface alone.
5. After the evaluations the individual results are aggregated.
6. A report is prepared which identifies a prioritized list of problems with the interface.
7. Action the findings of evaluation

RESOURCES

1. A panel of experts
2. A list of heuristic criteria for evaluation.

REFERENCES

1. Nielsen, J., and Molich, R. (1990). Heuristic evaluation of user interfaces, Proc. ACM CHI'90 Conf. (Seattle, WA, 1–5 April), 249-256
2. Nielsen, J. (1994). Heuristic evaluation. In Nielsen, J., and Mack, R.L. (Eds.), Usability Inspection Methods, John Wiley & Sons, New York, NY

idiographic approach

WHAT IS IT?

This method is an intense study of a person emphasizing that person's uniqueness. This differs from research that concentrates on common or repeated forms of behavior

WHO INVENTED IT?

Piaget 1953

WHY USE THIS METHOD?

1. May provide a more in depth understanding of an individual.

CHALLENGES

1. Difficult to generalize findings
2. Freud and Paiget created universal theories on the basis of unrepresentative individuals.

WHEN TO USE THIS METHOD

1. Know Context
2. Know User
3. Frame insights

HOW TO USE THIS METHOD

1. Use case studies
2. Use flexible long term procedures.

RESOURCES

1. Video camera
2. Camera
3. Digital voice recorder
4. Note pad
5. Pens

REFERENCES

1. Cone, J. D. (1986). Idiographic, nomothetic, and related perspectives in behavioral assessment. In R. O. Nelson & S. C. Hayes (Eds.): Conceptual foundations of behavioral assessment (pp. 111–128). New York: Guilford.

cultural immersion

WHAT IS IT?

The design team spends a period of time exploring a location or environment to gain a deeper understanding of the design context.

WHY USE THIS METHOD?

1. To gain a deeper understanding of the design context
2. To gain empathy

RESOURCES

1. Note book
2. Digital camera
3. Video Camera
4. Digital Voice recorder

WHEN TO USE THIS METHOD

1. Define intent
2. Know Context
3. Know User
4. Frame insights

HOW TO USE THIS METHOD

Activities may involve

1. Interviews
2. Photography
3. Observations
4. Video
5. Note taking
6. Sketching
7. Recordings
8. Collecting objects.

172

innovation diagnostic

WHAT IS IT?

An innovation diagnostic is an evaluation of an organization's innovation capabilities. It reviews practices by stakeholders which may help or hinder innovation. An innovation diagnostic is the first step in preparing an implementing a strategy to create an organizational culture that supports innovation.

WHY USE THIS METHOD?

1. It helps organizations develop sustainable competitive advantage.
2. Helps identify innovation opportunities
3. Helps develop innovation strategy.

WHEN TO USE THIS METHOD

1. Know Context
2. Know User
3. Frame insights
4. Explore Concepts
5. Make Plans

HOW TO USE THIS METHOD

An innovation diagnostic reviews organizational and stakeholder practices using both qualitative and quantitative methods including

1. The design and development process
2. Strategic practices and planning.
3. The ability of an organization to monitor and respond to relevant trends.
4. Technologies
5. Organizational flexibility
6. Ability to innovate repeatedly and consistently

interview methods

WHAT IS IT?

An interview is a conversation where questions are asked to obtain information.

WHY USE THIS METHOD?

Contextual interviews uncover tacit knowledge about people's context that the people may not be consciously aware of. The information gathered can be detailed.

CHALLENGES

1. Keep control
2. Be prepared
3. Be aware of bias
4. Be neutral
5. Select location carefully

RESOURCES

6. Note pad
7. Confidentiality agreement
8. Digital voice recorder
9. Video camera
10. Digital still camera

WHEN TO USE THIS METHOD

1. Know Context
2. Know User
3. Frame insights

HOW TO USE THIS METHOD

1. Contextual inquiry may be structured as 2 hour one on one interviews.
2. The researcher does not usually impose tasks on the user.
3. Go to the user's context. Talk, watch listen and observe.
4. Understand likes and dislikes.
5. Collect stories and insights.
6. See the world from the user's point of view.
7. Take permission to conduct interviews.
8. Do one-on-one interviews.
9. The researcher listens to the user.
10. 2 to 3 researchers conduct an interview.
11. Understand relationship between people, product and context.
12. Document with video, audio and notes.

RESOURCES

1. Computer
2. Notebook
3. Pens
4. Video camera
5. Release forms
6. Interview plan or structure
7. Questions, tasks and discussion items
8. Confidentiality agreement

REFERENCES

1. Kvale, Steinar. Interviews: An Introduction to Qualitative Research Interviewing, Sage Publications, 1996
2. Foddy, William. Constructing Questions for Interviews, Cambridge University Press, 1993

interviews
contextual inquiry

WHAT IS IT?
Contextual inquiry involves one-on-one observations and interviews of activities in the context. Contextual inquiry has four guiding principles:
1. Context
2. Partnership with users.
3. Interpretation
4. Focus on particular goals.

WHO INVENTED IT?
Whiteside, Bennet, and Holtzblatt 1988

WHY USE THIS METHOD?
1. Contextual interviews uncover tacit knowledge about people's context.
2. The information gathered can be detailed.
3. The information produced by contextual inquiry is relatively reliable

CHALLENGES
1. End users may not have the answers
2. Contextual inquiry may be difficult to challenge even if it is misleading.

SEE ALSO
1. Questionnaire
2. Interview
3. Affinity diagram
4. Scenario
5. Persona
6. Ethnography
7. Contextual design

WHEN TO USE THIS METHOD
1. Know Context
2. Know User
3. Frame insights

HOW TO USE THIS METHOD
1. Contextual inquiry may be structured as 2 hour one on one interviews.
2. The researcher does not usually impose tasks on the user.
3. Go to the user's context. Talk, watch listen and observe.
4. Understand likes and dislikes.
5. Collect stories and insights.
6. See the world from the user's point of view.
7. Take permission to conduct interviews.
8. Do one-on-one interviews.
9. The researcher listens to the user.
10. 2 to 3 researchers conduct an interview.
11. Understand relationship between people, product and context.
12. Document with video, audio and notes.

REFERENCES
1. Beyer, H. and Holtzblatt, K., Contextual Design: Defining Customer-Centered Systems, Morgan Kaufmann Publishers Inc., San Francisco (1997).
2. Wixon and J. Ramey (Eds.), Field Methods Case Book for Product Design. John Wiley & Sons, Inc., NY, NY, 1996.

interviews
contextual interviews

WHAT IS IT?

A contextual interview is conducted with people in their own environment. Contextual interviews with users can be conducted in environments such as homes, offices, trains, hospitals or factories. People and researchers collaborate to understand the context.

WHO INVENTED IT?

Whiteside, Bennet, and Holtzblatt 1988

WHY USE THIS METHOD?

Contextual interviews uncover tacit knowledge about people's context that the people may not be consciously aware of. The information gathered can be detailed.

CHALLENGES

1. Keep control
2. Be prepared
3. Be aware of bias
4. Be neutral
5. Select location carefully

WHEN TO USE THIS METHOD

1. Know Context
2. Know User
3. Frame insights

HOW TO USE THIS METHOD

Contextual inquiry is often structured as 2 hour one on one interviews. The researcher does not usually impose tasks on the user. The researcher listens to the user. A contextual interview has three phases:

1. The introduction. The researcher gives information about the length of the interview, content, confidentiality and method of recording.
2. The body of the interview. The researcher investigates the user in context and documents the information gathered.
3. Wrap up. The researcher goes through the data gathered for verification and clarification by the person being interviewed.

RESOURCES

1. Computer
2. Notebook
3. Pens
4. Video camera
5. Release forms
6. Interview plan or structure
7. Questions, tasks and discussion items
8. Confidentiality agreement

REFERENCES

1. Rubin, Herbert and Irene Rubin. Qualitative Interviewing: The Art of Hearing Data. 2nd edition. Thousand Oaks, CA: Sage Publications, 2004. Print.

interviews
contextual laddering

WHAT IS IT?

Contextual laddering is a one-on-one interviewing technique done in context. Answers are further explored by the researcher to uncover root causes or core values.

WHO INVENTED IT?

Gutman 1982, Olsen and Reynolds 2001.

WHY USE THIS METHOD?

1. Laddering can uncover underlying reasons for particular behaviors.
2. Laddering may uncover information not revealed by other methods.
3. Complement other methods
4. Link features and product attributes with user/customer values

CHALLENGES

1. Analysis of data is sometimes difficult.
2. Requires a skilled interviewer who can keep the participants engaged.
3. Laddering can be an unpleasant experience for participants because of it's repetitive nature.
4. Sometimes information may not be represented hierarchically.

WHEN TO USE THIS METHOD

1. Know Context
2. Know User
3. Frame insights
4. Explore Concepts

HOW TO USE THIS METHOD

1. Interviews typically take 60 to 90 minutes.
2. The introduction. The researcher gives information about the length of the interview, content, confidentiality and method of recording.
3. The body of the interview. The researcher investigates the user in context and documents the information gathered.
4. Ask participants to describe what kinds of features would be useful in or distinguish different products.
5. Ask why.
6. If this answer doesn't describe the root motivation ask why again.
7. Repeat step 3. until you have reached the root motivation.
8. Wrap up. Verification and clarification

RESOURCES

1. Note pad
2. Confidentiality agreement
3. Digital voice recorder
4. Video camera
5. Digital still camera
6. Interview plan or structure
7. Questions, tasks and discussion items

interviews
conversation cards

WHAT IS IT?
Cards used for initiating conversation in a contextual interview and to help subjects explore.

WHO INVENTED IT?
Originator unknown. Google Ngram indicates the term first appeared around 1801 in England for a collection of "Moral and Religious Anecdotes particularly adapted for the entertainment and instruction of young persons, and to support instead of destroying serious conversation"

WHY USE THIS METHOD?
1. Questions are the springboard for conversations.
2. Can be used to initiate sensitive conversations.

CHALLENGES
1. How will data from the cards be used?
2. How will cards be evaluated?
3. How many cards are necessary to be representative?
4. What are potential problems relating card engagement
5. Use one unit of information per question.

WHEN TO USE THIS METHOD
1. Know Context
2. Know User
3. Frame insights

HOW TO USE THIS METHOD
1. Decide on goal for research.
2. Formulate about 10 questions related to topic
3. Create the cards.
4. Recruit the subjects.
5. Undertake pre interview with sample subject to test.
6. Use release form if required.
7. Carry light equipment.
8. Record answers verbatim.
9. Communicate the purpose and length of the interview.
10. Select location. It should not be too noisy or have other distracting influences
11. Work through the cards.
12. Video or record the sessions for later review.
13. Analyze
14. Create Insights

RESOURCES
1. Conversation Cards.
2. Notebook
3. Video Camera
4. Pens
5. Interview plan or structure
6. Questions, tasks and discussion items

REFERENCES
1. Kvale, Steinar. Interviews: An Introduction to Qualitative Research Interviewing, Sage Publications, 1996

interviews
emotion cards

WHAT IS IT?

Emotion cards are a field method of analyzing and quantifying peoples emotional response to a design. The method classifies emotions into sets of emotions which each can be associated with a specific recognizable facial expression.

The emotion card tool consists of sixteen cartoon-like faces, half male and half female, each representing distinct emotions. Each face
represents a combination of two emotion dimensions,Pleasure and Arousal. Based on these dimensions, the emotion cards can be divided into four quadrants: Calm-Pleasant, Calm-Unpleasant, Excited-Pleasant, and Excited-Unpleasant.

WHO INVENTED IT?

Bradley 1994
Pieter Desmet 2001

WHY USE THIS METHOD?

1. It is an inexpensive method.
2. The results are easy to analyze.
3. Emotion cards is a cross-cultural tool.
4. Facial emotions are typically universally recognized

CHALLENGES

1. Emotions of male and female faces are interpreted differently.
2. Sometimes users want to mark more than one picture to express a more complex emotional response.

WHEN TO USE THIS METHOD

1. Know Context
2. Know User
3. Frame insights
4. Explore Concepts

HOW TO USE THIS METHOD

1. Decide the goal of the study.
2. Recruit the participants.
3. Brief the participants.
4. When each interaction is complete the researcher asks the participant to select one of a number of cards that shows facial expressions that they associate with the interaction.

RESOURCES

1. Emotion cards
2. Notebook
3. Pens
4. Video camera
5. Release forms
6. Interview plan or structure
7. Questions, tasks and discussion items

REFERENCES

1. Bradley and Lang. Measuring emotion: the Self-Assessment Manikin and the Semantic Differential. Journal of Behavior Therapy and Experimental Psychiatry, 25, 1 (1994).
2. Desmet, P.M.A. Emotion through expression;designing mobile telephones with an emotional fit. Report of Modeling the Evaluation Structure of KANSEI, 3 (2000), 103-110.

179

interviews
e-mail

WHAT IS IT?
With this method an interview is conducted via an e-mail exchange.

WHY USE THIS METHOD?
1. Extended access to people.
2. Background noises are not recorded.
3. Interviewee can answer the questions at his or her own convenience
4. It is not necessary to take notes
5. It is possible to use online translators.
6. Interviewees do not have to identify a convenient time to talk.

CHALLENGES
1. Interviewer may have to wait for answers.
2. Interviewer is disconnected from context.
3. Lack of communication of body language.

WHEN TO USE THIS METHOD
1. Know Context
2. Know User
3. Frame insight

HOW TO USE THIS METHOD
1. Choose a topic
2. Identify a subject.
3. Contact subject and obtain approval.
4. Prepare interview questions.
5. Conduct interview
6. Analyze data.

RESOURCES
1. Computer
2. Internet connection
3. Notebook
4. Pens
5. Interview plan or structure
6. Questions, tasks and discussion items
7. Confidentiality agreement

REFERENCES
1. Foddy, William. Constructing Questions for Interviews, Cambridge University Press, 1993

interviews
extreme user

WHAT IS IT?

Interview experienced or inexperienced users of a product or service. in order to discover useful insights that can be applied to the general users.

WHY USE THIS METHOD?

Extreme user's solutions to problems can inspire solutions for general users. Their behavior can be more exaggerated than general users so it is sometimes easier to develop useful insights from these groups.

CHALLENGES

1. Keep control
2. Be prepared
3. Be aware of bias
4. Be neutral
5. Select location carefully

WHEN TO USE THIS METHOD

1. Know Context
2. Know User
3. Frame insights
4. Explore Concepts

HOW TO USE THIS METHOD

1. Do a timeline of your activity and break it into main activities
2. Identify very experienced or very inexperienced users of a product or service in an activity area.
3. Explore their experiences through interview.
4. Discover insights that can inspire design.
5. Refine design based on insights.

RESOURCES

1. Computer
2. Notebook
3. Pens
4. Video camera
5. Release forms
6. Interview plan or structure
7. Questions, tasks and discussion items
8. Confidentiality agreement

REFERENCES

1. Rubin, Herbert and Irene Rubin. Qualitative Interviewing: The Art of Hearing Data. 2nd edition. Thousand Oaks, CA: Sage Publications, 2004. Print.
2. Kvale, Steinar. Interviews: An Introduction to Qualitative Research Interviewing, Sage Publications, 1996
3. Foddy, William. Constructing Questions for Interviews, Cambridge University Press, 1993

interviews group

WHAT IS IT?

This method involves interviewing a group of people.

WHY USE THIS METHOD?

People will often give different answers to questions if interviewed one-on-one and in groups. If resources are available it is useful to interview people in both situations.

CHALLENGES

1. Group interview process is longer than an individual interview

WHEN TO USE THIS METHOD

1. Know Context
2. Know User
3. Frame insight

RESOURCES

1. Computer
2. Notebook
3. Pens
4. Video camera
5. Release forms
6. Interview plan or structure
7. Questions, tasks and discussion items
8. Confidentiality agreement

HOW TO USE THIS METHOD

1. Welcome everyone and introduce yourself
2. Describe the process.
3. Ask everyone to introduce themselves.
4. Conduct a group activity or warming-up exercise.
5. Break the larger group into smaller groups of 4 or 5 people and give them a question to answer. Ask each participant to present their response to the larger group.
6. Allow about 25 minutes.
7. Ask each interviewee to write a summary
8. Collect the summaries.
9. Ask if have any further comments.
10. Thank everyone and explain the next steps.
11. Give them your contact details.

REFERENCES

12. Kvale, Steinar. Interviews: An Introduction to Qualitative Research Interviewing, Sage Publications, 1996
13. Foddy, William. Constructing Questions for Interviews, Cambridge University Press, 1993

interviews
guided storytelling

WHAT IS IT?

Also called directed storytelling.
Guided storytelling is interview technique,
where the designer asks a participant to walk
you through a scenario of use for a concept.
Directed story telling guides participants to
describe their experiences and thoughts on a
specific topic.

WHO INVENTED IT?

Whiteside, Bennet, and Holtzblatt 1988

WHY USE THIS METHOD?

1. Guided storytelling uncovers tacit
   knowledge.

CHALLENGES

1. Keep control
2. Be prepared
3. Be aware of bias
4. Be neutral
5. Select location carefully

WHEN TO USE THIS METHOD

1. Know Context
2. Know User
3. Frame insight

RESOURCES

1. Computer
2. Notebook
3. Pens
4. Video camera
5. Release forms
6. Interview plan or structure
7. Confidentiality agreement

HOW TO USE THIS METHOD

1. Contextual inquiry may be structured
   as 2 hour one on one interviews.
2. The researcher does not usually impose
   tasks on the user.
3. Go to the user's context. Talk, watch
   listen and observe.
4. Understand likes and dislikes.
5. Collect stories and insights.
6. See the world from the user's point of
   view.
7. Take permission to conduct interviews.
8. Do one-on-one interviews.
9. The researcher listens to the user.
10. 2 to 3 researchers conduct an interview.
11. Understand relationship between
    people, product and context.

REFERENCES

1. Rubin, Herbert and Irene Rubin.
   Qualitative Interviewing: The Art of
   Hearing Data. 2nd edition. Thousand
   Oaks, CA: Sage Publications, 2004.
   Print.
2. Kvale, Steinar. Interviews: An
   Introduction to Qualitative Research
   Interviewing, Sage Publications, 1996
3. Foddy, William. Constructing Questions
   for Interviews, Cambridge University
   Press, 1993

interviews
man in the street

WHAT IS IT?

Man in the street interviews are impromptu interviews usually recorded on video. They are usually conducted by two people, a researcher and a cameraman.

WHY USE THIS METHOD?

1. Contextual interviews uncover tacit knowledge.
2. The information gathered can be detailed.

CHALLENGES

1. Keep control
2. Be prepared
3. Be aware of bias
4. Be neutral
5. Ask appropriate questions
6. Select location carefully
7. Create a friendly atmosphere, interviewee to feel relaxed.
8. Clearly convey the purpose of the interview.
9. This method results in accidental sampling which may not be representative of larger groups.

WHEN TO USE THIS METHOD

1. Know Context
2. Know User
3. Frame insights

HOW TO USE THIS METHOD

1. Decide on goal for research.
2. Formulate about 10 questions related to topic
3. Use release form if required.
4. Conduct a preliminary interview.
5. Select location. It should not be too noisy or have other distracting influences
6. Approach people, be polite. Say, "Excuse me, I work for [your organization] and I was wondering if you could share your opinion about [your topic]."
7. If someone does not wish to respond, select another subject to interview.
8. Limit your time. Each interview should be no be longer than about 10 minutes.
9. Conduct 6 to 10 interviews

RESOURCES

1. Video camera
2. release forms

REFERENCES

1. Rubin, Herbert and Irene Rubin. Qualitative Interviewing: The Art of Hearing Data. 2nd edition. Thousand Oaks, CA: Sage Publications, 2004. Print.
2. Kvale, Steinar. Interviews: An Introduction to Qualitative Research Interviewing, Sage Publications, 1996

interviews
naturalistic group

WHAT IS IT?

Naturalistic group interview is an interview method where the participants know each other prior to the interview and so have conversations that are more natural than participants who do not know each other.

WHY USE THIS METHOD?

1. This method has been applied in research in Asia where beliefs are informed by group interaction.
2. Can help gain useful data in cultures where people are less willing to share their feelings.

CHALLENGES

1. Familiarity of participants can lead to groupthink.

WHEN TO USE THIS METHOD

2. Know Context
3. Know User

HOW TO USE THIS METHOD

1. The interview context should support natural conversation.
2. Select participants who have existing social relationships.
3. Group the participants in natural ways so that the conversation is as close as possible to the type of discussion they would have in their everyday life.
4. Groups should be no larger than four people for best results.

RESOURCES

1. Video camera
2. Note pad
3. Pens
4. Use local moderator

REFERENCES

1. Bengtsson, Anders, and Giana M. Eckhardt. "Naturalistic Group Interviewing in China." Qualitative Market Research: An International Journal. 12:1 (2010): 36-44.

interviews
one-on-one

WHAT IS IT?

The one-on-one interview is an interview that is between a researcher and one participant in a face-to-face situation.

WHY USE THIS METHOD?

1. The best method for personal information
2. Works well with other methods in obtaining information to inform design.
3. Can be used to exchange ideas or to gather information to inform design

CHALLENGES

1. Keep control
2. Be prepared
3. Be aware of bias
4. Be neutral
5. Select location carefully
6. Record everything
7. Combine one on one interviews with group interviews.

WHEN TO USE THIS METHOD

1. Know Context
2. Know User
3. Frame insights

RESOURCES

4. Notebook
5. Pens
6. Video camera
7. Release forms
8. Interview plan
9. Questions, and tasks

HOW TO USE THIS METHOD

1. May be structured as 2 hour one on one interviews.
2. Select the questions and the subjects carefully.
3. Create interview guide,
4. Conduct a preinterview to refine the guide.
5. The researcher does not usually impose tasks on the user.
6. Go to the user's context. Talk, watch listen and observe.
7. Understand likes and dislikes.
8. Collect stories and insights.
9. See the world from the user's point of view.
10. Take permission to conduct interviews.
11. Understand relationship between person, product and context.
12. Document with video, audio and notes.

REFERENCES

1. Rubin, Herbert and Irene Rubin. Qualitative Interviewing: The Art of Hearing Data. 2nd edition. Thousand Oaks, CA: Sage Publications, 2004. Print.
2. Kvale, Steinar. Interviews: An Introduction to Qualitative Research Interviewing, Sage Publications, 1996
3. Foddy, William. Constructing Questions for Interviews, Cambridge University Press, 1993

interviews
photo elicitation

WHAT IS IT?

Photos are used by a researcher as a focus to discuss the experiences, thoughts and feelings of participants.

WHY USE THIS METHOD?

1. A method sometimes used to interview children.
2. Photos can make staring a conversation with a participant easier.
3. Photos can uncover meaning which is not uncovered in a face to face interview.

CHALLENGES

1. Photos can create ethical questions for the researcher.
2. A researcher may show bias in selecting subject of photos.

RESOURCES

1. Note pad
2. Pens
3. Camera
4. Video camera
5. Digital voice recorder

WHEN TO USE THIS METHOD

1. Know Context
2. Know User

HOW TO USE THIS METHOD

1. Define the context.
2. Select the participants
3. Either researcher or participant may take the photos.
4. Researcher analyses photos and plans the interview process
5. Researcher shows the photos to the participant and discusses their thoughts in relation to the photographs.
6. The interview is analyzed by the researcher.
7. The researcher creates a list of insights.

REFERENCES

1. M. Clark-Ibáñez. Framing the social world with photo-elicitation interviews. American Behavioral Scientist,47(12):1507--1527, 2004.

interviews
structured

WHAT IS IT?

In a structured interview the researcher prepares a list of questions, script or an interview guide that they follow during the interview. Most interviews use a structured method.

WHY USE THIS METHOD?

1. A structured interview is often used for phone interviews.
2. It is easy to analyze the results.
3. Structured interviews are often used by quantitative researchers.

CHALLENGES

1. Respondents may be less likely to discuss sensitive experiences.

WHEN TO USE THIS METHOD

1. Know Context
2. Know User
3. Frame insight

HOW TO USE THIS METHOD

1. The researcher should follow the script exactly.
2. The interviewer is required to show consistency in behavior across all interviews

RESOURCES

1. Computer
2. Notebook
3. Pens
4. Video camera
5. Release forms
6. Interview plan
7. Questions, and tasks
8. Confidentiality agreement

REFERENCES

1. Rubin, Herbert and Irene Rubin. Qualitative Interviewing: The Art of Hearing Data. 2nd edition. Thousand Oaks, CA: Sage Publications, 2004. Print.
2. Kvale, Steinar. Interviews: An Introduction to Qualitative Research Interviewing, Sage Publications, 1996
3. Foddy, William. Constructing Questions for Interviews, Cambridge University Press, 1993

interviews
unstructured

WHAT IS IT?

Unstructured interviews are interviews where questions can be modified as needed by the researcher during the interview.

WHY USE THIS METHOD?

1. A useful technique for understanding how a subject may perform under pressure.
2. Unstructured interviews are used in ethnographies and case studies
3. Respondents may be more likely to discuss sensitive experiences.

CHALLENGES

1. Interviewer bias is unavoidable

WHEN TO USE THIS METHOD

1. Know Context
2. Know User
3. Frame insight

HOW TO USE THIS METHOD

1. Researchers need a list of topics to be covered during the interview

RESOURCES

1. Computer
2. Notebook
3. Pens
4. Video camera
5. Release forms
6. Interview plan
7. Questions, and tasks
8. Confidentiality agreement

REFERENCES

1. Rubin, Herbert and Irene Rubin. Qualitative Interviewing: The Art of Hearing Data. 2nd edition. Thousand Oaks, CA: Sage Publications, 2004. Print.
2. Kvale, Steinar. Interviews: An Introduction to Qualitative Research Interviewing, Sage Publications, 1996
3. Foddy, William. Constructing Questions for Interviews, Cambridge University Press, 1993

interviews telephone

WHAT IS IT?

With this method an interview is conducted via telephone.

WHY USE THIS METHOD?

1. Wide geographical access
2. Allows researcher to reach hard to reach people.
3. Allows researcher to access closed locations.
4. Access to dangerous or politically sensitive sites

CHALLENGES

1. Lack of communication of body language.
2. Interviewer is disconnected from context.

WHEN TO USE THIS METHOD

1. Know Context
2. Know User
3. Frame insight

HOW TO USE THIS METHOD

1. Choose a topic
2. Identify a subject.
3. Contact subject and obtain approval.
4. Prepare interview questions.
5. Conduct interview
6. Analyze data.

RESOURCES

7. Computer
8. Notebook
9. Pens

REFERENCES

1. Rubin, Herbert and Irene Rubin. Qualitative Interviewing: The Art of Hearing Data. 2nd edition. Thousand Oaks, CA: Sage Publications, 2004. Print.
2. Kvale, Steinar. Interviews: An Introduction to Qualitative Research Interviewing, Sage Publications, 1996
3. Foddy, William. Constructing Questions for Interviews, Cambridge University Press, 1993

mobile diary study

WHAT IS IT?

A mobile diary studies is a method that uses portable devices to capture a person's experiences in context when and where they happen such as their work place or home. Participants can create diary entries from their location on mobile phones or tablets.

WHY USE THIS METHOD?

1. Most people carry a mobile phone.
2. It is a convenient method of recording diary entries.
3. It is easier to collect the data than collecting written diaries.
4. Collection of data happens in real time.
5. Mobile devices have camera, voice and written capability.

CHALLENGES

1. Can miss non verbal feedback.
2. Technology may be unreliable

WHEN TO USE THIS METHOD

1. Know Context
2. Know User
3. Frame insights

HOW TO USE THIS METHOD

1. Define intent
2. Define audience
3. Define context
4. Define technology
5. Automated text messages are sent to participants to prompt an entry.
6. Analyze data

RESOURCES

1. Smart phones,
2. Cameras,
3. Laptops and
4. Tablets

REFERENCES

1. Coover, R. (2004) 'Using Digital Media Tools and Cross-Cultural Research,Analysis and Representation', Visual Studies19(1): 6–25.
2. Dicks, B., B. Mason, A. Coffey and P. Atkinson (2005) Qualitative Research and Hypermedia: Ethnography for the Digital Age. London: SAGE.
3. Kozinets R.V. (2010a), Netnography. Doing Ethnographic Research Online, Sage, London.

191

longitudinal analysis

WHAT IS IT?

Some research requires long term studies. Longitudinal analysis focuses on studying a group of people over a long period of time The study may continue over decades. This method allows insights into a person's long term development. Longitudinal studies allow designers and researchers to distinguish short from long-term phenomena.

WHY USE THIS METHOD?

1. Longitudinal studies allow design researchers to distinguish short from long-term phenomena, such as poverty or aging.
2. Allows researchers to look at changes over tim

CHALLENGES

1. There is the risk of bias due to incomplete follow up,
2. Longitudinal studies are expensive
3. Participants drop out of the study

RESOURCES

1. Note pad
2. Computer
3. Video camera
4. Camera

WHEN TO USE THIS METHOD

1. Know Context
2. Know User
3. Frame insights

HOW TO USE THIS METHOD

Three types of longitudinal studies:

1. Panel Study: Involves sampling diverse individuals.
2. Cohort Study: Involves selecting a group based on factors such as their age or where they live.
3. Retrospective Study: Involves looking at historical records

REFERENCES

1. Carlson, Neil and et al. "Psychology the Science of Behavior", p. 361. Pearson Canada

mobile ethnography

WHAT IS IT?

Widespread use of mobile devices including laptops, tablets and digital cameras smart phone has enabled new ways of undertaking research and connecting with people with people in their everyday context.

WHY USE THIS METHOD?

1. Can be faster and less expensive than non-digital methods.
2. Data collected real time
3. Access to people may be easier
4. People carry digital devices such as smart phones, cameras, laptops and tablets
5. Data can be gathered in context

CHALLENGES

1. Can miss non verbal feedback.
2. Technology may be unreliable
3. Devices may be expensive

WHEN TO USE THIS METHOD

4. Define intent
5. Know Context
6. Know User
7. Frame insights
8. Explore Concepts
9. Make Plans
10. Deliver Offering

HOW TO USE THIS METHOD

There are many different methods which use or access:

1. Audio conferences
2. Web conferences
3. Virtual in depth interviews
4. Virtual Focus groups
5. Mobile diaries

RESOURCES

1. Smart phones,
2. Cameras,
3. Laptops and tablets
4. Mobile software applications

REFERENCES

1. Coover, R. (2004) 'Using Digital Media Tools and Cross-Cultural Research,Analysis and Representation', Visual Studies19(1): 6–25.
2. Dicks, B., B. Mason, A. Coffey and P. Atkinson (2005) Qualitative Research and Hypermedia: Ethnography for the Digital Age. London: SAGE.
3. Kozinets R.V. (2010a), Netnography. Doing Ethnographic Research Online, Sage, London.

MIND MAP

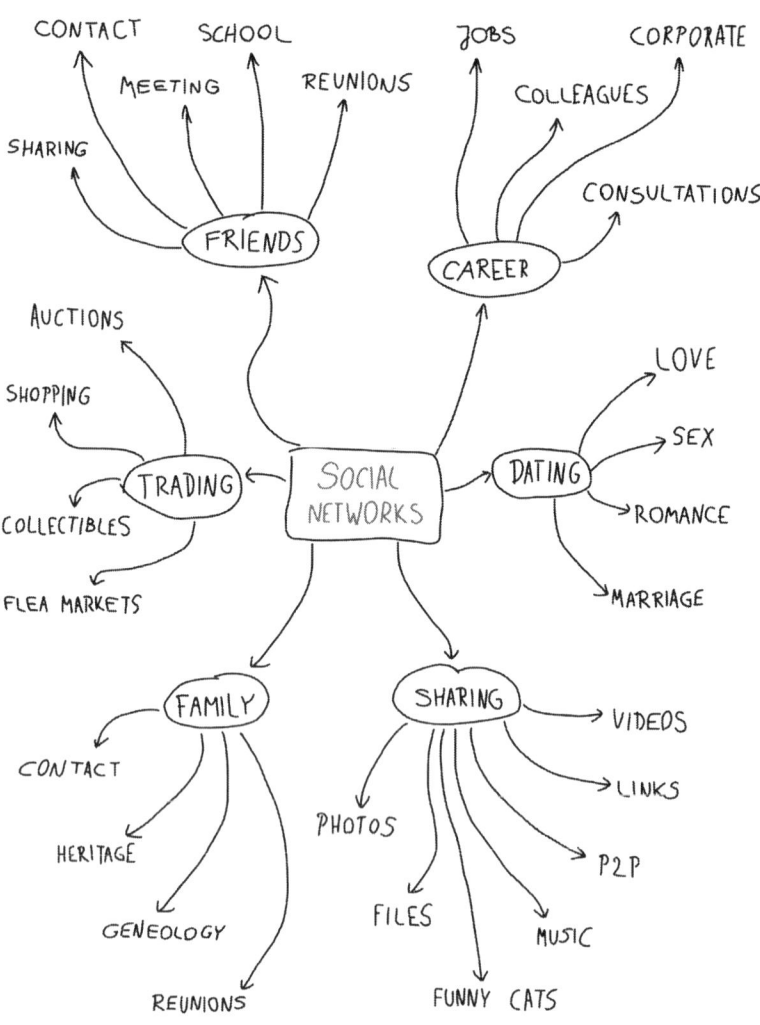

mind map

WHAT IS IT?

A mind map is a diagram used to represent the affinities or connections between a number of ideas or things. Understanding connections is the starting point for design. Mind maps are a method of analyzing information and relationships.

WHO INVENTED IT?

Porphry of Tyros 3rd century BC.
Allan Collins, Northwestern University 1960, USA

WHY USE THIS METHOD?

1. The method helps identify relationships.
2. There is no right or wrong with mind maps. They help with they help with memory and organization.
3. Problem solving and brainstorming
4. Relationship discovery
5. Summarizing information
6. Memorizing information

CHALLENGES

Print words clearly, use color and images for visual impact.

WHEN TO USE THIS METHOD

1. Know Context
2. Know User
3. Frame insights
4. Explore Concepts
5. Make Plans

HOW TO USE THIS METHOD

1. Start in the center with a key word or idea. Put box around this node.
2. Use images, symbols, or words for nodes.
3. Select key words.
4. Keep the key word names of nodes s simple and short as possible.
5. Associated nodes should be connected with lines to show affinities.
6. Make the lines the same length as the word/image they support.
7. Use emphasis such as thicker lines to show the strength of associations in your mind map.
8. Use radial arrangement of nodes.

RESOURCES

1. Paper
2. Pens
3. White board
4. Dry-erase markers

REFERENCES

1. Mind maps as active learning tools', by Willis, CL. Journal of computing sciences in colleges. ISSN: 1937-4771. 2006. Volume: 21 Issue: 4
2. Mind Maps as Classroom Exercises John W. Budd The Journal of Economic Education, Vol. 35, No. 1 (Winter, 2004), pp. 35-46 Published by: Taylor & Francis, Ltd.

method bank

WHAT IS IT?

A Method Bank is a central bank where design methods are documented by an organization's employees and can be accessed and applied by other employees.

WHO INVENTED IT?

1. Lego have compiled a Design Practice and emerging methods bank. Microsoft have a methods bank in their Online User Experience best practice intranet.
2. Starbucks have a methods bank in their online workflow management tool

WHY USE THIS METHOD?

1. This approaches helps document tacit knowledge within an organization.

WHEN TO USE THIS METHOD

1. Define intent
2. Know Context
3. Know User
4. Frame insights
5. Explore Concepts
6. Make Plans
7. Deliver Offering

HOW TO USE THIS METHOD

1. Methods are uploaded to the intranet bank.
2. The bank may include descriptions, video, images charts or sketches.

RESOURCES

1. Intranet
2. Camera
3. Video camera
4. Templates
5. Data base.
6. Computers

196

mystery shopper

WHAT IS IT?

Mystery shopping tool used to collect information about products and services. Mystery shoppers perform tasks including purchasing a product, submitting complaints, and then produce feedback.

Mystery shopping is also known as:

1. Secret Shopping
2. Experience Evaluation
3. Mystery Customers
4. Spotters
5. Digital Customers
6. Evaluations of employee interactions
7. Audits of employee performance
8. Telephone Checks

WHO INVENTED IT?

It was first used around 1953

WHY USE THIS METHOD?

1. Provides information performance
2. Produces actionable insights.
3. Increases employee and customer levels of satisfaction

CHALLENGES

1. Can be expensive, time consuming and not supported by employees.
2. Ethical issues

WHEN TO USE THIS METHOD

1. Know Context
2. Know User
3. Frame insights

HOW TO USE THIS METHOD

1. Form objectives
2. Create evaluation form for mystery shopper
3. Recruit mystery shoppers. Can be internal or external personnel.
4. Train mystery shoppers
5. Conduct evaluation.
6. Analyze results.
7. Formulate conclusions and actions needed.
8. Implement Actions.

RESOURCES

1. Evaluation form
2. Video camera
3. Notebook
4. Digital still camera.

REFERENCES

1. Health Care Taps 'Mystery Shoppers' at Wall Street Journal, August 8, 2006
2. C. Erlich, "Mystery Shopping," Competitive Intelligence Magazine 10(2007): 43-44.
3. Ton Van Der Wiele, Martin Hesselink, and Jos Van Iwaarden, "Mystery Shopping: A Tool to Develop Insight into Customer Service Provision," Total Quality Management 16(2005): 529-541.

network map

WHAT IS IT?

This is a method which maps and helps the researcher understand systems or services that involve many stakeholders. The map identifies the stakeholders, their links, influence and goals.

WHO INVENTED IT?

Eva Schiffer 2004 to 2008

WHY USE THIS METHOD?

1. Inexpensive and fast.
2. Connects to existing research tools and methods
3. Makes implicit knowledge explicit
4. Structures complex reality
5. Flexible for use in different contexts.

RESOURCES

1. Large sheets of paper for network map
2. Felt pens for drawing links
3. Adhesive paper as actor cards
4. Flat discs for building Influence-towers
5. Actor figurines

WHEN TO USE THIS METHOD

1. Know Context
2. Know User
3. Frame insights

HOW TO USE THIS METHOD

1. Define problems and goals.
2. Recruit participants
3. Define interview questions
4. Define network links to study
5. Ask participant to go through the process in detail.
6. Make a card with the name and description of each stakeholder. Place the cards on your map.
7. Show links between the stakeholders as lines on the map.
8. Number the links.
9. Create a legend describing each link.
10. Setting up influence towers:
11. Describe the influence of each stakeholder.?
12. Quantify the strength of influence of each stakeholder.
13. Stack discs next to each stakeholder card showing the relative level of influence.
14. Write descriptions of perceived problems next to each stakeholder.

REFERENCES

1. Eva Schiffer http://netmap.wordpress.com/process-net-map

INTERVIEW PROCESS

Question 1: Who is involved?

Ask: "Who is involved in this process?"Write names on actor cards (with different colors of cards for different groups of actors) and distribute on empty Net-Map sheet.

Question 2: How are they linked?

Ask: "Who is linked to whom?" Go through the different kinds of links one by one Draw arrows between actor cards according to interviewee directions. If two actors exchange something draw double headed arrows. If actors exchange more than one thing, add differently colored arrow heads to existing links.

Question 3: How influential are they?

Ask: "How strongly can actors influence (our complex issue)?" Explain / agree on a definition of influence with your interviewee, clarify that this is about influence only and not influence in the world at large. Ask interviewee to assign influence towers to actors: The higher the influence on the issue at stake, the higher the tower. Towers of different actors can be of the same height. Actors with no influence can be put on ground level. Towers can be as high as participants want. Place influence towers next to actor cards. Verbalize set-up and give interviewee the chance to adjust towers before noting height of tower on the Net-Map.

Question 4: What are their goals?

Ask according to pre-defined goals, actor by actor, e.g. "Does this actor support environmental, developmental goals or both?"
Note abbreviations for goals next to actor cards, allow for multiple goals where appropriate, by noting more than one goal next to the actor.

Discussion

Discuss the result with your interview partners. Depending on the goal of this specific mapping process, you might ask your participants to think strategically about the network and develop ideas to improve the situation in the future.

Source: Eva Schiffer http://netmap. wordpress.com/process-net-map

observation methods

WHAT IS IT?

This method involves observing people in their natural activities and usual context such as work environment. With direct observation the researcher is present and indirect observation the activities may be recorded by means such as video or digital voice recording.

WHY USE THIS METHOD?

1. Allows the observer to view what users actually do in context.
2. Indirect observation uncovers activity that may have previously gone unnoticed

CHALLENGES

1. Observation does not explain the cause of behavior.
2. Obtrusive observation may cause participants to alter their behavior.
3. Analysis can be time consuming.
4. Observer bias can cause the researcher to look only where they think they will see useful information.

WHEN TO USE THIS METHOD

1. Know Context
2. Know User
3. Frame insights

HOW TO USE THIS METHOD

1. Define objectives
2. Define participants and obtain their cooperation.
3. Define The context of the observation: time and place.
4. In some countries the law requires that you obtain written consent to video people.
5. Define the method of observation and the method of recording information. Common methods are taking written notes, video or audio recording.
6. Run a test session.
7. Hypothesize an explanation for the phenomenon
8. Predict a logical consequence of the hypothesis
9. Test your hypothesis by observation
10. Analyze the data gathered and create a list of insights derived from the observations.

RESOURCES

1. Note pad
2. Pens
3. Camera
4. Video camera
5. Digital voice recorder

REFERENCES

1. Kosso, Peter (2011). A Summary of Scientific Method. Springer. pp. 9. ISBN 9400716133,

observation: covert

WHAT IS IT?

Covert observation is to observe people without them knowing. The identity of the researcher and the purpose of the research are hidden from the people being observed.

WHY USE THIS METHOD?

1. This method may be used to reduce the effect of the observer's presence on the behavior of the subjects.
2. To capture behavior as it happens.
3. Researcher is more likely to observe natural behavior

CHALLENGES

1. The method raises serious ethical questions.
2. Observation does not explain the cause of behavior.
3. Can be difficult to gain access and maintain cover
4. Analysis can be time consuming.
5. Observer bias can cause the researcher to look only where they think they will see useful information.

RESOURCES

1. Camera
2. Video Camera
3. Digital voice recorder

WHEN TO USE THIS METHOD

1. Know Context
2. Know User

HOW TO USE THIS METHOD

1. Define objectives.
2. Define participants and obtain their cooperation.
3. Define The context of the observation: time and place.
4. In some countries the law requires that you obtain written consent to video people.
5. Define the method of observation and the method of recording information. Common methods are taking written notes, video or audio recording.
6. Run a test session.
7. Hypothesize an explanation for the phenomenon.
8. Predict a logical consequence of the hypothesis.
9. Test your hypothesis by observation
10. Analyze the data gathered and create a list of insights derived from the observations.

REFERENCES

1. Ethical Challenges in Participant Observation: A Reflection on Ethnographic Fieldwork By Li, Jun Academic journal article from The Qualitative Report, Vol. 13, No. 1

201

observation: direct

WHAT IS IT?

Direct observation is a method in which a researcher observes and records behavior events, activities or tasks while something is happening recording observations as they are made.

WHO INVENTED IT?

Radcliff-Brown 1910
Bronisław Malinowski 1922
Margaret Mead 1928

WHY USE THIS METHOD?

1. To capture behavior as it happens.

CHALLENGES

1. Observation does not explain the cause of behavior.
2. Analysis can be time consuming.
3. Observer bias can cause the researcher to look only where they think they will see useful information.
4. Obtain a proper sample for generalization.
5. Observe average workers during average conditions.
6. The participant may change their behavior because they are being watched.

RESOURCES

1. Note pad
2. Pens
3. Camera
4. Video Camera
5. Digital voice recorder

WHEN TO USE THIS METHOD

6. Know Context
7. Know User

HOW TO USE THIS METHOD

1. Define objectives.
2. Make direct observation plan
3. Define participants and obtain their cooperation.
4. Define The context of the observation: time and place.
5. In some countries the law requires that you obtain written consent to video people.
6. Define the method of observation and the method of recording information. Common methods are taking written notes, video or audio recording.
7. Run a test session.
8. Hypothesize an explanation for the phenomenon.
9. Predict a logical consequence of the hypothesis.
10. Test your hypothesis by observation
11. Analyze the data gathered and create a list of insights derived from the observations.

REFERENCES

1. Zechmeister, John J. Shaughnessy, Eugene B. Zechmeister, Jeanne S. (2009). Research methods in psychology (8th ed. ed.). Boston [etc.]: McGraw-Hill. ISBN 9780071283519.

observation: indirect

WHAT IS IT?

This is a method where the observer is unobtrusive and is sometimes used for sensitive research subjects.

WHY USE THIS METHOD?

1. To capture behavior as it happens in it's natural setting.
2. Indirect observation uncovers activity that may have previously gone unnoticed
3. May be inexpensive
4. Can collect a wide range of data

CHALLENGES

1. Observation does not explain the cause of behavior.
2. Analysis can be time consuming.
3. Observer bias can cause the researcher to look only where they think they will see useful information.
4. Obtain a proper sample for generalization.
5. Observe average workers during average conditions.
6. The participant may change their behavior because they are being watched.

REFERENCES

1. Zechmeister, John J. Shaughnessy, Eugene B. Zechmeister, Jeanne S. (2009). Research methods in psychology (8th ed. ed.). Boston [etc.]: McGraw-Hill. ISBN 9780071283519.

WHEN TO USE THIS METHOD

1. Know Context
2. Know User

HOW TO USE THIS METHOD

1. Define objectives.
2. Make indirect observation plan
3. Define participants
4. Define The context of the observation: time and place.
5. Define the method of observation and the method of recording information. Common methods are taking written notes, video or audio recording.
6. Run a test session.
7. Hypothesize an explanation for the phenomenon.
8. Predict a logical consequence of the hypothesis.
9. Test your hypothesis by observation
10. Analyze the data gathered and create a list of insights derived from the observations.

RESOURCES

1. Note pad
2. Pens
3. Camera
4. Video Camera
5. Digital voice recorder

observation:
non participant

WHAT IS IT?

The observer does not become part of the situation being observed or intervene in the behavior of the subjects. Used when a researcher wants the participants to behave normally. Usually this type of observation occurs in places where people normally work or live

WHY USE THIS METHOD?

1. Use this method when it is desirable not to influence the subject's behavior.

CHALLENGES

1. Observation does not explain the cause of behavior.
2. Analysis can be time consuming.
3. Observer bias can cause the researcher to look only where they think they will see useful information.
4. Obtain a proper sample for generalization.
5. Observe average workers during average conditions.
6. The participant may change their behavior because they are being watched.

WHEN TO USE THIS METHOD

1. Know Context
2. Know User

HOW TO USE THIS METHOD

1. Determine research goals.
2. Select a research context
3. The site should allow clear observation and be accessible.
4. Select participants
5. Seek permission.
6. Gain access
7. Gather research data.
8. Analyze data
9. Find common themes
10. Create insights

RESOURCES

1. Note pad
2. Pens
3. Camera
4. Video Camera
5. Digital voice recorder

REFERENCES

1. Zechmeister, John J. Shaughnessy, Eugene B. Zechmeister, Jeanne S. (2009). Research methods in psychology (8th ed. ed.). Boston [etc.]: McGraw-Hill. ISBN 9780071283519.

observation: participant

WHAT IS IT?

Participant observation is an observation method where the researcher participates. The researcher becomes part of the situation being studied. The researcher may live or work in the context of the participant and may become an accepted member of the participant's community. This method was used extensively by the pioneers of field research.

WHO INVENTED IT?

Radcliff-Brown 1910
Bronisław Malinowski 1922
Margaret Mead 1928

WHY USE THIS METHOD?

1. The goal of this method is to become close and familiar with the behavior of the participants.
2. To capture behavior as it happens.

CHALLENGES

1. My be time consuming
2. May be costly
3. The researcher may influence the behavior of the participants.
4. The participants may not show the same behavior if the observer was not present.
5. May be language barriers
6. May be cultural barriers
7. May be risks for the researcher.
8. Be open to possibilities.
9. Be sensitive to privacy, and confidentiality.

WHEN TO USE THIS METHOD

1. Know Context
2. Know User

HOW TO USE THIS METHOD

1. Determine research goals.
2. Select a research context
3. The site should allow clear observation and be accessible.
4. Select participants
5. Seek permission.
6. Gain access
7. Gather research data.
8. Analyze data
9. Find common themes
10. Create insights

RESOURCES

1. Note pad
2. Pens
3. Camera
4. Video Camera
5. Digital voice recorder

REFERENCES

1. Malinowski, Bronisław (1929) The sexual life of savages in north-western Melanesia: an ethnographic account of courtship, marriage and family life among the natives of the Trobriand Islands, British New Guinea. New York: Halcyon House.
2. Marek M. Kaminski. 2004. Games Prisoners Play. Princeton University Press. ISBN 0-691-11721-7

observation: structured

WHAT IS IT?

Particular types of behavior are observed and counted like a survey. The observer may create an event so that the behavior can be more easily studied. This approach is systematically planned and executed.

WHY USE THIS METHOD?

1. Allows stronger generalizations than unstructured observation.
2. May allow an observer to study behavior that may be difficult to study in unstructured observation.
3. To capture behavior as it happens.
4. A procedure is used which can be replicated.

CHALLENGES

1. Observation does not explain the cause of behavior.
2. Analysis can be time consuming.
3. Observer bias can cause the researcher to look only where they think they will see useful information.

RESOURCES

1. Note pad
2. Pens
3. Camera
4. Video Camera
5. Digital voice recorder

WHEN TO USE THIS METHOD

1. Know Context
2. Know User

HOW TO USE THIS METHOD

1. Define objectives.
2. Define participants and obtain their cooperation.
3. Define The context of the observation: time and place.
4. In some countries the law requires that you obtain written consent to video people.
5. Define the method of observation and the method of recording information. Common methods are taking written notes, video or audio recording.
6. Run a test session.
7. Hypothesize an explanation for the phenomenon.
8. Predict a logical consequence of the hypothesis.
9. Test your hypothesis by observation
10. Analyze the data gathered and create a list of insights derived from the observations.

REFERENCES

1. Zechmeister, John J. Shaughnessy, Eugene B. Zechmeister, Jeanne S. (2009). Research methods in psychology (8th ed. ed.). Boston [etc.]: McGraw-Hill. ISBN 9780071283519.

observation: unstructured

WHAT IS IT?

This method is used when a researcher wants to see what is naturally occurring without predetermined ideas. We use have an open-ended approach to observation and record all that we observe

WHY USE THIS METHOD?

1. To capture behavior as it happens.
2. This form of observation is appropriate when the problem has yet to be formulated precisely and flexibility is needed in observation to identify key components of the problem and to develop hypotheses
3. Observation is the most direct measure of behavior

CHALLENGES

1. Replication may be difficult.
2. Observation does not explain the cause of behavior.
3. Analysis can be time consuming.
4. Observer bias can cause the researcher to look only where they think they will see useful information.
5. Data cannot be quantified
6. In this form of observation there is a higher probability of observer's bias.

WHEN TO USE THIS METHOD

1. Know Context
2. Know User

HOW TO USE THIS METHOD

1. Select a context to explore
2. Take a camera, note pad and pen
3. Record things and questions that you find interesting
4. Record ideas as you form them
5. Do not reach conclusions.
6. Ask people questions and try to understand the meaning in their replies.

RESOURCES

1. Note pad
2. Pens
3. Camera
4. Video Camera
5. Digital voice recorder

REFERENCES

1. Zechmeister, John J. Shaughnessy, Eugene B. Zechmeister, Jeanne S. (2009). Research methods in psychology (8th ed. ed.). Boston [etc.]: McGraw-Hill. ISBN 9780071283519.

online methods: experiments

WHAT IS IT?

A internet based experiment is an experiment that is conducted over the Internet.

WHO INVENTED IT?

Early study by Reips and Bosnjak, 2001

WHY USE THIS METHOD?

1. Researchers can collect large amounts of research material from a wide range of locations and people at relatively low expense.

CHALLENGES

1. Web-based experiments may have weaker experimental controls

WHEN TO USE THIS METHOD

1. Know Context
2. Know User

HOW TO USE THIS METHOD

1. Consider using a web-based software tool
2. Pretest your experiment for clarity of instructions and availability on different platforms.
3. Check your Web experiment for configuration errors
4. Run your experiment both online and offline,for comparison.
5. Ask filter questions
6. Check for obvious naming of files,conditions,and,if applicable,passwords.
7. Perform consistency checks.
8. Report and analyze dropout curves

Source [1]

online methods: online ethics

HOW TO USE THIS METHOD
Below are some guidelines for online research.

1. Participant should not be obliged to answer questions
2. Incentives to take a survey should be used as little as possible.
3. Questionnaires should allow respondents to remain anonymous.
4. Sensitive questionnaires should be confidential.
5. Questions should have the option of "I don't know" or an option that denotes neutrality
6. Questions should not trick the participant.
7. Participant should know why the questionnaire is taking place
8. Participant should know what the information will be used for.
9. In sensitive cases, the questionnaire should be reviewed by an ethics committee or outside party.

REFERENCES

1. Reips, Ulf-Dietrich . (2007). The methodology of Internet-based experiments. In A. Joinson, K. McKenna, T. Postmes, & U.-D. Reips (Eds.), The Oxford Handbook of Internet Psychology (pp. 373-390). Oxford: Oxford University Press.
1. Reips Ulf-Dietrich Standards for Internet-Based Experimenting Experimental and Developmental Psychology, 2002 University of Zürich, Switzerland
2. Reips, U.-D. (2002). Standards for Internet-based experimenting. Experimental Psychology, 49 (4), 243-256.

observation: overt

WHAT IS IT?
A method of observation where the subjects are aware that they are being observed

WHO INVENTED IT?
Radcliff-Brown 1910
Bronisław Malinowski 1922
Margaret Mead 1928

WHY USE THIS METHOD?
1. To capture behavior as it happens.

CHALLENGES
1. Observation does not explain the cause of behavior.
2. Analysis can be time consuming.
3. Observer bias can cause the researcher to look only where they think they will see useful information.

RESOURCES
1. Note pad
2. Pens
3. Camera
4. Video Camera
5. Digital voice recorder

REFERENCES
1. Zechmeister, John J. Shaughnessy, Eugene B. Zechmeister, Jeanne S. (2009). Research methods in psychology (8th ed. ed.). Boston [etc.]: McGraw-Hill. ISBN 9780071283519.

WHEN TO USE THIS METHOD
1. Know Context
2. Know User

HOW TO USE THIS METHOD
1. Define objectives.
2. Define participants and obtain their cooperation.
3. Define The context of the observation: time and place.
4. In some countries the law requires that you obtain written consent to video people.
5. Define the method of observation and the method of recording information. Common methods are taking written notes, video or audio recording.
6. Run a test session.
7. Hypothesize an explanation for the phenomenon.
8. Predict a logical consequence of the hypothesis.
9. Test your hypothesis by observation
10. Analyze the data gathered and create a list of insights derived from the observations.

nomothetic approach

WHAT IS IT?

Nomothetic approach is the approach of investigating a large group of people to find general laws of behavior that apply to everybody. The term "nomothetic" comes from the Greek word "nomos" meaning "law"

WHO INVENTED IT?

Wilhelm Windelband (1848–1915), M.T. Conner 1986, R.P.J. Freeman 1993 and O. Sharpe 2005

WHY USE THIS METHOD?

1. Useful for designing mass produced products or services.

CHALLENGES

1. Individuals are unique.
2. Superficial understanding of any single person.

WHEN TO USE THIS METHOD

1. Define intent
2. Know Context
3. Know User
4. Frame insights

REFERENCES

1. Butterworth-Heinemann, Elsevior (2005). Research Methods. British Library: Elsevior Ltd. pp. 32.
2. Cone, J. D. (1986). Idiographic, nomothetic, and related perspectives in behavioral assessment. In R. O. Nelson & S. C. Hayes (Eds.): Conceptual foundations of behavioral assessment (pp. 111–128). New York: Guilford.
3. Thomae, H. (1999). The nomothetic-idiographic issue: Some roots and recent trends. International Journal of Group Tensions, 28(1), 187–215.

online methods

WHAT IS IT?

Online testing is a method of obtaining feedback for a design relatively quickly and cost effectively. It is an emerging area of design research.

Some areas are:

1. Online ethnography
2. Online focus groups
3. Online interviews
4. Online questionnaires
5. Web-based experiments
6. Online clinical trials

WHY USE THIS METHOD?

1. You can reach a large number of people
2. Flexible
3. Time and cost effective
4. New media seem to offer the hope of reaching different populations of research subjects in new ways
5. Access to populations
6. May be more acceptable method for participants.

CHALLENGES

1. May not be the fastest method of getting feedback.
2. Participants may lose interest quickly.
3. High drop out rates.
4. Participant's input from senses is limited to vision
5. Is a method that is still being adopted.
6. Sensitivity is required in internet research for legal, practical and ethical reasons.

WHEN TO USE THIS METHOD

1. Know Context
2. Know User

HOW TO USE THIS METHOD

This is a complex and growing area of research. Some guidelines are

1. E-mail can be used for online focus groups using the copy all function.
2. Because participants can reply at any time moderation may be more difficult than a face to face focus group.
3. Group interaction may be less than in a face to face interview or focus group.
4. Social networks can be useful in generating lively discussions and allowing interaction within the social context of a group

RESOURCES

1. Computer
2. Text editor
3. Internet connection
4. Social network connections

REFERENCES

1. Fischer, M., Lyon, S. and Zeitlyn, D. (2008) The internet and the future of social science research. In Fielding, N., Lee, R. M. and Blank, G. (Eds.), The SAGE handbook of Online Research Methods. London. SAGE. pp. 519-536.
2. Hewson, C., Yule, P., Laurent, D. and Vogel, C. (2003) Internet Research Methods. London. Sage.

online methods
ethnography

WHAT IS IT?
Online ethnography refers to a number of related online research methods that adapt ethnographic methods to the study of the communities and cultures created through computer-mediated social interaction

WHO INVENTED IT?
One of the early published articles identifying emerging online ethnography was by Arnould and Wallendorf 1994

WHY USE THIS METHOD?
1. New level of access to people
2. Access to more people
3. Easier access than traditional ethnography
4. Less expensive Than traditional ethnography.
5. Faster than traditional methods

CHALLENGES
1. Some believe that new methods need to be developed that are distinctively different than face to face ethnographic methods.

WHEN TO USE THIS METHOD
1. Know Context
2. Know User

HOW TO USE THIS METHOD
There are diverse methods developing for ethnographic study via the internet.
1. Netnography
2. Online Interviews
3. Online focus groups
4. Online Communities and Cultures

RESOURCES
1. Computer
2. Web browser
3. Internet connection

REFERENCES
1. Wilson, Samuel M.; Peterson, Leighton C. (2002). "The Anthropology of Online Communities". Annual Review of Anthropology 31: 449–467.
2. Domínguez, Daniel; Beaulieu, Anne; Estalella, Adolfo; Gómez, Edgar; Schnettler, Bernt & Read, Rosie (2007). Virtual Ethnography. Forum Qualitative Sozialforschung / Forum: Qualitative Social Research, 8(3), http://nbn-resolving.de/urn:nbn:de:0114-fqs0703E19.

online methods:
interviews

WHAT IS IT?

With this method an interview is conducted via internet.

WHY USE THIS METHOD?

1. Possible to access a geographically dispersed population;
2. Possible savings in costs to the researcher
3. Reduce issues of interviewer effect as participants cannot 'see' each other

CHALLENGES

1. Lack of communication of body language.
2. Establishing a good rapport may be more difficult.
3. Higher drop out rate.
4. Lack of visibility of distractions.

RESOURCES

1. Computer
2. Internet connection
3. Notebook
4. Pens
5. Interview plan or structure
6. Questions, tasks and discussion items
7. Confidentiality agreement

WHEN TO USE THIS METHOD

1. Know Context
2. Know User

HOW TO USE THIS METHOD

Technologies include news groups and forums and e-mail.

1. Choose a topic
2. Identify a subject.
3. Contact subject and obtain approval.
4. An asynchronous online interview is one where the researcher and the researched are not necessarily online at the same time.
5. Prepare interview questions.
6. Conduct interview
7. Analyze data.

REFERENCES

1. Mann and Stewart (2005) Internet Communication and Qualitative Research: A Handbook for Researching Online London: Sage

214

online methods: questionnaires

WHAT IS IT?

An online questionnaire is a questionnaire conducted via the internet.

WHY USE THIS METHOD?

1. Web surveys are faster, simpler and cheaper
2. Data collection period is significantly shortened
3. Simple to compile data
4. Complex skip patterns can be implemented in ways that are mostly invisible to the respondent
5. According to ESOMAR online survey research accounted for 20% of global data-collection expenditure in 2006.

CHALLENGES

1. Response rates are generally low
2. Sample selection bias that is out of research control

REFERENCES

1. Burns, A. C., & Bush, R. F. (2010). Marketing Research. Upper Saddle River, NJ: Pearson Education.
2. Foddy, W. H. (1994). Constructing questions for interviews and questionnaires: Theory and practice in social research (New ed.). Cambridge, UK: Cambridge University Press.

WHEN TO USE THIS METHOD

1. Know Context
2. Know User

HOW TO USE THIS METHOD

1. It is recommended that the time taken to complete an online questionnaire should not exceed 5 minutes.
2. Pretest the questionnaire with at least 5 people, prior to publication on the web.
3. The questionnaire should begin with a short introduction that explains to the participant why it is being conducted and what the information will be used for.
4. Use "smart branching" to lessen complexity. Jump to the next relevant question based on a particular answer.
5. Include a "Thank you" statement at the end.
6. Use statements which are interpreted in the same way by different cultures.
7. Use statements where people that have different opinions will give different answers.
8. Use positive statements and avoid negatives or double negatives.
9. Do not make assumptions about the respondent.
10. Use clear and comprehensible wording, easily understandable for all educational levels
11. Avoid items that contain more than one question per item

215

PERCEPTUAL MAP

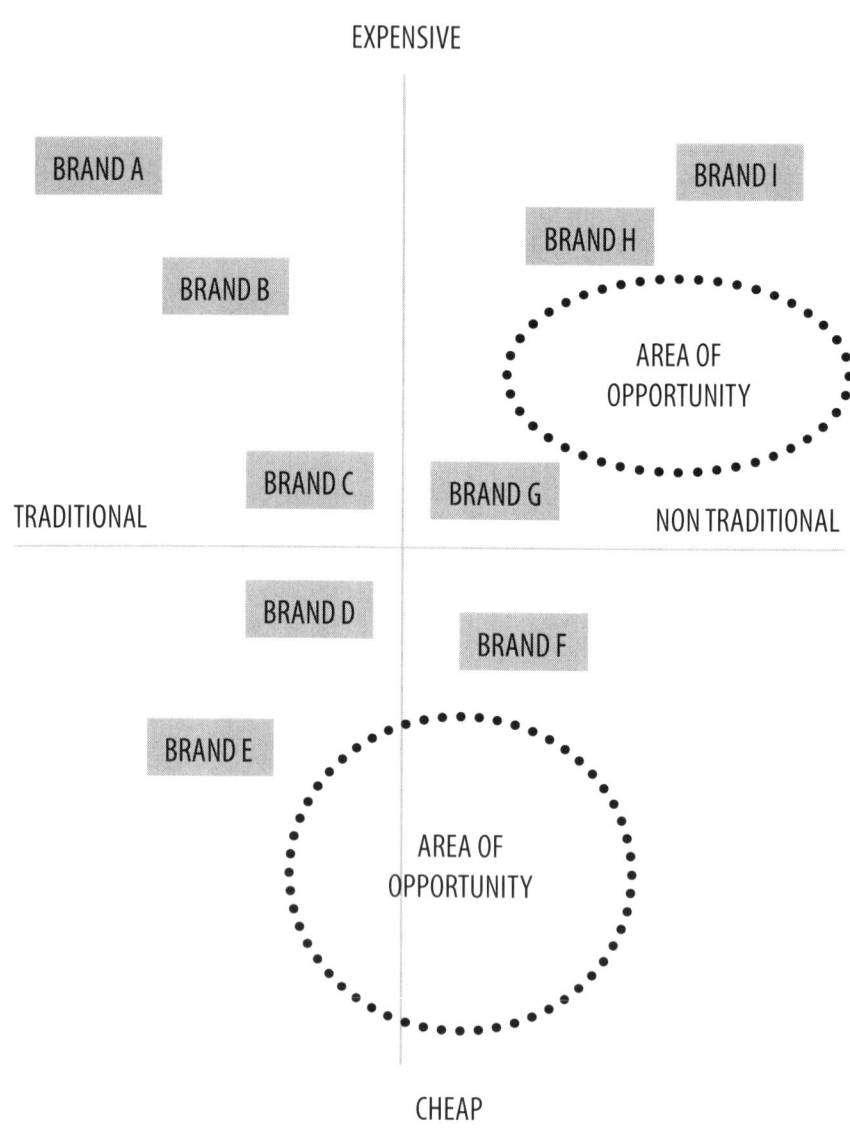

perceptual map

WHAT IS IT?

Perceptual mapping is a method that creates a map of the perceptions of people of competing alternatives to be compared.

WHO INVENTED IT?

Unknown

WHY USE THIS METHOD?

1. Aids communication and discussion within the organization
2. To gain competitive advantage,
3. Helps build competitive strategy
4. Helps build communication strategy
5. Helps identify potential new products
6. Helps build brand strategy

CHALLENGES

1. Because the position of a product or service on the map is subjective, you can ask several people to locate the position through group discussion.
2. Works well for clearly defined functional attributes such as price, product features

WHEN TO USE THIS METHOD

1. Know Context
2. Know User
3. Frame insights
4. Explore Concepts

HOW TO USE THIS METHOD

1. Define characteristics of product or service to map.
2. Identify competing brands, services or products to map.
3. Map individual items.
4. Interpret the map.
5. Create strategy.

RESOURCES

1. Pen
2. Paper
3. White board
4. Dry erase markers

217

PERSONA TEMPLATE

PERSONA NAME

....

DEMOGRAPHICS

....
....
....
....

CHARACTERISTIC STATEMENT

....
....
....
....
....

GOALS

....
....
....
....

AMBITIONS

....
....
....
....

INFLUENCERS AND ACTIVITIES

....
....
....
....

SCENARIOS

....
....
....
....

OTHER CHARACTERISTICS

TYPE: TYPE: TYPE: TYPE: TYPE: TYPE: TYPE: TYPE: TYPE: TYPE:

personas

WHAT IS IT?

"A persona is a archetypal character that is meant to represent a group of users in a role who share common goals, attitudes and behaviors when interacting with a particular product or service Personas are user models that are presented as specific individual humans. They are not actual people, but are synthesized directly from observations of real people."(Cooper)

WHO INVENTED IT?

Alan Cooper 1998

WHY USE THIS METHOD?

1. Helps create empathy for users and reduces self reference.
2. Use as tool to analyze and gain insight into users.
3. Help in gaining buy-in from stake holders.

CHALLENGES

1. Portigal (2008) has claimed that personas give a "cloak of smug customer-centricity" while actually distancing a team from engagement with real users and their needs

REFERENCES

1. Pruitt, John & Adlin, Tamara. The Persona Lifecycle : Keeping People in Mind Throughout Product Design. Morgan Kaufmann, 2006. ISBN 0-12-566251-3

WHEN TO USE THIS METHOD

1. Know Context
2. Know User
3. Frame insights
4. Explore Concept

HOW TO USE THIS METHOD

1. Inaccurate personas can lead to a false understandings of the end users. Personas need to be created using data from real users.
2. Collect data through observation, interviews, ethnography.
3. Segment the users or customers
4. Create the Personas
5. Avoid Stereotypes
6. Each persona should be different. Avoid fringe characteristics. Personas should each have three to four life goals which are personal aspirations,
7. Personas are given a name, and photograph.
8. Design personas can be followed by building customer journeys

RESOURCES

1. Raw data on users from interviews or other research
2. Images of people similar to segmented customers.
3. Computer
4. Graphics software

personal inventory

WHAT IS IT?

This method involves studying the contents of a research subject's purse, or wallet. Study the things that they carry everyday.

WHO INVENTED IT?

Rachel Strickland and Doreen Nelson 1998

WHY USE THIS METHOD?

1. To provide insights into the user's lifestyle, activities, perceptions, and values.
2. to understand the needs priorities and interests

WHEN TO USE THIS METHOD

1. Know Context
2. Know User
3. Frame insights

HOW TO USE THIS METHOD

1. Formulate aims of research
2. Recruit participants carefully.
3. "the participant is asked to bring their 'most often carried bag' and lay the objects they carry on a flat surface, talking through the purpose and last-use of each item. Things to look out for where the bag is kept in the home and what is clustered around it, what is packed/repacked on arrival/departure, and the use of different bags for different activities." *Jan Chipchase*
4. Document the contents with photographs and notes
5. ask your research subject to talk about the objects and their meaning.
6. Analyze the data.

RESOURCES

1. Camera
2. Note pad

picture cards

WHAT IS IT?

Picture cards is a method that involves using a collection of cards with images and words that help people talk about their life experiences

WHY USE THIS METHOD?

1. Helps people discuss their experiences and feelings relevant to the research topic.
2. It is relatively inexpensive and fast.
3. The cards may make staring in depth conversations easier.

WHEN TO USE THIS METHOD

4. Know Context
5. Know User
6. Frame insights

HOW TO USE THIS METHOD

1. 100 to 150 cards are created with images and words relevant to the research topic.
2. Prepare question guide
3. In the participant session the researcher asks the participant to recall a story about an experience to start a conversation.
4. Include cards that help the participant discuss issues relevant to proposed design.
5. Can video the session with permission.
6. Analyze the data

RESOURCES

1. Deck of picture cards
2. Video camera
3. Note pad

221

POWERGRAM

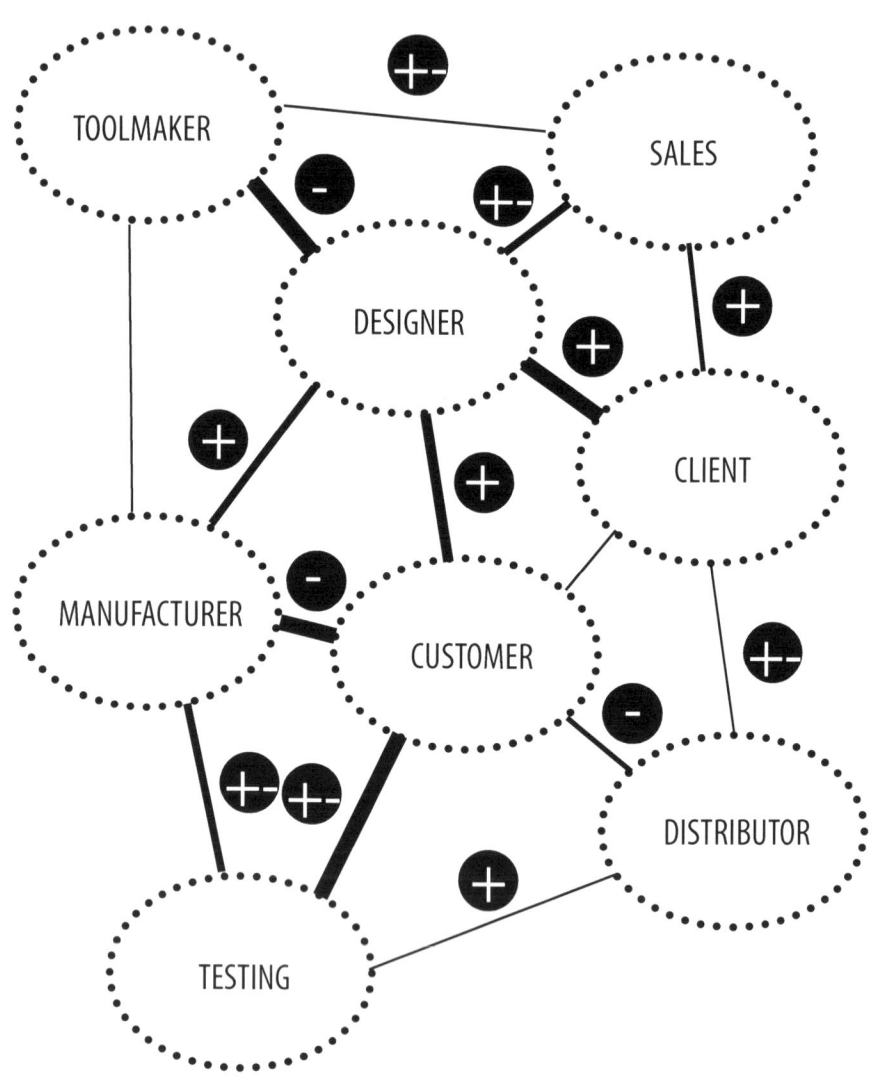

powergram

WHAT IS IT?

"A powergram is a graphical representation of the power dynamics, and power positions, within an account. It shows the true power structure, which is usually different than the account's organizational chart. It provides useful insights about an account's decision making process." *Source: Greg Alexander*

WHO INVENTED IT?

Greg Alexander

WHY USE THIS METHOD?

1. A more descriptive method than an organizational chart.
2. Can illustrate unofficial power structures.
3. Can be used to generate debate and discussion on roles and responsibilities.

CHALLENGES

1. Can be subjective.
2. Rank does not equal power.

WHEN TO USE THIS METHOD

1. Define intent
2. Know Context

HOW TO USE THIS METHOD

1. "Identify the formal lines of reporting and authority.
2. A circle represents a person
3. Identify the stakeholders you like to include
4. The larger the circle, the more power '
5. A line denotes a relationship
6. The heavier the line, the stronger the relationship
7. A strike through a line means a negative relationship
8. A shorter line represents a closer relationship,or frequent contact
9. A longer line represents a more distant the relationship"

Source: Greg Alexander

RESOURCES

1. Pen
2. Paper
3. Post-it-notes
4. White board
5. Dry erase pens

REFERENCES

1. Brill, Peter L. and Richard Worth. The four levers of corporate change. New York : AMACOM, 1997.

RADAR CHART

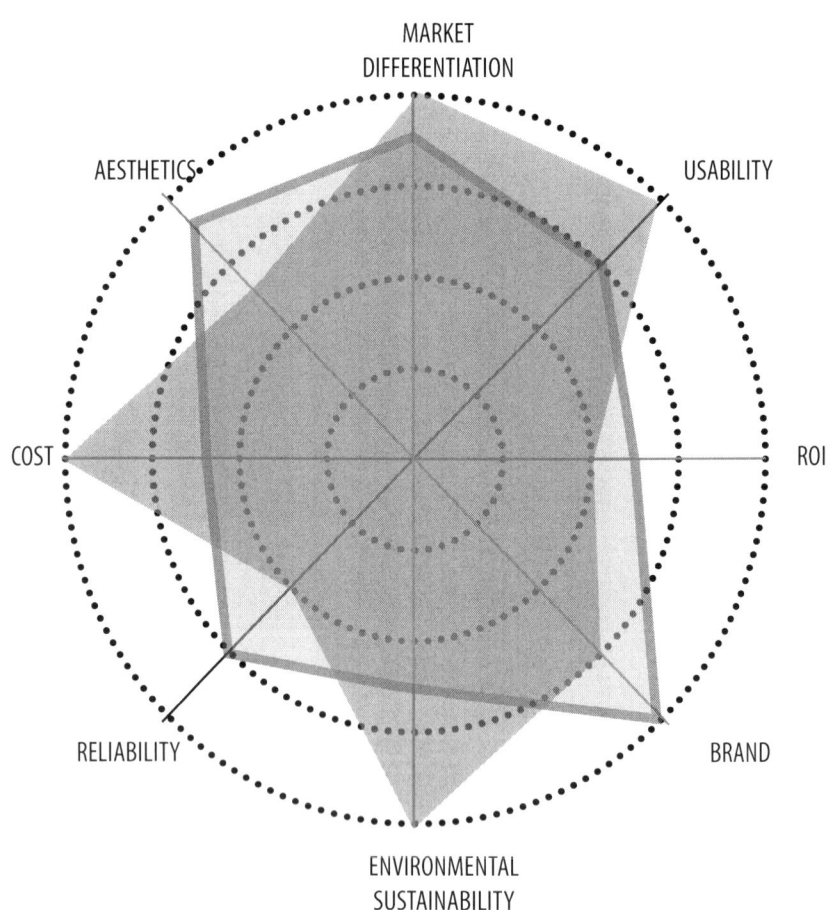

MARKET
DIFFERENTIATION

USABILITY

AESTHETICS

ROI

COST

BRAND

RELIABILITY

ENVIRONMENTAL
SUSTAINABILITY

radar chart

WHAT IS IT?

The radar chart is a star shape chart that allows information to be logged radially for a number of variables. The radar chart is also known as a web chart, spider chart, star chart, star plot, cobweb chart, irregular polygon, polar chart, or kiviat diagram.

WHO INVENTED IT?

Georg von Mayr 1877

CHALLENGES

1. Radar charts may not provide information for trade off decisions.

WHY USE THIS METHOD?

1. A spider diagram is a way of displaying a great deal of information in a condensed form,

WHEN TO USE THIS METHOD

1. Know Context
2. Know User
3. Frame insights

HOW TO USE THIS METHOD

1. Draw a circle on a flipchart paper
2. For each item to evaluate draw a line from the center to the circle.
3. Write the item on the intersection between the line and the circle.
4. Draw spider lines from the inside to the outside of the circle (see photo).
5. Gather the participants around the flipchart.
6. Ask them to put one dot for each item: If highly ranked the dot should be close top the center; if poorly ranked the dot should be close to the circle.
7. Present and discuss the result with the group.

RESOURCES

1. Paper
2. Pens
3. Computer
4. Graphic software

REFERENCES

1. Chambers, John, William Cleveland, Beat Kleiner, and Paul Tukey, (1983). Graphical Methods for Data Analysis. Wadsworth. pp. 158-162

questionnaires

WHAT IS IT?

A questionnaire is a research tool made up of a number of questions. Questionnaires may be designed for statistical analysis. This is a primary research method.

WHY USE THIS METHOD?

1. Easy to analyze
2. Large sample at relatively low cost.
3. Simple to manage
4. Familiar format
5. Quick to complete
6. Can be used for sensitive topics
7. Respondents have flexibility in time to complete.

WHO INVENTED IT?

Sir Francis Galton 1800s

WHEN TO USE THIS METHOD

1. Know Context
2. Know User
3. Frame insights

CHALLENGES

1. Avoid complex questions
2. Avoid leading questions
3. Avoid jargon
4. Avoid bias
5. Have standard procedure
6. Ask one information at a time
7. Be as simple as possible
8. Adjust the style of the questions to the target audience

HOW TO USE THIS METHOD

1. Define the questions to research
2. Select the participants
3. Prepare the questions
4. Use closed questions with multiple predefined choices or open questions to allow respondents to respond in their own words.
5. Two common closed formats are: the Likert 7 point format: strongly agree, agree, undecided, disagree, strongly disagree. Or 4 point Forced choice format, Strongly agree, agree, disagree, strongly disagree.
6. Pretest the questionnaire
7. Refine the questionnaire
8. Questions should flow logically

REFERENCES

1. Gillham, B. (2008). Developing a questionnaire (2nd ed.). London, UK: Continuum International Publishing Group Ltd
2. Oppenheim, A. N. (2000). Questionnaire design, interviewing and attitude measurement (New ed.). London, UK: Continuum International Publishing Group Ltd.

remote evaluation

WHAT IS IT?

Remote evaluation is any usability testing method where the researcher and participant are not in the same location. Remote evaluation may be moderated, or unmoderated.

WHO INVENTED IT?

First published Hartson Castillo Kelson and Neale 1996

WHY USE THIS METHOD?

1. Captures rich feedback
2. Users are in own context
3. Can use for single or multiple participants.
4. May be less expensive and faster.
5. Good for Geographically dispersed user groups.
6. The participant records the data.
7. Face to face evaluation can be expensive, It may be difficult to access participants. and requires a dedicated space.

CHALLENGES

1. You can read body language with in person testing.
2. Difficult to build relationship with participants.
3. Difficult to ensure security of information.
4. Technology can present problems.

HOW TO USE THIS METHOD

1. Define focus of study.
2. Recruit participants.
3. Typically 5 to 5 participants are used in each iteration of testing.
4. Schedule the evaluation.
5. Brief the participants
6. Run a pilot test.
7. Instruct the participants to say what they are thinking and doing doing and why out loud repeatedly.
8. Users undertake the tasks.
9. Participants undertake a short questionnaire.
10. Researcher review the data and analyzes most common participant problems.
11. Designer implements the changes to the the design based on participant feedback.

RESOURCES

1. Computers
2. Research software

REFERENCES

1. Chalil Madathil, Kapil; Joel S. Greenstein (May 2011). "Synchronous remote usability testing: a new approach facilitated by virtual worlds". Proceedings of the 2011 annual conference on Human factors in computing systems. CHI '11: 2225–2234.

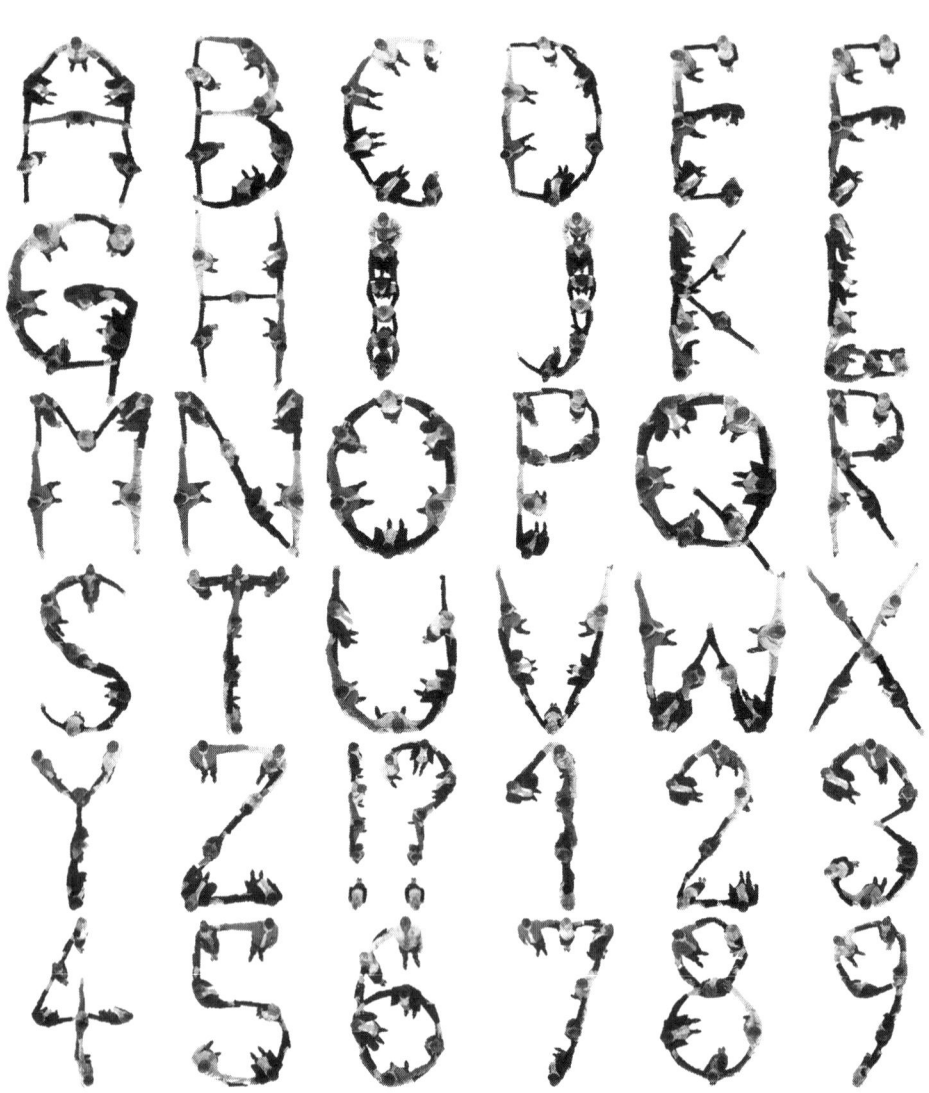

228

sampling: cluster

WHAT IS IT?

This sampling method is often used to save time and cost when a population is widely dispersed. Dividing a geographic area into clusters is a first step. Following this step, clusters are then sampled.

WHY USE THIS METHOD?

1. May reduce the average cost per interview.

CHALLENGES

1. Higher sampling error than some other methods.

WHEN TO USE THIS METHOD

2. Know Context
3. Know User
4. Frame insights

HOW TO USE THIS METHOD

1. Define the population to be sampled.
2. Divide the population into groups or clusters.
3. Determine the sample size.
4. Select a representative sample from the targeted population.
5. Collect the data from each group.
6. Analyze the data

REFERENCES

1. Kerry and Bland (1998). Statistics notes: The intracluster correlation coefficient in cluster randomisation. British Medical Journal, 316, 1455-1460.
2. Babbie, E. (2001). The Practice of Social Research: 9th Edition. Belmont, CA: Wadsworth Thomson.

sampling: convenience

WHAT IS IT?

A sampling method that uses people who are easily available to sample. Convenience sampling is also known as Opportunity Sampling, Accidental Sampling or Haphazard Sampling.

WHO INVENTED IT?

Pierre Simon Laplace pioneered sampling 1786

WHY USE THIS METHOD?

1. Use when time is limited
2. Use when budgets are limited

CHALLENGES

3. Use as many people as possible.

WHEN TO USE THIS METHOD

1. Know Context
2. Know User

HOW TO USE THIS METHOD

1. Use people in the street, friends, work colleagues, customers, fellow students.

REFERENCES

1. Cochran, William G. (1977). Sampling techniques (Third ed.). Wiley. ISBN 0-471-16240-X
2. Robert Groves, et alia. Survey methodology (2010) Second edition of the (2004) first edition ISBN 0-471-48348-6.
3. Chambers, R L, and Skinner, C J (editors) (2003), Analysis of Survey Data, Wiley, ISBN 0-471-89987-9

sampling: random

WHAT IS IT?

With random also called probability sampling, all people in the population being studied have some opportunity of being included in the sample, and the mathematical probability that any one of them will be selected can be calculated.

WHO INVENTED IT?

Pierre Simon Laplace pioneered sampling 1786

WHY USE THIS METHOD?

1. Applicable when population is small, homogeneous & readily available
2. Each person has an equal probability of selection.
3. Estimates are easy to calculate.

CHALLENGES

1. Minority subgroups of interest in population may not be present in sample in sufficient numbers for study.
2. Requires selection of relevant stratification variables which can be difficult.
3. Is not useful when there are no homogeneous subgroups.
4. Can be expensive to implement.

WHEN TO USE THIS METHOD

1. Know Context
2. Know User

HOW TO USE THIS METHOD

1. Define the population to be sampled.
2. Specifying a sampling frame, a set of items or events possible to measure
3. Determine the sample size.
4. Select a representative sample from the targeted population.
5. Implement the sampling plan. A table of random numbers or lottery system is used to determine which are to be selected.
6. Carefully collect required data.

REFERENCES

1. Cochran, William G. (1977). Sampling techniques (Third ed.). Wiley. ISBN 0-471-16240-X
2. Robert Groves, et alia. Survey methodology (2010) Second edition of the (2004) first edition ISBN 0-471-48348-6.
3. Chambers, R L, and Skinner, C J (editors) (2003), Analysis of Survey Data, Wiley, ISBN 0-471-89987-9

sampling: situation

WHAT IS IT?

Situation sampling involves observation of behavior in different locations, circumstances and conditions.

WHO INVENTED IT?

Pierre Simon Laplace pioneered sampling 1786

WHY USE THIS METHOD?

1. Situation sampling enhances the external validity of findings.
2. By sampling behavior in several different situations, you are able to determine whether the behavior in question changes as a function of the context in which you observed it.
3. Your ability to generalize any behavioral consistencies across the various situations is increased.

WHEN TO USE THIS METHOD

1. Know Context
2. Know User

HOW TO USE THIS METHOD

1. When two individuals observe the same behavior, it is possible to see how well their observations agree.

REFERENCES

1. Cochran, William G. (1977). Sampling techniques (Third ed.). Wiley. ISBN 0-471-16240-X
2. Robert Groves, et alia. Survey methodology (2010) Second edition of the (2004) first edition ISBN 0-471-48348-6.
3. Chambers, R L, and Skinner, C J (editors) (2003), Analysis of Survey Data, Wiley, ISBN 0-471-89987-9

232

shadowing

WHAT IS IT?

Shadowing is observing people in context. The researcher accompanies the user and observes user experiences and activities. It allows the researcher and designer to develop design insights through observation and shared experiences with users.

WHO INVENTED IT?

Alex Bavelas 1944
Lucy Vernile, Robert A. Monteiro 1991

WHY USE THIS METHOD?

1. This method can help determine the difference between what subjects say they do and what they really do.
2. It helps in understanding the point of view of people. Successful design results from knowing the users.
3. Define intent
4. Can be used to evaluate concepts.

CHALLENGES

1. Selecting the wrong people to shadow.
2. Hawthorne Effect, The observer can influence the daily activities under being studied.

WHEN TO USE THIS METHOD

1. Know Context
2. Know User
3. Frame insights
4. Generate Concepts

HOW TO USE THIS METHOD

1. Prepare
2. Select carefully who to shadow.
3. Observe people in context by members of your design team.
4. Capture behaviors that relate to product function.
5. Identify issues and user needs.
6. Create design solutions based on observed and experienced user needs.
7. Typical periods can be one day to one week.

RESOURCES

1. Video camera
2. Digital still camera
3. Note pad
4. Laptop Computer

SEE ALSO

1. Day in the life
2. Fly on the wall

REFERENCES

1. McDonald, Seonaidh. "Studying Actions in Context: A Qualitative Shadowing Method for Organizational Research." Qualitative Research. The Robert Gordon University. SAGE Publications. London. 2005. p455-473.
2. Alan Bryman, Emma Bell. Business Research Meythods. Oxford University Press 2007 ISBN 978-0-19-928498-6

PATIENT STAKEHOLDER MAP

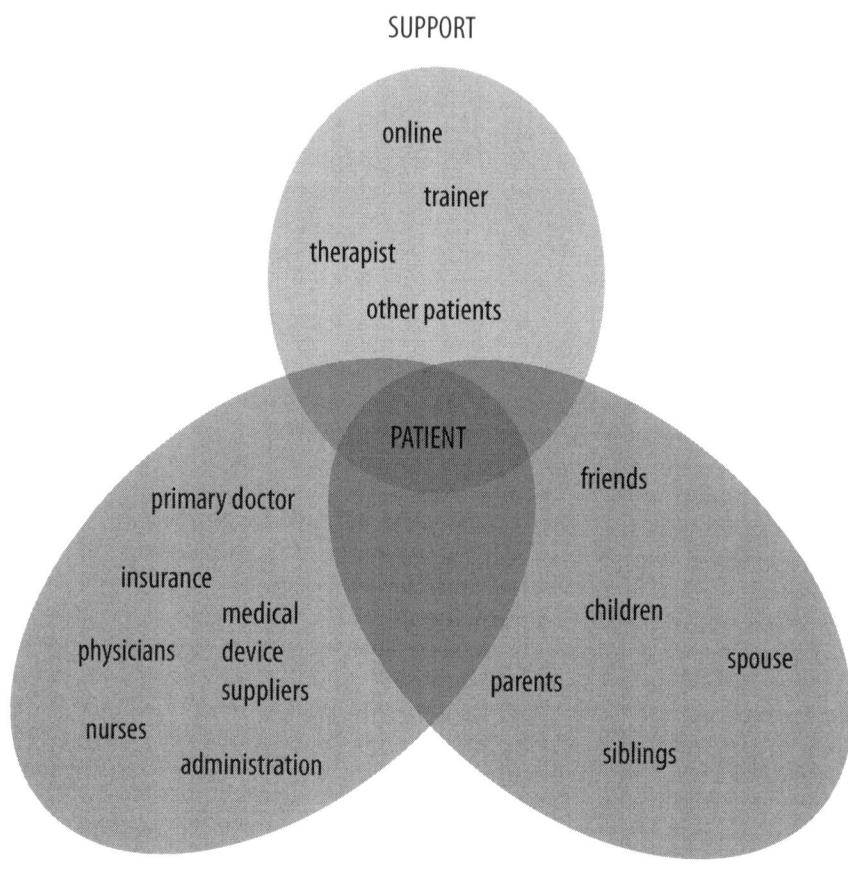

SUPPORT

online

trainer

therapist

other patients

PATIENT

friends

primary doctor

insurance

medical
device
suppliers

physicians

children

spouse

parents

nurses

siblings

administration

HEALTH CARE

FAMILY & FRIENDS

stakeholder map

WHAT IS IT?

Stakeholders maps are used to document the key stake holders and their relationship. They can include end users, those who will benefit, those who may be adversely affected, those who hold power and those who may sabotage design outcomes. At the beginning of a design project it is important to identify the key stake holders and their relationships. The map serves as a reference for the design team.

WHO INVENTED IT?

Mitchell 1997

WHY USE THIS METHOD?

1. Stakeholder mapping helps discover ways to influence other stakeholders.
2. Stakeholder mapping helps discover risks.
3. Stakeholder mapping helps discover positive stakeholders to involve in the design process.

CHALLENGES

1. Stakeholder mapping helps discover negative stakeholders and their associated risks.

RESOURCES

1. White board
2. Post-it-notes
3. Pens
4. Dry-erase markers
5. Interview data

WHEN TO USE THIS METHOD

1. Define intent
2. Know Context
3. Know User
4. Frame insights

HOW TO USE THIS METHOD

1. Develop a categorized list of the members of the stakeholder community.
2. Assign priorities
3. Map the 'highest priority' stakeholders.
4. Can initially be documented on a white board, cards, post-it-notes and consolidated as a diagram through several iterations showing hierarchy and relationships.

Some of the commonly used 'dimensions' include:
1. Power (three levels)
2. Support (three levels)
3. Influence (three levels)
4. Need (three levels)

REFERENCES

1. Mitchell, R. K., B. R. Agle, and D.J. Wood. (1997). "Toward a Theory of Stakeholder Identification and Salience: Defining the Principle of Who and What really Counts." in: Academy of Management Review 22(4): 853 - 888
2. Savage, G. T., T. W. Nix, Whitehead and Blair. (1991). "Strategies for assessing and managing organizational stakeholders." In: Academy of Management Executive 5(2): 61 – 75.

INTERNAL STAKEHOLDERS

FUNCTION	NAME 1	NAME 2	NAME 3	NAME 4
MARKETING				
SALES				
CUST. SERVICE				
HR				
IT				
ENGINEERING				
DESIGN				
MANAGEMENT				
FINANCE				
EMPLOYEES				
REPS				

Out of scope [ ]   In scope [ ]   Highest priority [ ]

EXTERNAL STAKEHOLDERS

FUNCTION	NAME 1	NAME 2	NAME 3	NAME 4
COMPETITORS				
GOVERNMENT				
CUSTOMERS				
SUPPLIERS				
MEDIA				
CLIENTS				

stakeholder scope matrix

WHAT IS IT?

A stakeholder scope map is a map that indicates the priority and scope of stakeholders in a project

WHO INVENTED IT?

Mel Silberman 2000

WHY USE THIS METHOD?

1. The map assists in identifying which stakeholders should be given priority during a project.

CHALLENGES

1. Should not be too detailed

REFERENCES

1. The Consultant's Toolkit: High-Impact Questionnaires, Activities and How-to. Guides for Diagnosing and Solving Client Problems, Mel Silberman (2000)

WHEN TO USE THIS METHOD

1. Define intent

HOW TO USE THIS METHOD

1. Brainstorm with your design team a list of internal stakeholders and a list of external stakeholders.
2. Determine which stakeholders are highest priority and which stakeholders are inside and outside the scope of the project management process.
3. Identify conflicts of interest.

RESOURCES

1. Pens
2. Paper
3. White board
4. Dry erase markers
5. Post-it-notes

STORYBOARD

PROJECT

NAME

DATE

PAGE

DIALOGUE

DIALOGUE

DIALOGUE

ACTION

ACTION

ACTION

238

storyboards

WHAT IS IT?

The storyboard is a narrative tool derived from cinema. A storyboard is a form of prototyping which communicates each step of an activity, experience or interaction. Used in films and multimedia as well as product and UX design. Storyboards consists of a number of 'frames' that communicate a sequence of events in context.

WHO INVENTED IT?

Invented by Walt Disney in 1927. Disney credited animator Webb Smith with creating the first storyboard. By 1937-38 all studios were using storyboards.

WHY USE THIS METHOD?

1. Can help gain insightful user feedback.
2. Conveys an experience.
3. Can use a storyboard to communicate a complex task as a series of steps.
4. Allows the proposed activities to be discussed and refined.
5. Storyboards can be used to help designers identify opportunities or use problems.

CHALLENGES

1. Interaction between the storyboard and a user is limited Participants may not be able to draw well.
2. There haven't been conclusive studies about the effectiveness of storyboards for some design activities.
3. Storyboarding is linear.
4. Not useful for detailed design.

WHEN TO USE THIS METHOD

1. Generate Concepts
2. Create Solutions

HOW TO USE THIS METHOD

1. Decide what story you want to describe.
2. Choose a story and a message: what do you want the storyboard to express?
3. Create your characters
4. Think about the whole story first rather than one panel at a time.
5. Create the drafts and refine them through an iterative process. Refine.
6. Illustrations can be sketches or photographs.
7. Consider: Visual elements, level of detail, text, experiences and emotions, number of frames, and flow of time.
8. Keep text short and informative.
9. 6 to 12 frames.
10. Tell your story efficiently and effectively.
11. Brainstorm your ideas.

RESOURCES

1. Pens
2. Digital camera
3. Storyboard templates
4. Comic books for inspiration

239

SUSTAINABILITY MAP

ENVIRONMENTALLY
SUSTAINABLE

ACTIVITY B

ACTIVITY I

ACTIVITY H

LOW BUSINESS
POTENTIAL

ACTIVITY G

HIGH BUSINESS
POTENTIAL

ACTIVITY F

ACTIVITY E

ACTIVITY C

ACTIVITY D

ACTIVITY A

NOT
ENVIRONMENTALLY
SUSTAINABLE

sustainability map

WHAT IS IT?

This method allows the team to assess the relative business potential and environmental impact of products and services.

WHY USE THIS METHOD?

1. Aids communication and discussion within the organization.
2. To gain competitive advantage with environmental sustainability,
3. Helps build competitive strategy
4. Helps build team alignment

CHALLENGES

1. Can be subjective

WHEN TO USE THIS METHOD

1. Know Context
2. Know User
3. Frame insights
4. Explore Concepts

HOW TO USE THIS METHOD

1. Moderator draws grid on whiteboard or flip chart.
2. Team brainstorms
3. Interpret the map.
4. Create strategy.
5. Products and services which have both high environmental sustainability and good business proposition are given priority.

RESOURCES

1. Pen
2. Paper
3. White board
4. Dry erase markers

SWIMLANES

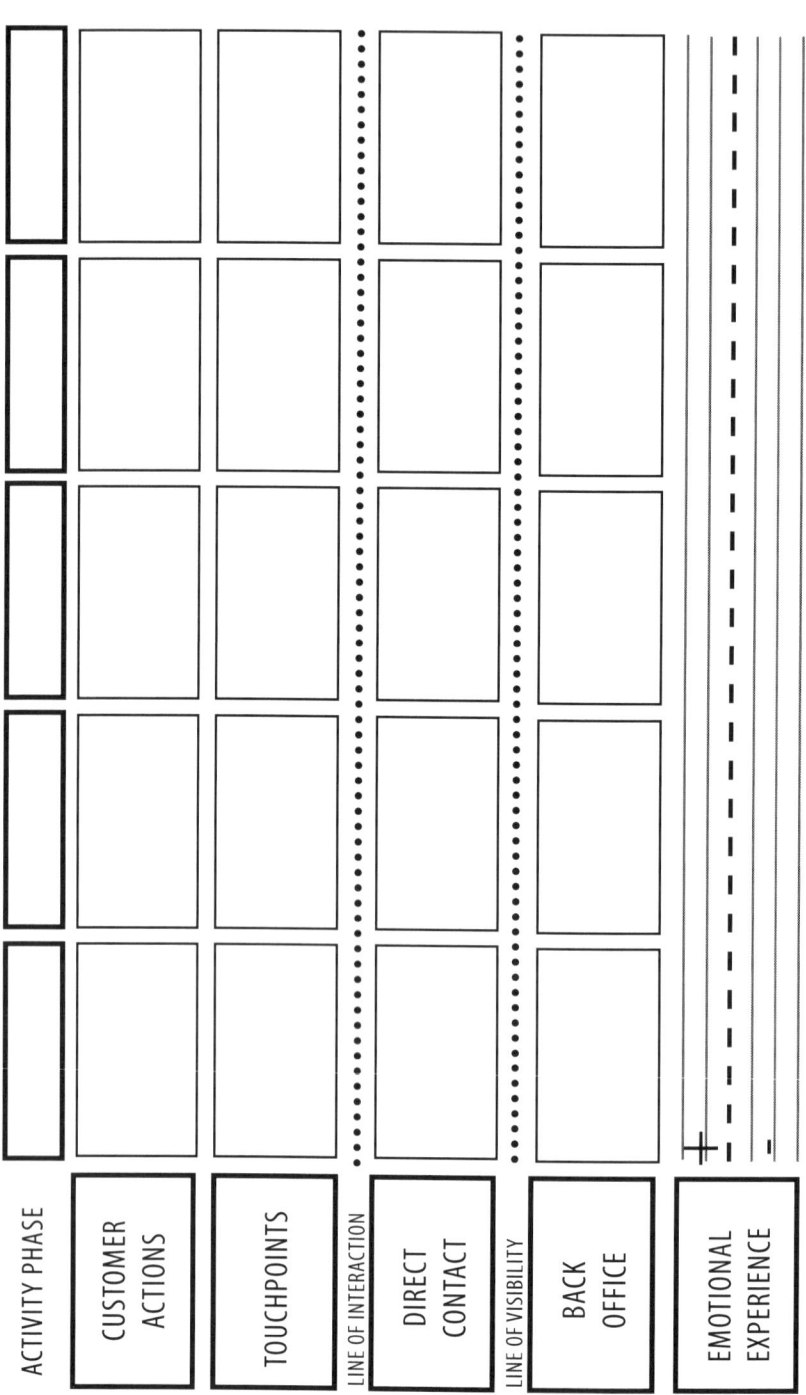

ACTIVITY PHASE

CUSTOMER ACTIONS

TOUCHPOINTS

LINE OF INTERACTION

DIRECT CONTACT

LINE OF VISIBILITY

BACK OFFICE

EMOTIONAL EXPERIENCE

swimlanes

WHAT IS IT?

Diagram that shows parallel streams for user, business, and technical process flows. You can include a storyboard lane. Create a blueprint for each persona, interaction or scenario. Provides a focus for discussion and refinement of services or experiences. They may document activities over time such as:

1. Customer Actions
2. Touch points
3. Direct Contact visible to customers
4. Invisible back office actions
5. Support Processes
6. Physical Evidence
7. Emotional Experience for customer.

WHO INVENTED IT?

Lynn Shostack 1983

WHY USE THIS METHOD?

1. Can be used for design or improvement of existing services or experiences.
2. Is more tangible than intuition.
3. Makes the process of service development more efficient.
4. A common point of reference for stakeholders for planning and discussion.
5. Tool to assess the impact of change.

WHEN TO USE THIS METHOD

1. Know Context
2. Know User
3. Frame insights

HOW TO USE THIS METHOD

1. Define the service or experience to focus on.
2. A blueprint can be created in a brainstorming session with stakeholders.
3. Define the customer demographic.
4. See though the customer's eyes.
5. Define the activities and phases of activity under each heading.
6. Link the contact or customer touchpoints to the needed support functions
7. Use post-it-notes on a white board for initial descriptions and rearrange as necessary drawing lines to show the links.
8. Create the blueprint then refine iteratively.

RESOURCES

1. Paper
2. Pens
3. White board
4. Dry-erase markers
5. Camera
6. Blueprint templates
7. Post-it-notes

REFERENCES

1. (1991) G. Hollins, W. Hollins, Total Design: Managing the design process in the service sector, Trans Atlantic Publications
2. (2004) R. Kalakota, M.Robinson, Services Blueprint: Roadmap for Execution, Addison-Wesley, Boston.

243

talk out loud protocol

WHAT IS IT?

Think aloud or thinking out loud protocols involve participants verbalizing their thoughts while performing a set of tasks. Users are asked to say whatever they are looking at, thinking, doing, and experiencing. A related method is the think-aloud protocol where subjects also explain their actions.

WHO INVENTED IT?

Clayton Lewis IBM 1993

WHY USE THIS METHOD?

1. Provides an understanding of the user's mental model and interaction with the product.
2. Enables observers to see first-hand the process of task completion
3. The terminology the user uses to express an idea or function the design or and documentation.
4. Allows testers to understand how the user approaches the system.

CHALLENGES

1. The design team needs to be composed of people with a variety of skills.

WHEN TO USE THIS METHOD

1. Know Context
2. Know User
3. Frame insights
4. Explore Concepts

HOW TO USE THIS METHOD

1. Identify users.
2. Choose representative tasks.
3. Create a mock-up or prototype.
4. Select participants.
5. Provide the test users with the system or prototype to be tested and tasks.
6. Brief participants.
7. Take notes of everything that users say, without attempting to interpret their actions and words.
8. Iterate
9. Videotape the tests, then analyze the videotapes.

RESOURCES

1. Computer
2. Video camera
3. Note pad
4. Pens

teachback

WHAT IS IT?

In the teachback method an expert explains a concept to a non-expert. The non-expert then tries to teach back what the expert had explained. During the teachback session, the expert corrects any misunderstandings.

WHY USE THIS METHOD?

1. Teachback is a way to confirm that you have explained what needs to be known in a manner that is understood.
2. The method can highlight concepts that are hard to understand.
3. Everyone benefits from clear information.
4. A chance to check for understanding and, if necessary, re-teach the information.

CHALLENGES

1. The teachback method is not highly structured.
2. It is hard to identify people at risk of misunderstanding.

WHEN TO USE THIS METHOD

1. Know Context
2. Know User
3. Frame insights
4. Deliver Offering

HOW TO USE THIS METHOD

1. Use Plain Language, avoid technical terms, talk slowly, break it down into short statements, focus on the 2 or 3 most important concepts.
2. Ask the subject to repeat in his or her own words how he or she understands the concept explained. If a process was demonstrated to the subject ask the subject to demonstrate it, "I want to be sure I explained everything clearly. Can you please explain it back to me so I can be sure I did?"
3. Ask the subject to verbalize their understanding to ensure that it is correct.
4. Repeat Steps 2 and 3 as necessary.
5. Ask the subject to explain or demonstrate how they will undertake an activity.

REFERENCES

1. Johnson, L. & Johnson, N.E., (1987). Knowledge Elicitation Involving Teachback Interviewing in Kidd, A.L., (Ed.), 1987, Knowledge Acquisition for Expert

other eyes

WHAT IS IT?

At several times during a design project it is useful to invite an outside group to review the state of the design and to tell your design team if they think that your design direction is real and good.

WHY USE THIS METHOD?

1. A design team can follow design directions that seem unworkable or unrealistic to end users because they may be remote from the end users of a product or service.

WHEN TO USE THIS METHOD

1. Explore concepts

RESOURCES

1. Pen
2. Paper
3. White board
4. Dry erase markers

HOW TO USE THIS METHOD

1. Define your design problem clearly
2. Select a group of outside people who are representative of the end users of a product or service.
3. Prepare a presentation that may include prototypes or images and statements that clearly communicate the favored concept direction.
4. Prepare a question guide to help your design team obtain useful feedback
5. Review your design with the outside group.
6. Refine your design based on the feedback
7. Provide feedback to the outside reviewers to let them know how their input has been useful.
8. It may be necessary to ask the external participants to sign a non disclosure agreement before to the design review.

unfocus group

WHAT IS IT?

Unfocus groups is a qualitative research method in which interviewers hold group interviews where the subjects are selected based on diverse viewpoints and backgrounds The participants may not be users of the product or service.

WHO INVENTED IT?

Uses methods pioneered by Liz Sanders and the consulting firm IDEO circa 2001

WHY USE THIS METHOD?

1.

WHEN TO USE THIS METHOD

1. Define intent
2. Know Context
3. Know User
4. Frame insights
5. Explore Concepts
6. Make Plans

HOW TO USE THIS METHOD

1. Assemble a diverse group of participants. Choose Diverse Participants Who:
- Are not likely to use the product or service,
- Are highly motivated.
- Are extreme users of the product
- Have a tangential connection with the product
- Don't want the product.
2. Select a good moderator.
3. Prepare a screening questionnaire.
4. Decide incentives for participants.
5. Select facility.
6. Recruit participants.
7. Provide refreshments.
8. Prepare the space. Participants should sit around a large table.
9. Describe rules.
10. First question should encourage talking and participation.
11. Provide simple materials such as paper and ask the participants to create crude prototypes for discussion.
12. Ask participants to act out ideas.
13. Record the feedback for idea generation phase.
14. Follow discussion guide.
15. At end of focus group summarize key points.
16. Moderator collects forms and debriefs focus group.

247

think out loud protocol

WHAT IS IT?

Think aloud or thinking out loud protocols involve participants verbalizing their thoughts while performing a set of tasks. Users are asked to say whatever they are looking at, thinking, doing, and feeling.

A related but method is the talk-aloud protocol where participants describe their activities but do not give explanations. This method is thought to be more objective

WHO INVENTED IT?

Clayton Lewis IBM 1993

WHY USE THIS METHOD?

1. Helps a researcher understand interaction with a product or service,.
2. Enables observers to see first-hand the process of task completion
3. The terminology the user uses to express an idea or function the design or and documentation.
4. Allows testers to understand how the user approaches the system.

CHALLENGES

1. The design team needs to be composed of persons with a variety of skills.
2. Pick a diverse, cross disciplinary team.

WHEN TO USE THIS METHOD

1. Know Context
2. Know User
3. Frame insights
4. Explore Concepts

HOW TO USE THIS METHOD

1. Identify users.
2. Choose Representative Tasks.
3. Create a Mock-Up or Prototype.
4. Select Participants.
5. Provide the test users with the system or prototype to be tested and tasks.
6. Brief participants.
7. Take notes of everything that users say, without attempting to interpret their actions and words.
8. Iterate
9. Videotape the tests, then analyze the videotapes.

RESOURCES

1. Computer
2. Video camera
3. Note pad
4. Pens

REFERENCES

1. Lewis, C. H. (1982). Using the "Thinking Aloud" Method In Cognitive Interface Design (Technical report). RC-9265.

triangulation

WHAT IS IT?

Triangulation is a research method where the researcher uses more than two research methods in one study to see if the different methods give similar findings. One example of triangulation is to compare observed behavior with the responses of a survey.

WHO INVENTED IT?

The comes from surveying where triangles are used to create a map.

WHY USE THIS METHOD?

1. Useful when analyzing large data sets.
2. It is employed in quantitative and qualitative research.
3. Helps overcome bias of a single method.
4. It may help the credibility of research conclusions.

CHALLENGES

1. There may be more than one valid conclusion from studying real world people and contexts.

WHEN TO USE THIS METHOD

1. Know Context
2. Know User
3. Frame insights

HOW TO USE THIS METHOD

Types of triangulation approaches include:
1. Dat triangulation where the researcher uses several different strategies for collecting data.
2. Researcher triangulation where more than one researcher is used
3. Method triangulation where more than one method is used to gather data.

REFERENCES

1. Denzin, N. (2006). Sociological Methods: A Sourcebook. Aldine Transaction. ISBN 978-0-202-30840-1. (5th edition).

VENN DIAGRAM

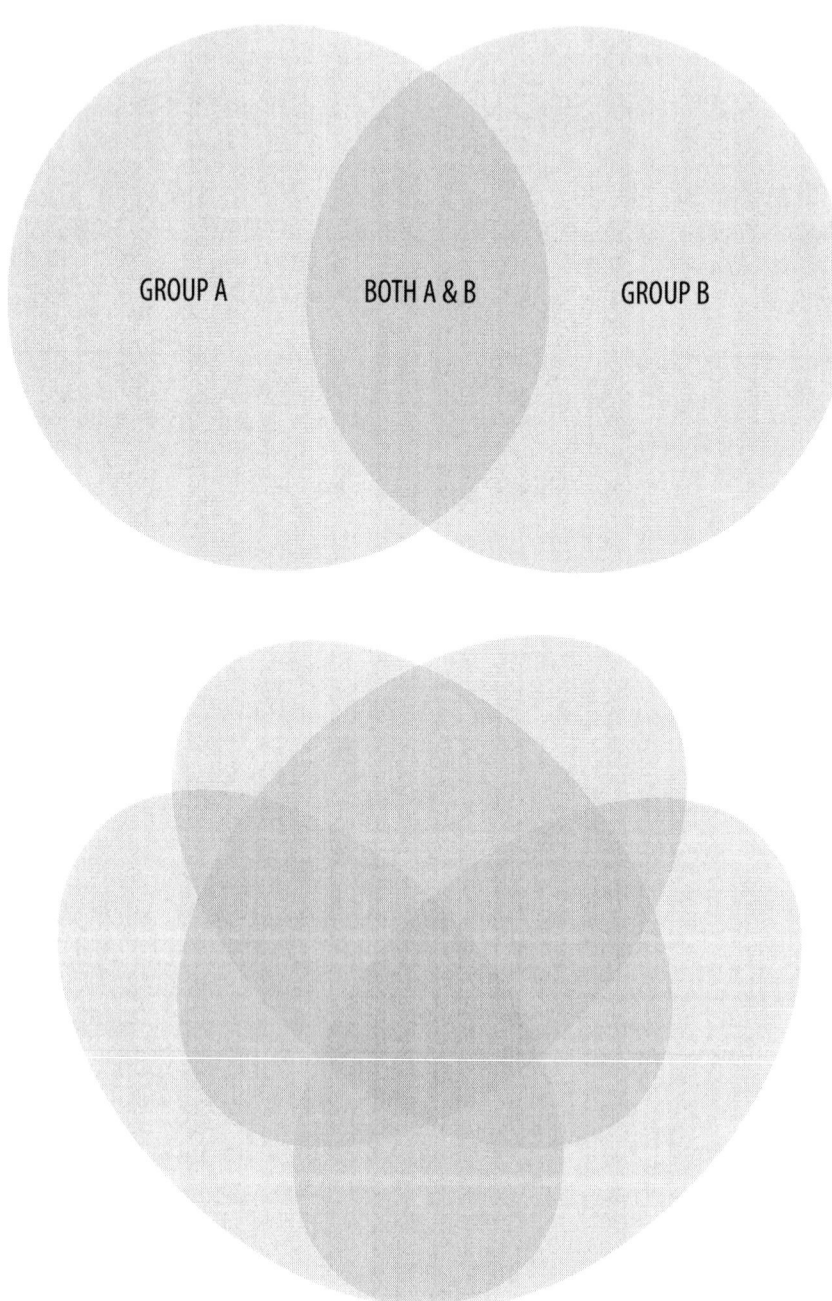

GROUP A BOTH A & B GROUP B

Venn's four-set diagram using ellipses

venn diagram

WHAT IS IT?

Venn diagrams normally are constructed from overlapping circles. The interior of the circle and the areas of overlap symbolically represents the elements of discreet sets.

WHO INVENTED IT?

John Venn 1880

WHY USE THIS METHOD?

1. A useful tool for simplifying and communicating data related to user populations and design features

WHEN TO USE THIS METHOD

1. Know Context
2. Know User
3. Frame insights

RESOURCES

1. Paper
2. Pens
3. Software

REFERENCES

1. Grimaldi, Ralph P. (2004). Discrete and combinatorial mathematics. Boston: Addison-Wesley. p. 143. ISBN 0-201-72634-3.
2. Edwards, A.W.F. (2004). Cogwheels of the mind: the story of Venn diagrams. JHU Press. ISBN 978-0-8018-7434-5.

surveys

WHAT IS IT?

Surveys are a method of collecting information. Surveys collect data usually from a large number of participants. A survey may be undertaken to study objects or animals as well as people. Surveys may take the form of a questionnaire or a face to face interview.

WHO INVENTED IT?

Sir Francis Galton 1800s

WHY USE THIS METHOD?

1. Easy to analyze
2. Large sample at relatively low cost.
3. Simple to manage
4. Familiar format
5. Quick to complete
6. Can be used for sensitive topics
7. Respondents have flexibility in time to complete.

CHALLENGES

1. Avoid complex questions
2. Avoid leading questions
3. Avoid jargon
4. Avoid bias
5. Have standard procedure
6. Ask one information at a time
7. Be as simple as possible
8. Adjust the style of the questions to the target audience

WHEN TO USE THIS METHOD

1. Know Context
2. Know User
3. Frame insights

HOW TO USE THIS METHOD

1. Define topics for research
2. Define the participants
3. Prepare the questions
4. Use closed questions with multiple predefined choices or open questions to allow respondents to respond in their own words.
5. Two common closed formats are: the Likert 7 point format: strongly agree, agree, undecided, disagree, strongly disagree. Or 4 point Forced choice format, Strongly agree, agree, disagree, strongly disagree.
6. Pretest the questionnaire
7. Refine the questionnaire
8. Questions should flow logically

REFERENCES

1. Gillham, B. (2008). Developing a questionnaire (2nd ed.). London, UK: Continuum International Publishing Group Ltd
2. Oppenheim, A. N. (2000). Questionnaire design, interviewing and attitude measurement (New ed.). London, UK: Continuum International Publishing Group Ltd.

wizard of oz

WHAT IS IT?

Wizard of Oz method is a research method in which research participants interact with a computer interface that subjects believe to be responding to their input, but which is being operated by an unseen person. The unseen operator is sometimes called the "wizard"

WHO INVENTED IT?

John F. Kelley
Johns Hopkins University. 1980 USA
Nigel Cross

WHY USE THIS METHOD?

1. Wizard of Oz is good for the testing of preliminary interface prototypes.
2. A relatively inexpensive type of simulation
3. Identify problems with an interface concept
4. Investigate visual affordance of an interface.

CHALLENGES

1. Requires training for the wizard.
2. It is difficult for wizards to provide consistent responses across sessions.
3. Computers respond differently than humans
4. It is difficult to evaluate systems with a complex interface using this method.

WHEN TO USE THIS METHOD

1. Know Context
2. Know User
3. Frame insights
4. Explore Concepts

HOW TO USE THIS METHOD

1. The wizard sits in a place not visible to the research participant.
2. The wizard observes the user's actions, and initiates the system's responses.
3. The "wizard" watches live video from a camera focused on the participant's hands and simulate the effects of the participant's actions.
4. Users are unaware that the actions of the system are being produced by the wizard.

RESOURCES

1. Video camera
2. Software interface prototype
3. Computers

REFERENCES

1. Höysniemi, J., Hämäläinen, P., and Turkki, L. 2004. Wizard of Oz prototyping of computer vision based action games for children. In Proceeding of the 2004 Conference on interaction Design and Children: Building A Community (Maryland, June 1–03, 2004). IDC '04. ACM Press, New York, NY, 27-34

wwwwwh

WHAT IS IT?

'Who, What, Where, When, Why, and How'? is a method for getting a thorough understanding of the problem, It is used to obtain basic information in police investigations. A well known golden rule of journalism is that if you want to know the full story about something you have to answer all the five W's. Journalists argue your story isn't complete until you answer all six questions.

1. Who is involved?
2. What occurred?
3. When did it happen?
4. Where did it happen?
5. Why did it occur?

"I keep six honest serving-men, They taught me all I knew; Their names are What and Why and When, And How and Where and Who" - *Rudyard Kipling*

WHO INVENTED IT?

Hermagoras of Temnos, Greece 1st century BC.

WHY USE THIS METHOD?

This method helps create a story that communicates clearly the nature of an activity or event to stakeholders.

CHALLENGES

1. The answers may be subjective.

WHEN TO USE THIS METHOD

1. Define intent
2. Know Context
3. Know User
4. Frame insights

HOW TO USE THIS METHOD

1. Ask the questions starting with the 5 w's and 1 h question words.
2. Identify the people involved
3. Identify the activities and make a list of them.
4. Identify all the places and make a list of them.
5. Identify all the time factors and make a list of them.
6. Identify causes for events of actions and make a list of them.
7. Identify the way events took place and make a list of them.
8. Study the relationships between the information.

RESOURCES

1. Pen
2. Paper

SOME SAMPLE
WWWWWH QUESTIONS

WHO

1. Is affected?
2. Who believes that the problem affects them?
3. Needs the problem solved?
4. Does not want the problem to be solved?
5. Could stand in the way of a solution?

WHEN

1. Does it happen
2. Doesn't it happen?
3. Did it start?
4. Will it end?
5. Is the solution needed?
6. Might it happen in the future?
7. Will it be a bigger problem?
8. Will it improve?

WHERE

1. Does it happen?
2. Doesn't it happen
3. Else does it happen?
4. Is the best place to solve the problem

WHY

1. Is this situation a problem?
2. Do you want to solve it?
3. Do you not want to solve it?
4. Does it not go away?
5. Would someone else want to solve it?
6. Can it be solved?
7. Is it difficult to solve?

WHAT

1. May be different in the future
2. Are its weaknesses?
3. Do you like?
4. Makes you unhappy about it?
5. Is flexible?
6. Is not flexible?
7. Do you know?
8. Do you not understand?
9. How have you solved similar problems?
10. Are the underlying ideas?
11. Are the values involved?
12. Are the elements of the problem and how are they related?
13. What can you assume to be correct
14. Is most important
15. Is least important
16. Are your goals?
17. Do you need to discover?

sampling: stratified

WHAT IS IT?

A sampling method that addresses the differences of subgroups, called strata, and ensures that a representative percentage is drawn from each stratum to form the sample.

WHO INVENTED IT?

Pierre Simon Laplace pioneered sampling 1786

WHY USE THIS METHOD?

1. Use when there are specific sub-groups to investigate.
2. May achieve greater statistical significance in a smaller sample.
3. May reduce standard error.

WHEN TO USE THIS METHOD

4. Know Context
5. Know User

HOW TO USE THIS METHOD

1. Divide the population up into a set of smaller non-overlapping sub-groups (strata), then do a simple random sample in each sub-group.
2. Strata can be natural groupings, such as age ranges or ethnic origins.

Source: changingminds.org

REFERENCES

1. Cochran, William G. (1977). Sampling techniques (Third ed.). Wiley. ISBN 0-471-16240-X
2. Robert Groves, et alia. Survey methodology (2010) Second edition of the (2004) first edition ISBN 0-471-48348-6.
3. Chambers, R L, and Skinner, C J (editors) (2003), Analysis of Survey Data, Wiley, ISBN 0-471-89987-9

sampling: systematic

WHAT IS IT?

A variation of random sampling in which members of a population are selected at a predetermined interval from a listing, time period, or space. Systematic sampling is also called systematic random sampling. Use when it is easiest to select every nth person.

WHO INVENTED IT?

Pierre Simon Laplace pioneered sampling 1786

WHY USE THIS METHOD?

1. Use when a stream of representative people are available.
2. Use when it is easiest to select every nth person.
3. Use when it is difficult to identify items using a simple random sampling method.

REFERENCES

1. Cochran, William G. (1977). Sampling techniques (Third ed.). Wiley. ISBN 0-471-16240-X
2. Robert Groves, et alia. Survey methodology (2010) Second edition of the (2004) first edition ISBN 0-471-48348-6.
3. Chambers, R L, and Skinner, C J (editors) (2003), Analysis of Survey Data, Wiley, ISBN 0-471-89987-9

WHEN TO USE THIS METHOD

1. Know Context
2. Know User

HOW TO USE THIS METHOD

1. "Identify your sample size, n. Divide the total number of items in the population, N, by n. Round the decimal down. This gives you your interval, k.
2. Thus for a population of 2000 and a sample of 100, k = 2000/100 = 20.
3. Put the population into a sequential order, ensuring the attribute being studied is randomly distributed.
4. Select a random number, x, between 1 and k.
5. The first sampled item is the x-th. Then select every k-th item.
6. Thus if k is 20 and x is 12, select the 12th item, then the 32nd, then the 52nd and so on.
7. In brief: select every nth item, starting with a random one"

Source: changingminds.org

257

sampling: time

WHAT IS IT?

Researchers choose time intervals for making observations.

WHO INVENTED IT?

Pierre Simon Laplace pioneered sampling 1786

WHY USE THIS METHOD?

The main advantages of sampling are:
1. The cost is lower,
2. Data collection is faster,
3. Time sampling is a useful way to collect and present observation data over a long period of time

CHALLENGES

1. Be careful to record events according to your plan.

WHEN TO USE THIS METHOD

1. Know Context
2. Know User

HOW TO USE THIS METHOD

1. Determine the goal of the research.
2. Select a place and participants.
3. Create a chart to record your data.
4. Carefully collect required data.

REFERENCES

1. Cochran, William G. (1977). Sampling techniques (Third ed.). Wiley. ISBN 0-471-16240-X
2. Robert Groves, et alia. Survey methodology (2010) Second edition of the (2004) first edition ISBN 0-471-48348-6.
3. Chambers, R L, and Skinner, C J (editors) (2003), Analysis of Survey Data, Wiley, ISBN 0-471-89987-9

sampling: expert

KNOW PEOPLE AND CONTEXT

WHAT IS IT?

A method of sampling where experts with a high level of knowledge are sampled.

WHO INVENTED IT?

Pierre Simon Laplace pioneered sampling 1786

WHY USE THIS METHOD?

1. The opinions of experts are respected.
2. May be credible with audience that accepts the people sampled as experts.

CHALLENGES

1. Not everyone will have the same definition of an expert.

WHEN TO USE THIS METHOD

1. Know Context
2. Know User

HOW TO USE THIS METHOD

1. If a pre study define the definition of an expert for the purpose of the sampling process.
2. Select those people who pass the definition of an expert for the sample.

REFERENCES

1. Cochran, William G. (1977). Sampling techniques (Third ed.). Wiley. ISBN 0-471-16240-X
2. Robert Groves, et alia. Survey methodology (2010) Second edition of the (2004) first edition ISBN 0-471-48348-6.
3. Chambers, R L, and Skinner, C J (editors) (2003), Analysis of Survey Data, Wiley, ISBN 0-471-89987-9

Chapter 5
Service Design Methods
Explore ideas

brainstorming methods

WHAT IS IT?

Brainstorming is one of the oldest,fastest and most widely used creativity methods. Brainstorming does need to be undertaken by experts. It can be undertaken as a group or individually. Osborn believed that brainstorming as a group was most effective. Recent research has questioned this assumption.

It should be used to address a single problem. Brainstorming is worthwhile when it is part of a larger process of design.

WHO INVENTED IT?

Alex Faickney Osborn 1953

WHY USE THIS METHOD?

1. It is useful for generating new types of solutions to problems.
2. Brainstorming allows each person in a group to better understand a problem.
3. It can be used to overcome creative blocks.
4. There is group buy-in to a design direction.

CHALLENGES

1. Groupthink
2. Not enough good ideas
3. Taking turns
4. Freeloading
5. Inhibition
6. Lack of critical thinking
7. A group that is too large competes for attention.

WHEN TO USE THIS METHOD

1. Explore Ideas

HOW TO USE THIS METHOD

1. A facilitator explains the problem to be explored and the process.
2. The problem can be written in a place where it can be seen by everyone participating
3. Defer judgment
4. Build on ideas to make them better.
5. Don't ridicule any idea.
6. One person speaking at a time.
7. Go for quantity the more ideas the better
8. No idea is too wild.
9. Stay focused on the problem
10. Be visual
11. Record everything.
12. Don't edit during a brainstorm
13. Preferred group size is from 2 to 12
14. A good facilitator should keep the ideas flowing.
15. Give a number of ideas to be generated for example 10 and time limit such as 30 minutes.
16. Analyze the results.

RESOURCES

1. Pens
2. Post-it-notes
3. A flip chart
4. White board or wall
5. Refreshments.

REFERENCES

1. Clark , Charles Hutchinson. The Dynamic New Way to Create Successful Ideas Publisher: Classic Business Bookshelf (November 23, 2010) ISBN-10: 1608425614 ISBN-13: 978-1608425617
2. Rawlinson J. Geoffrey Creative Thinking and Brainstorming. Jaico Publishing House (April 30, 2005) ISBN-10: 8172243480 ISBN-13: 978-8172243487

101 method

WHAT IS IT?

This is a brainstorming method focuses on creating volumes of ideas

WHY USE THIS METHOD?

1. Leverages the diverse experiences of a team.
2. A large volume of ideas helps overcome people's inhibitions to innovating.
3. Makes group problem solving fun.
4. Helps build team cohesion.
5. Everyone can participate.

CHALLENGES

1. Because the focus is on volume some ideas will not be useful.
2. Best used with other creativity methods

REFERENCES

1. Clark , Charles Hutchinson. The Dynamic New Way to Create Successful Ideas Publisher: Classic Business Bookshelf (November 23, 2010) ISBN-10: 1608425614 ISBN-13: 978-1608425617
2. Rawlinson J. Geoffrey Creative Thinking and Brainstorming. Jaico Publishing House (April 30, 2005) ISBN-10: 8172243480 ISBN-13: 978-8172243487

WHEN TO USE THIS METHOD

1. Explore Ideas

HOW TO USE THIS METHOD

1. Define a problem
2. Select a moderator
3. Select a diverse design team of 4 to 12 people and a moderator.
4. The moderator asks the team to each generate 101 solutions to the design problem in a defined time. Allow 30 to 60 minutes.
5. Analyze results and prioritize.
6. Develop actionable ideas.

RESOURCES

1. Pens
2. Post-it-notes
3. A flip chart
4. White board or wall
5. Refreshments

method 635

WHAT IS IT?

Method 635 is a structured form of brain-storming. "

Here six participant gain a thorough under-standing of the task at hand and them sepa-rately writes three rough ideas for solution. These three ideas are then passed on the one of the other participants who read and add three additional ideas or modifications. This process continues until all participants have expanded or revised all original ideas. Six participants, three ideas, five rounds of supplements"
(Löwgren and Stolterman 2004).

WHO INVENTED IT?

Professor Bernd Rohrbach 1968

WHY USE THIS METHOD?

1. Can generate a lot of ideas quickly
2. Participants can build on each others ideas
3. Ideas are recorded by the participants
4. Democratic method.
5. Ideas are contributed privately.

SEE ALSO

1. Brainwriting
2. Dot voting

WHEN TO USE THIS METHOD

1. Frame insights
2. Explore Ideas

HOW TO USE THIS METHOD

1. Your team should sit around a table.
2. Each team member is given a sheet of paper with the design objective written at the top.
3. Each team member is given three minutes to generate three ideas.
4. Your participants then pass the sheet of paper to the person sitting on their left.
5. Each participant must come up with three new ideas.
6. The process can stop when sheets come around the table.
7. Repeat until ideas are exhausted. No discussion at any stage.
8. No discussion.
9. Analyze ideas as a group,

RESOURCES

1. Paper
2. Pens
3. White board
4. Large table

REFERENCES

1. Rohrbach, Bernd: Creativity by rules - Method 635, a new technique for solv-ing problems first published in the Ger-man sales magazine "Absatzwirtschaft", Volume 12, 1969. p73-75 and Volume 19, 1 October 1969.

alpha brainstorming

WHAT IS IT?

A brainstorming method that uses the alphabet for inspiration.

WHO INVENTED IT?

WHY USE THIS METHOD?

1. There is a hierarchy of ideas
2. This method generates many ideas.
3. This method highlights the connections between ideas which is the starting point for a design solution.

CHALLENGES

1. Groupthink
2. Not enough good ideas
3. Taking turns
4. Freeloading
5. Inhibition
6. Lack of critical thinking
7. A group that is too large competes for attention.

RESOURCES

1. Paper
2. Pens
3. White board
4. Dry-erase markers
5. Post-it-notes.

WHEN TO USE THIS METHOD

1. Explore Ideas

HOW TO USE THIS METHOD

1. The moderator introduces the method to the group.
2. The problem is defined by the moderator.
3. The larger group is broken down into groups of 4 or 5 participants.
4. One participant is asked to offer a solution to the design problem that starts with the letter A
5. The moderator records the ideas on a white board.
6. The person to the left of the first participant to present is asked to define a solution that starts with the letter B.
7. Continue until participants have proposed solutions starting with each letter of the alphabet.
8. The participants are asked to vote for their three preferred solutions.
9. Select the top ideas for further development.

aoki method

WHAT IS IT?

The Aoki or MBS method is a structured brainstorming method that stresses input by all team members.

WHO INVENTED IT?

Sadami Aoki. Used by Mitsubishi

WHY USE THIS METHOD?

1. There is a hierarchy of ideas
2. This method requires that a quantity of ideas is generated.
3. shifts you from reacting to a static snapshot of the problem and broadens your perspective toward the problem and the relationships and connections between its components

CHALLENGES

1. Groupthink
2. Not enough good ideas
3. Taking turns
4. Freeloading
5. Inhibition
6. Lack of critical thinking
7. A group that is too large competes for attention.

WHEN TO USE THIS METHOD

1. Explore Ideas

RESOURCES

1. Paper
2. Pens
3. White board
4. Dry-erase markers
5. Post-it-notes.

HOW TO USE THIS METHOD

6. Warm Up: Participants generate ideas for 15 minutes.
7. Participants present their ideas verbally to the larger group.
8. The larger group continues to generate ideas during the individual presentations.
9. For one hour the individual team members further explain their ideas to the group
10. Idea maps are created by the moderator.

REFERENCES

1. Clark , Charles Hutchinson. The Dynamic New Way to Create Successful Ideas Publisher: Classic Business Bookshelf (November 23, 2010) ISBN-10: 1608425614 ISBN-13: 978-1608425617
2. Rawlinson J. Geoffrey Creative Thinking and Brainstorming. Jaico Publishing House (April 30, 2005) ISBN-10: 8172243480 ISBN-13: 978-8172243487

analogies and metaphors

WHAT IS IT?

A method to help clarify an issue when exploring complex ideas. An analogy is a way of showing similarities between two different things. a metaphor is a representation of something.

WHO INVENTED IT?

Ava S, Butler 1996

WHY USE THIS METHOD?

1. Unstructured meetings waste time by trying to discuss all aspects of an issue at once.
2. This method saves time and improves the outcomes and efficiency of meetings.
3. Useful when discussing complex issues

RESOURCES

1. Paper
2. Pens
3. Whiteboard
4. Dry erase markers

WHEN TO USE THIS METHOD

1. Know Context
2. Know User
3. Frame insights
4. Explore Ideas

HOW TO USE THIS METHOD

1. Define the problem to be addressed.
2. The moderator introduces the problem and the method.
3. The moderator gives the group five minutes to consider appropriate analogies and metaphors.
4. Each participant presents their best analogies and metaphors to the group.
5. The group selects the best analogies and metaphors.
6. Summarize learnings.

REFERENCES

1. Butler, Ava S. (1996) Teamthink Publisher: Mcgraw Hill ISBN 0070094330
2. Clark , Charles Hutchinson. The Dynamic New Way to Create Successful Ideas Publisher: Classic Business Book-shelf (November 23, 2010) ISBN-10: 1608425614 ISBN-13: 978-1608425617
3. Rawlinson J. Geoffrey Creative Thinking and Brainstorming. Jaico Publish-ing House (April 30, 2005) ISBN-10: 8172243480 ISBN-13: 978-8172243487

backcasting

WHAT IS IT?

Backcasting is a method for planning the actions necessary to reach desired future goals. This method is often applied in a workshop format with stakeholders participating. The future scenarios are developed for periods of between 1 and 20 years in the future.

The participants first identify their goals and then work backwards to identify the necessary actions to reach those goals.

WHO INVENTED IT?

AT&T 1950s, Shel 1970s

WHY USE THIS METHOD?

1. It is inexpensive and fast
2. Backcasting is a tool for identifying, planning and reaching future goals.
3. Backcasting provides a strategy to reach future goals.

CHALLENGES

1. Need a good moderator
2. Needs good preparation

RESOURCES

1. Post-it-notes
2. White board
3. Pens
4. Dry-erase markers
5. Cameras

WHEN TO USE THIS METHOD

1. Define intent
2. Know Context
3. Know User
4. Frame insights
5. Explore Ideas
6. Make Plans
7. Deliver Offering

HOW TO USE THIS METHOD

A typical backcasting question is "How would you define success for yourself in 2015?

1. Define a framework
2. Analyze the present situation in relation to the framework
3. Prepare a vision and a number of desirable future scenarios.
4. Back-casting: Identify the steps to achieve this goal.
5. Further elaboration, detailing
6. Step by step strategies towards achieving the outcomes desired.
7. Ask do the strategies move us in the right direction? Are they flexible strategies?. Do the strategies represent a good return on investment?
8. Implementation, policy, organization embedding, follow-up

REFERENCES

1. Quist, J., & Vergragt, P. 2006. Past and future of backcasting: The shift to stakeholder participation and a proposal for a methodological framework. Futures Volume 38, Issue 9, November 2006, 1027-1045

banned

WHAT IS IT?

Banned is a method involving creating future scenarios based on imagining a world if a product, service system or experience did not exist and how people would possibly adapt.

WHO INVENTED IT?

Herman Kahn, Rand Corporation 1950, US

WHY USE THIS METHOD?

1. May uncover new design directions and possibilities not dependent on existing products services and systems.
2. Expose problems and opportunities.
3. Banned Scenarios become a focus for discussion related to a user experience. which helps evaluate and refine concepts. They can be used to challenge concepts through prototyping user interactions.

REFERENCES

1. "Scenarios," IDEO Method Cards. ISBN 0-9544132-1-0
2. Carroll, John M. Making Use: Scenario-based design of human-computer interactions. MIT Press, 2000.
3. Carroll J. M. Five Reasons for Scenario Based Design. Elsevier Science B. V. 2000.
4. Carroll, John M. Scenario-Based Design: Envisioning Work and Technology in System Development.

WHEN TO USE THIS METHOD

1. Know Context
2. Know User
3. Frame insights
4. Explore Ideas

HOW TO USE THIS METHOD

This exercise can be done individually or in group.

1. Decide the question to investigate.
2. Decide time and scope for the scenario process.
3. Identify stake holders.
4. Identify uncertainties.
5. Define the scenarios.
6. Can use with personas. Who is the persona? What is the experience? What is the outcome?
7. Create storyboards.
8. Analyze the scenarios through discussion.
9. Iterate as necessary.
10. Summarize insights

RESOURCES

1. Storyboard templates
2. Post-it-notes
3. Pens
4. Dry-erase markers
5. Video cameras
6. Empathy tools
7. Props

269

bodystorming

WHAT IS IT?

Bodystorming is method of prototyping experiences. It requires setting up an experience - complete with necessary artifacts and people - and physically "testing" it. A design team play out scenarios based on design concepts that they are developing. The method provides clues about the impact of the context on the user experience.

WHO INVENTED IT?

Buchenau, Fulton 2000

WHY USE THIS METHOD?

1. You are likely to find new possibilities and problems.
2. Generates empathy for users.
3. This method is an experiential design tool. Bodystorming helps design ideation by exploring context.
4. It is fast and inexpensive.
5. It is a form of physical prototyping
6. It is difficult to imagine misuse scenarios

CHALLENGES

1. Some team members may find acting a difficult task.

RESOURCES

1. Empathy tools
2. A large room
3. White board
4. Video camera

WHEN TO USE THIS METHOD

1. Know Context
2. Know User
3. Frame insights
4. Explore Ideas

HOW TO USE THIS METHOD

1. Select team.
2. Define the locations where a design will be used.
3. Go to those locations and observe how people interact. the artifacts in their environment.
4. Develop the prototypes and props that you need to explore an idea. Identify the people, personas and scenarios that may help you with insight into the design directions.,
5. Bodystorm the scenarios.
6. Record the scenarios with video and analyze them for insights.

REFERENCES

Understanding contexts by being there: case studies in bodystorming. Personal and Ubiquitous Computing, Vol. 7, No. 2. (July 2003), pp. 125-134, doi:10.1007/s00779-003-0238-7 by Antti Oulasvirta, Esko Kurvinen, Tomi Kankainen

freewriting

WHAT IS IT?

WHO INVENTED IT?

Alex Faickney Osborn 1953 is often credited with inventing brainstorming.

WHY USE THIS METHOD?

1. There is a hierarchy of ideas
2. This method generates many ideas.
3. This method highlights the connections between ideas which is the starting point for a design solution.

CHALLENGES

1. Groupthink
2. Not enough good ideas
3. Taking turns
4. Freeloading
5. Inhibition
6. Lack of critical thinking
7. A group that is too large competes for attention.

RESOURCES

1. Paper
2. Pens
3. White board
4. Dry-erase markers
5. Post-it-notes.

WHEN TO USE THIS METHOD

1. Explore Ideas

HOW TO USE THIS METHOD

1. The moderator introduces the method to the group.
2. The problem is defined by the moderator.
3. The moderator instructs the participants to begin writing about the design problem and not to stop until the time is up.
4. Allow ten minutes and give each participant 10 to 20 pages of blank copy paper.
5. After ten minutes each participant passes the pages that they have written to the participant on their left.
6. Each participant reviews the written material, underlines ideas that they find interesting and is asked to provide a one sentence summary of the content
7. Allow ten minutes.
8. After ten minutes each participant presents their underlined ideas and summary to the group.
9. The group selects the most interesting ideas for further development.

271

brainwriting

WHAT IS IT?

Brainwriting is an alternative to brainstorming generating ideas by asking people to write down their ideas rather than presenting them verbally.

WHO INVENTED IT?

Brahm & Kleiner, 1996

WHY USE THIS METHOD?

1. Moderation of Brainwriting is easier than brainstorming.
2. Brainwriting tends to produce more ideas than brainstorming
3. Can be conducted in 15 to 30 minutes
4. Brainwriting is better if participants are shy or from cultures where group interaction is more guarded.
5. Brainwriting reduces the problems of groupthink.

CHALLENGES

1. Not enough good ideas
2. Freeloading
3. Inhibition
4. Lack of critical thinking

WHEN TO USE THIS METHOD

1. Explore Ideas

HOW TO USE THIS METHOD

1. Define the problem
2. Each participant should brainstorm three solutions in two minutes in written form.
3. Then have them pass the sheet of paper to their left.
4. Have the participants add to or build upon the existing suggestions by writing their own ideas underneath the original solutions. Allow 3 minutes.
5. The process should be repeated as many times as there are people around the table allowing an additional minute each time.
6. When you've finished post the ideas on a wall.
7. Get the group to vote on the most promising ideas.

RESOURCES

1. Pens
2. Post-it-notes
3. A flip chart
4. White board or wall
5. Refreshments.

REFERENCES

1. Clark , Charles Hutchinson. The Dynamic New Way to Create Successful Ideas Publisher: Classic Business Bookshelf (November 23, 2010) ISBN-10: 1608425614 ISBN-13: 978-1608425617
2. Rawlinson J. Geoffrey Creative Thinking and Brainstorming. Jaico Publishing House (April 30, 2005) ISBN-10: 8172243480 ISBN-13: 978-8172243487

dark horse prototype

WHAT IS IT?

A dark horse prototype is your most creative idea built as a fast prototype. The innovative approach serves as a focus for finding the optimum real solution to the design problem.

WHO INVENTED IT?

One of the methods taught at Stanford University.

WHY USE THIS METHOD?

1. This method is a way of breaking free of average solutions and exploring unknown territory
2. A way of challenging assumptions.

CHALLENGES

1. Fear of unexplored directions
2. Fear of change
1. Designers can become too attached to their prototypes and allow them to become jewelry that stands in the way of further refinement.
2. Client may believe that system is real.

WHEN TO USE THIS METHOD

1. Explore Ideas

HOW TO USE THIS METHOD

1. After initial brainstorming sessions select with your team the most challenging, interestingly or thought provoking idea.
2. Create a low resolution prototype of the selected idea.
3. With your team analyze and discuss the prototype.
4. Brainstorm ways of bringing back the dark horse concept into a realizable solution.

REFERENCES

1. Constantine, L. L., Windl, H., Noble, J., and Lockwood, L. A. D. "From Abstraction to Realization in User Interface Design: Abstract Prototypes Based on Canonical Components." Working Paper, The Convergence Colloquy, July 2000.

273

crawford slip method

WHAT IS IT?

The Crawford Slip method is a form of brainstorming that was developed in the 1920s and may have been the inspiration for most forms of brainstorming today. It was the origin of the method of brainstorming most common today. A moderator defines a problem statement, then participants record their ideas on 3 × 5 index cards.

WHO INVENTED IT?

The Crawford slip method was developed in the late 1920's by Dr. C. Crawford of the University of Southern California

WHY USE THIS METHOD?

1. Any size group
2. Commonly used for 50 to 200 participants but can be used for up to 5,000 people.
3. Any seating arrangement.
4. Broader participation (includes less expressive participants).
5. Large quantity of ideas.
6. Good for sensitive topics since participants' input is anonymous, without team interaction.
7. Easier process of sorting ideas.

CHALLENGES

1. Written ideas may need to be explained verbally.
2. Written ideas may be stated as a word if a detailed description would be too long.
3. All members participate.

WHEN TO USE THIS METHOD

1. Explore Ideas

HOW TO USE THIS METHOD

1. Define the problem
2. Distribute 3 inch by 5 inch blank index cards to each team member. 20 cards each may be a suitable number.
3. The moderator writes the problem statement on a white board.
4. Participants spend 20 minutes to 40 minutes generating ideas and describing one idea per index card with sketches or written descriptions. One sentence or idea per card.
5. The cards are returned to the moderator and spread out on a large table.
6. The cards are sorted into between 3 and 10 large categories. The categories depend on the problem and are generated by the team through discussion.
7. The categories are prioritized.

RESOURCES

1. Pens
2. Paper
3. 3 X 5 inch index cards

REFERENCES

1. Dettmer H, W. Brainpower Networking Using the Crawford Slip Method. Publisher: Trafford (October 2003) ISBN-10: 141200909X ISBN-13: 978-1412009096

digital method

WHAT IS IT?

This brainstorming method uses an electronic meeting system or e-mail.

WHY USE THIS METHOD?

1. Ideas are automatically recorded.
2. This method requires that a quantity of ideas is generated.
3. The session can be a short duration such as 30 minutes or over a long duration such as 2 weeks.
4. Enables much larger groups to brainstorm on a topic than would normally be productive in a traditional brainstorming session

CHALLENGES

1. Groupthink
2. Not enough good ideas
3. Taking turns
4. Freeloading
5. Inhibition
6. Lack of critical thinking

WHEN TO USE THIS METHOD

1. Explore Ideas

RESOURCES

1. Computer
2. Internet connection
3. Brainstorming software
4. E-mail
5. Electronic meeting system.

HOW TO USE THIS METHOD

1. Define a problem to be explored
2. Appoint a moderator.
3. Each participant connects through an electronic meeting system
4. Participants share ideas
5. Ideas are immediately visible to the group
6. Ideas are often anonymously posted or through avatars.
7. Review the contributions.

disney method

WHAT IS IT?

The Disney method is a parallel thinking technique. It allows a team to discuss an issue from four perspectives. It involves parallel thinking to analyze a problem, generate ideas, evaluate ideas, and to create a strategy. It is a method used in workshops. The four thinking perspectives are - Spectators,
Dreamers, Realist's and Critics.

WHO INVENTED IT?

Dilts, 1991

WHY USE THIS METHOD?

1. Allows the group top discuss a problem from four different perspectives

CHALLENGES

1. An alternative to De Bono Six hat Method.
2. Will deliver a workable solution quickly.

WHEN TO USE THIS METHOD

1. Explore Ideas

HOW TO USE THIS METHOD

1. At the end of each of the four sessions the participants leave the room and then at a later time reenter the room then assuming the personas and perspectives of the next group. Time taken is often 60 to 90 minutes in total.
2. The spectator's view. Puts the problem in an external context. How would a consultant, a customer or an outside observer view the problem?
3. The Dreamers view. Looking for an ideal solution. What would our dream solution for this be? What if? Unconstrained brainstorm. Defer judgement. Divergent thinking. What do we desire? If we could have unlimited resources what would we do? They list their ideas on the white board.
4. Realists view. The realists are convergent thinkers. How can we turn the dreamer's views into reality? Looking for ideas that are feasible, profitable, customer focused and can be implemented within 18 months. They look through the dreamer's ideas on the white board and narrow them down to a short list, discuss them and choose the single best idea and create an implementation plan. What steps are necessary to implement this idea? Who can approve it, how much funding is needed? They draw the plan on the whiteboard and then leave the room.
5. The Critics view. What are the risks and obstacles? Who would oppose this plan? What could go wrong? Refine, improve or reject. Be constructive. This group defines the risks and obstacles, make some suggestions and write down these ideas on the white board.

RESOURCES

1. White board
2. Dry erase markers.
3. Pens

five points

WHAT IS IT?

This method is a way of selecting a concept direction from a number of alternatives based on the preferences of your design team. Each participant is given five points to distribute between the concepts they like the most.

WHY USE THIS METHOD?

1. It is a fast and effective way of selecting the best concepts to develop.

CHALLENGES

1. Can be subjective
2. Team members can influence voting by the strength of their personality.

WHEN TO USE THIS METHOD

1. Explore Ideas

RESOURCES

1. Pen
2. Paper
3. White board
4. Dry erase markers

HOW TO USE THIS METHOD

1. Assemble your design team.
2. Brainstorm concepts
3. Pin the concepts on a wall
4. Team members present their ideas to the group.
5. Each team member is given five points to allocate to the concepts
6. This method works best if your team is between 4 and 12 people and a diverse cross disciplinary team
7. Each team member has five points to allocate.
8. They can allocate them all to one idea or distribute the points between several ideas.
9. Team members shouldn't vote for their own ideas.
10. Total the points and develop the ideas with most points in a further brainstorming session.

dot voting

WHAT IS IT?

This method is a collective way of prioritizing and converging on a design solution that uses group wisdom. Concepts can be individually scored against selection criteria such as the business proposition, ease of manufacturing, cost and usability. Each participant scores each concept against a list of assessment criteria and the scores are totaled to determine the favored ideas.

WHY USE THIS METHOD?

It is a method of selecting a favored idea by collective rather than individual judgment. It is a fast method that allows a design to progress. It leverages the strengths of diverse team member viewpoints and experiences.

CHALLENGES

1. The assessment is subjective.
2. Groupthink
3. Not enough good ideas
4. Inhibition
5. Lack of critical thinking

RESOURCES

1. Large wall
2. Adhesive dots

REFERENCES

1. Dotmocracy handbook Jason Diceman Version 2.2 March 2010 ISBN 45152708X EAN-13 9781451527087

Image Copyright, avian 2013
Used under license from Shutterstock.com

WHEN TO USE THIS METHOD

1. Define intent
2. Know Context
3. Know User
4. Frame insights
5. Explore Ideas
6. Make Plans
7. Deliver Offering

HOW TO USE THIS METHOD

1. Select a team of between 4 and 20 cross disciplinary participants.
2. Brainstorm ideas for example ask each team member to generate six ideas as sketches.
3. Each idea should be presented on one post it note or page.
4. Each designer should quickly explain each idea to the group before the group votes.
5. Spread the ideas over a wall or table.
6. Ask the team to group the ideas by similarity or affinity.
7. Ask the team to vote on their two or three favorite ideas and total the votes. You can use sticky dots or colored pins to indicate a vote or a moderator can tally the scores.
8. Rearrange the ideas so that the ideas with the dots are grouped together, ranked from most dots to least.
9. Talk about the ideas that received the most votes and see if there is a general level of comfort with taking one or more of those ideas to the next step.

DOUBLE REVERSAL PROCESS

1
PREVIOUSLY BRAINSTORMED IDEAS

2
REVERSE THE PROBLEM
BRAINSTORM NEW IDEAS

3
REVERSE THE REVERSED
PROBLEM IDEAS

4
ADD NEW IDEAS TO PREVIOUSLY
BRAINSTORMED IDEAS

double reversal

WHAT IS IT?

The double reversal is a reversed thinking process that allows teams to continue with idea generating after they have run out of ideas or simply have found no novel way of looking at the problem. This tool requires an issue, idea, or goal to be reversed or stated in a negative form in order to gain more ideas of what could cause the problem. Reversing again each reversed idea should produce potential action steps to consider in the problem solution phase.

WHY USE THIS METHOD?

1. To identify new solutions for a design problem.
1. To expaand a list of previously brainstormed ideas.
1. To take a new perspective after an unproductive brainstorming effort.

WHEN TO USE THIS METHOD

1. Explore Ideas

HOW TO USE THIS METHOD

1. Start with a collection of previously brainstormed ideas.
2. Display the ideas and discuss them with your team.
3. Reverse the objective.
4. Your team brainstorms how to make the problem worse with each idea.
5. Record the ideas on a white board the double reversal process.
6. The team reverses the ideas. A double reversal.
7. Add the new set of ideas to the original set.

RESOURCES

1. Pens
2. Paper
3. White board
4. Dry erase markers
5. Post it notes.

go and no go

WHAT IS IT?

A method to determine when your team is ready to move on to the next discussion item in a meeting.

WHO INVENTED IT?

Ava S, Butler 1996

WHY USE THIS METHOD?

1. Unstructured meetings waste time by trying to discuss all aspects of an issue at once.
2. This method saves time and improves the outcomes and efficiency of meetings.
3. Useful when discussing complex issues

RESOURCES

1. Paper
2. Pens
3. Whiteboard
4. Dry erase markers

WHEN TO USE THIS METHOD

1. Define intent
2. Make Plans

HOW TO USE THIS METHOD

1. When the moderator thinks that it is time to move on to the next agenda item ask:
- "All in favor of moving on to the next agenda item say Go"
- "All in favor of not moving forward say No Go"
2. If there are more no go votes the moderator asks "what needs to happen before we will feel comfortable moving forward?"
3. Iterate if necessary.

REFERENCES

1. Butler, Ava S. (1996) Teamthink Publisher: Mcgraw Hill ISBN 0070094330

crowd sourcing

WHAT IS IT?

Crowd sourcing involves out sourcing a task to a dispersed group of people. It usually refers to tasks undertaken by an undefined public group rather than paid employees. Types of crowd sourcing include:

1. Crowd funding
2. Crowd purchasing
3. Micro work

The incentives for crowd sourcing can include: immediate payoffs, delayed payoffs, and social motivation, skill variety, task identity, task autonomy, direct feedback from the job

WHO INVENTED IT?

Jeff Howe first used the term in a June 2006 Wired magazine article "The Rise of Crowd sourcing"

WHY USE THIS METHOD?

1. Crowd sourcing can obtain large numbers of alternative solutions.
2. It is relatively fast
3. Inexpensive.
4. Diverse solutions.
5. group of people is sometimes more intelligent than an individual

CHALLENGES

1. A faulty results caused by targeted, malicious work efforts
2. Ethical concerns
3. Difficulties in collaboration and team activity of crowd members.
4. Lack of monetary motivation

WHEN TO USE THIS METHOD

1. Define intent
2. Know Context
3. Know User
4. Frame insights
5. Explore Ideas
6. Make Plans
7. Deliver Offering

HOW TO USE THIS METHOD

1. Define your problem
2. Define your use of the crowd
3. Identify incentives.
4. Identify mechanism to reach the crowd.
5. Inspire your users to create
6. Distribute brief to the crowd
7. Analyze results.
8. Create preferred design solution.
9. Repeat above stages as necessary to refine the design.

RESOURCES

1. A social or other network
2. Crowd sourcing site or interface
3. A mechanism to reach the crowd.
4. An incentive for the crowd.
5. A crowd

REFERENCES

1. Howe, Jeff (2008), "Crowd sourcing: Why the Power of the Crowd is Driving the Future of Business", The International Achievement Institute.

OBJECTS	ACTIONS
remote control	smell
button	hear
computer	touch
phone	see
car	walk
sailboat	sing
camera	talk
television	dance
internet	vision
gps	laugh
mp3 player	magic
book	swim
	play
	tell a story

heuristic ideation

WHAT IS IT?

Heuristic ideation method is used to create new concepts, ideas, products or solutions.

WHY USE THIS METHOD?

1. To create new connections and insights for products, services and experiences

WHO INVENTED IT?

Couger 1995, McFadzean 1998, McFadzean, Somersall, and Coker 1998, VanGundy 1988

RESOURCES

1. Pens
2. Markers
3. White board or flip chart
4. Dry erase markers

WHEN TO USE THIS METHOD

1. Explore Ideas

HOW TO USE THIS METHOD

1. The group will first make two lists of words
2. Each team member selects three words from the first list and connects each word to a different word in the second list.
3. Each team members develops these ideas into concepts and illustrates or describes each concept on an index card.
4. The index cards are places on a pin board and each concept is briefly described by the team member who generated the idea.
5. The team votes to prioritize the ideas

REFERENCES

1. McFadzean, E. Creativity in MS / OR: Choosing the Appropriate Technique Interfaces 29: 5 September October 1999 (pp 110 122)

greeting cards

WHAT IS IT?

This is a group creativity method that uses greeting cards as a focus to stimulate ideas.

WHO INVENTED IT?

James Pickens 1981

WHY USE THIS METHOD?

1. It is a way to build team collaboration and stimulate ideas.

RESOURCES

2. Paste
3. Scissors
4. Magazines
5. Thick A3 or A4 or letter sized paper
6. Felt-tipped pens

REFERENCES

1. Clark , Charles Hutchinson. The Dynamic New Way to Create Successful Ideas Publisher: Classic Business Book-shelf (November 23, 2010) ISBN-10: 1608425614 ISBN-13: 978-1608425617
2. Rawlinson J. Geoffrey Creative Thinking and Brainstorming. Jaico Publishing House (April 30, 2005) ISBN-10: 8172243480 ISBN-13: 978-8172243487

WHEN TO USE THIS METHOD

1. Explore Ideas

HOW TO USE THIS METHOD

1. The moderator introduces the method
2. Break the large group into smaller groups of 3 to 5 people.
3. Supply each group with the materials listed under "resources"
4. Each participant cuts out 10 pictures that they like
5. Each group creates 2 or 3 greeting cards with their own message using the images and materials.
6. Each group presents their cards to the larger group.
7. The moderator introduces a problem statement and the groups use their cards to stimulate ideas for solutions.
8. Pass cards to next group and repeat.
9. When this process is complete review all the solutions with the larger group and select preferred directions.

idea advocate

WHAT IS IT?

This method involves appointing advocates for ideas that were previously created during a brainstorming session.

WHO INVENTED IT?

Battelle Institute in Frankfurt, Germany

WHY USE THIS METHOD?

1. Idea advocate is a simplified form of the dialectical approach
2. To ensure fair examination of all ideas.
3. To give every presented idea equal chance of being selected.
4. To uncover the positive aspects of ideas

CHALLENGES

1. Consideration should be given to also assigning a devil 's advocate for a more balanced assessment of certain proposed ideas.
2. There should be little difference in status amongst the idea advocates.

WHEN TO USE THIS METHOD

1. Explore Ideas

HOW TO USE THIS METHOD

1. The team reviews a list of previously generated ideas.
2. Assign idea advocate roles to:
3. A team member who proposed an idea, will implement an idea, or argues for the selection of a design direction.
4. The idea advocates present arguments to the design team on why the idea is the best direction.
5. After the advocates have presented the team votes on their preferred idea.

RESOURCES

1. Pens
2. Markers
3. White board or flip chart
4. Dry erase markers

if i were you

WHAT IS IT?

This is a method used to explore scenarios based on methods used by actors that allows refinement of ideas by a design team.

WHO INVENTED IT?

Gerber, E 2009

WHY USE THIS METHOD?

1. Does not require a lot of training.
2. Can take ideas into new areas.

CHALLENGES

1. Needs good moderator.

WHEN TO USE THIS METHOD

1. Know Context
2. Know User
3. Frame insights
4. Explore Ideas

HOW TO USE THIS METHOD

1. Moderator defines scenario.
2. Can use props or empathy tools.
3. Can videotape session.
4. Group sits around a table or on chairs in a circle.
5. Moderator introduces idea or scenario. Each participant in turn adds something to the idea prefixed by the statement "If I was you I would."
6. Statements should be positive

inside the box

WHAT IS IT?

Sometimes people have better ideas if they have some constraints. This brainstorming technique uses constraints to help develop new ideas.

WHO INVENTED IT?

Alex Faickney Osborn 1953 is often credited with inventing brainstorming.

WHY USE THIS METHOD?

1. Leverages the diverse experiences of a team.
2. Makes group problem solving fun.
3. Helps build team cohesion.
4. Everyone can participate.

CHALLENGES

1. Groupthink
2. Not enough good ideas
3. Taking turns
4. Freeloading
5. Inhibition
6. Lack of critical thinking
7. A group that is too large competes for attention.

WHEN TO USE THIS METHOD

1. Explore Ideas

HOW TO USE THIS METHOD

1. The moderator introduces the method to the group.
2. The problem is defined by the moderator.
3. The larger group is broken down into groups of 4 or 5 participants
4. The moderator assigns a limitation to each group
5. The moderator instructs each group to come up with a number of ideas if the limitation that they have been assigned is the only limitation that they have.
6. Allow 20 minutes to brainstorm ideas.
7. Participants should record one idea on each index card or post-it-note
8. After 20 minutes display the ideas on a wall organized by the limitation given.
9. The ideas are discussed by the group
10. The moderator groups related ideas.
11. Elect favored concepts and prioritize for further development.

RESOURCES

1. Pens
2. Post-it-notes
3. A flip chart
4. White board or wall
5. Refreshments

journey method

WHAT IS IT?

This is a brainstorming method that uses flexible geographic perspectives to look at a design problem.

WHO INVENTED IT?

Alex Faickney Osborn 1953

WHY USE THIS METHOD?

1. Leverages the diverse experiences of a team.
2. Makes group problem solving fun.
3. Helps build team cohesion.
4. Everyone can participate.

CHALLENGES

1. Some ideas that you generate using the tool may be impractical.
2. Best used with other creativity methods

WHEN TO USE THIS METHOD

1. Explore Ideas

HOW TO USE THIS METHOD

1. Define a problem
2. Select a diverse design team of 4 to 12 people and a moderator.
3. Ask team how they would deal with the problem if they were in a different place.
4. Analyze results and prioritize.
5. Develop actionable ideas.

RESOURCES

1. Pens
2. Post-it-notes
3. A flip chart
4. White board or wall
5. Refreshments

REFERENCES

1. Clark , Charles Hutchinson. The Dynamic New Way to Create Successful Ideas Publisher: Classic Business Bookshelf (November 23, 2010) ISBN-10: 1608425614 ISBN-13: 978-1608425617
2. Rawlinson J. Geoffrey Creative Thinking and Brainstorming. Jaico Publishing House (April 30, 2005) ISBN-10: 8172243480 ISBN-13: 978-8172243487

kj method

WHAT IS IT?

The KJ method is a form of brainstorming. The KJ method places emphasis on the most important ideas. It is one of the seven tools of Japanese quality management and incorporates the Buddhist value of structured meditation.

WHO INVENTED IT?

Kawakita Jiro

WHY USE THIS METHOD?

1. There is a hierarchy of ideas
2. This method generates many ideas.
3. This method highlights the connections between ideas which is the starting point for a design solution.

CHALLENGES

1. Groupthink
2. Not enough good ideas
3. Taking turns
4. Freeloading
5. Inhibition
6. Lack of critical thinking
7. A group that is too large competes for attention.

RESOURCES

1. Paper
2. Pens
3. White board
4. Dry-erase markers
5. Post-it-notes.

WHEN TO USE THIS METHOD

1. Explore Ideas

HOW TO USE THIS METHOD

1. The moderator frames the design challenge.
2. Team members generate ideas in up to 25 words on post-it notes.
3. Cards are shuffled and then handed out again to the participants.
4. Each participant should not gat any of their own cards back.
5. Each post-it note is read out by the participants, and all participants review the post-it notes that they hold to find any that seem to go with the one read out, so building a 'group'.
6. Organise post-it notes into groups.
7. Group the groups until you have no more than ten groups.
8. Sort categories into subcategories of 20-30 cards.
9. Refine groups into 10 post-it notes or less.
10. Use a white board or smooth wall.
11. Write the individual post-it notes arranged in groups on the white board or arrange the post-it notes on a wall.
12. The moderator will read out the groups and record the participant's ideas about the relationships and meaning of the information gathered.

LOTUS BLOSSOM

A1	A2	A3	B1	B2	B3	C1	C2	C3
A4	**A**	A5	B4	**B**	B5	C4	**C**	C5
A6	A7	A8	B6	B7	B8	C6	C7	C8
D1	D2	D3	**A**	**B**	**C**	E1	E2	E3
D4	**D**	D5	**D**		**E**	E4	**E**	E5
D6	D7	D8	**F**	**G**	**H**	E6	E7	E8
F1	F2	F3	G1	G2	G3	H1	H2	H3
F4	**F**	F5	G4	**G**	G5	H4	**H**	H5
F6	F7	F8	G6	G7	G8	H6	H7	H8

lotus blossom

WHAT IS IT?

The lotus blossom is a creativity technique that consists a framework for idea generation that starts by generating eight concept themes based on a central theme. Each concept then serves as the basis for eight further theme explorations or variations.

WHO INVENTED IT?

Yasuo Matsumura, Director of the Clover Management Research

WHY USE THIS METHOD?

1. There is a hierarchy of ideas
2. This method requires that a quantity of ideas is generated.
3. shifts you from reacting to a static snapshot of the problem and broadens your perspective toward the problem and the relationships and connections between its components

CHALLENGES

1. It is a somewhat rigid model. Not every problem will require the same number of concepts to be developed.

WHEN TO USE THIS METHOD

1. Explore Ideas

HOW TO USE THIS METHOD

1. Draw up a lotus blossom diagram made up of a square in the center of the diagram and eight circles surrounding the square;
2. Write the problem in the center box of the diagram.
3. Write eight related ideas around the center.
4. Each idea then becomes the central idea of a new theme or blossom.
5. Follow step 3 with all central ideas.

RESOURCES

1. Paper
2. Pens
3. White board
4. Dry-erase markers
5. Post-it-notes.

REFERENCES

1. Michalko M., Thinkpak, Berkeley, California, Ten Speed Press, 1994.
2. Michalko, Michael, Thinkertoys: A handbook of creative-thinking techniques, Second Edition, Ten Speed Press, 2006, Toronto;
3. Sloane, Paul. The Leader's Guide to Lateral Thinking Skills: Unlocking the Creativity and Innovation in You and Your Team (Paperback - 3 Sep 2006);

low fidelity prototyping

WHAT IS IT?

Cardboard prototyping is a quick and cheap way of gaining insight and informing decision making without the need for costly investment. Simulates function but not aesthetics of proposed design. Prototypes help compare alternatives and help answer questions about interactions or experiences.

WHY USE THIS METHOD?

1. May provide the proof of concept
2. It is physical and visible
3. Inexpensive and fast.
4. Useful for refining functional and perceptual interactions.
5. Assists to identify any problems with the design.
6. Helps to reduce the risks
7. Helps members of team to be in alignment on an idea.
8. Helps make abstract ideas concrete.
9. Feedback can be gained from the user

CHALLENGES

1. Producer might get too attached to prototype and it becomes jewelry because it is beautiful rather than a design tool.

WHEN TO USE THIS METHOD

1. Know Context
2. Know User
3. Frame insights
4. Explore Ideas

HOW TO USE THIS METHOD

1. Construct models, not illustrations
2. Select the important tasks, interactions or experiences to be prototyped.
3. Build to understand problems.
4. If it is beautiful you have invested too much.
5. Make it simple
6. Assemble a kit of inexpensive materials
7. Preparing for a test
8. Select users
9. Conduct test
10. Record notes on the 8x5 cards.
11. Evaluate the results
12. Iterate

RESOURCES

1. Paper
2. Cardboard
3. Wire
4. Foam board,
5. Post-it-notes
6. Hot melt glue

REFERENCES

1. Sefelin, R., Tscheligi, M., & Gukker, V. (2003). Paper Prototyping What is it good for? A Comparison of paper and Computer based Low fidelity Prototyping, CHI 2003, 778-779
2. Snyder, Carolyn (2003). Paper Prototyping: the fast and easy way to design and refine user interfaces. San Francisco, CA: Morgan Kaufmann

misuse scenarios

WHAT IS IT?

This is a method that focuses on possible misuse, both unintentional and malicious, of a product or service. The method involves use of scenarios and personas to envision possible misuse cases. These may be:

1. Typical scenarios
2. Atypical scenarios
3. Extreme scenarios

WHO INVENTED IT?

Ian Alexander 2003

WHY USE THIS METHOD?

1. Considering misuse reduces the possibility that a product will fail in use.
2. Consider on projects where there is potential for misuse.
3. High volume manufactured products have high potential for misuse.

CHALLENGES

1. Use customer service feedback to construct misuse scenarios.
2. It is sometimes hard to envision misuse scenarios for new products.

WHEN TO USE THIS METHOD

1. Know Context
2. Know User
3. Frame insights
4. Explore Ideas

HOW TO USE THIS METHOD

1. Think of various types of scenarios and when they may become misuse scenarios.
2. Talk to experts and ask them to provide scenarios of misuse.
3. Consider the context of use and how that may influence misuse.
4. Brainstorm with team to create scenarios of misuse.
5. Create a list of misuse scenarios.
6. Brainstorm remedies for misuse and modify design to remedy misuse.

RESOURCES

1. Pen
2. Paper
3. White board
4. Dry-erase markers
5. Camera

REFERENCES

1. Alexander, Ian, Use/Misuse Case Analysis Elicits Non-Functional Requirements, Computing & Control Engineering Journal, Vol 14, 1, pp 40-45, February 2003
2. Sindre, Guttorm and Andreas L. Opdahl, Templates for Misuse Case Description, Proc. 7th Intl Workshop on Requirements Engineering, Foundation for Software Quality (REFSQ'2001), Interlaken, Switzerland, 4-5 June 2001

merlin

WHAT IS IT?

The merlin method is a brainstorming method that seeks to develop ideas for improving a product, service or experience by imagining changes in size use or function.

WHY USE THIS METHOD?

1. There is a hierarchy of ideas
2. This method generates many ideas.
3. This method highlights the connections between ideas which is the starting point for design solutions.

WHO INVENTED IT?

Alex Faickney Osborn 1953

CHALLENGES

1. Groupthink
2. Not enough good ideas
3. Taking turns
4. Freeloading
5. Inhibition
6. Lack of critical thinking
7. A group that is too large competes for attention.

WHEN TO USE THIS METHOD

1. Explore Ideas

HOW TO USE THIS METHOD

1. The moderator frames the design challenge.
2. On a whiteboard or flipchart write four headings: enlarge reduce eliminate, reverse.
3. Work for ten minutes with your team under each heading
4. Review the lists, create hierarchy of solutions.

RESOURCES

1. Paper
2. Pens
3. White board
4. Dry-erase markers
5. Post-it-notes.

REFERENCES

1. Clark , Charles Hutchinson. The Dynamic New Way to Create Successful Ideas Publisher: Classic Business Bookshelf (November 23, 2010) ISBN-10: 1608425614 ISBN-13: 978-1608425617
2. Rawlinson J. Geoffrey Creative Thinking and Brainstorming. Jaico Publishing House (April 30, 2005) ISBN-10: 8172243480 ISBN-13: 978-8172243487

nhk method

WHAT IS IT?

The NHK method is a rigorous iterative process of brainstorming of ideas following a predetermined structure.

WHO INVENTED IT?

Hiroshi Takahashi

WHY USE THIS METHOD?

1. This method requires that a quantity of ideas is generated.

CHALLENGES

1. Groupthink
2. Not enough good ideas
3. Taking turns
4. Freeloading
5. Inhibition
6. Lack of critical thinking
7. A group that is too large competes for attention.

WHEN TO USE THIS METHOD

1. Explore Ideas

RESOURCES

1. Paper
2. Pens
3. White board
4. Dry-erase markers
5. Post-it-notes.

HOW TO USE THIS METHOD

1. Define problem statement.
1. Each participant writes down five ideas on five separate cards.
2. Create groups of five participants
3. While each person explains their ideas, the others continue to record new ideas.
4. Collect, and create groups of related concepts.
5. Form new groups of two or three people Brainstorm for half an hour.
6. Groups organize ideas and present them to the larger group.
7. Record all ideas on the white board.
8. Form larger groups of ten people and work further brainstorm each of the ideas on the white board.

REFERENCES

1. Clark , Charles Hutchinson. The Dynamic New Way to Create Successful Ideas Publisher: Classic Business Book-shelf (November 23, 2010) ISBN-10: 1608425614 ISBN-13: 978-1608425617
2. Rawlinson J. Geoffrey Creative Thinking and Brainstorming. Jaico Publish-ing House (April 30, 2005) ISBN-10: 8172243480 ISBN-13: 978-8172243487

nominal group method

WHAT IS IT?

The nominal group method is a brainstorming method that is designed to encourage participation of all members of the team and minimizes the possibility of more vocal members from dominating the discussion.

WHO INVENTED IT?

William Fox

WHY USE THIS METHOD?

1. To define and prioritize problems or opportunities
2. To understand the best solution to a problem
3. To create a plan to implement an opportunity

RESOURCES

1. White board
2. Dry erase markers
3. Blank postcards

WHEN TO USE THIS METHOD

1. Frame insights
2. Explore Ideas

REFERENCES

1. The Memory Jogger II: A Pocket Guide of Tools for Continuous Improvement and Effective Planning Michael Brassard (Author), Diane Ritter (Author), Francine Oddo (Editor) 1st edition (January 15, 1994)

HOW TO USE THIS METHOD

1. Distribute information about the process to participants before the meeting.
2. Participants drop anonymous suggestions into an unmonitored suggestion box written on blank postcards.
3. The suggestions are distributed to participants before the meeting so that they can think about them.
4. In the meeting the moderator writes the suggestions on to a white board
5. Each participant has the opportunity to speak in support or against any of the suggestions.
6. The moderator leads the team in to clarify each idea,
7. The moderator instructs each person to work silently and independently for five minutes, recording as many ideas, thoughts, or answers as possible on paper.
8. The moderator asks the group to list 5 to 10 ideas that the like the most, in order of importance, and to pass them to the moderator.
9. The moderator counts up the number of votes for each idea.
10. Each participant is given a number of votes that they record on blank postcards which are collected face down and tallied.

nyaka

WHAT IS IT?

The Nyaka method is a form of brainstorming. The Nyaka method places emphasis on exploring problems and solutions to problems.

WHY USE THIS METHOD?

1. There is a hierarchy of ideas
2. This method generates many ideas.

CHALLENGES

1. Groupthink
2. Not enough good ideas
3. Taking turns
4. Freeloading
5. Inhibition
6. Lack of critical thinking
7. A group that is too large competes for attention.

RESOURCES

1. Paper
2. Pens
3. White board
4. Dry-erase markers
5. Post-it-notes.

WHEN TO USE THIS METHOD

1. Explore Ideas

HOW TO USE THIS METHOD

1. Define a moderator
2. The moderator draws a vertical line on a whiteboard.
3. Time limit of 30 minutes
4. The moderator asks the team to define as many things that are wrong with a design or service or experience as possible.
5. The moderator asks the team to define solutions for as many of the problems defined as possible.
6. Create a hierarchy of problems and a hierarchy of solutions for each problem.
7. A group size of 4 to 20 people is optimum.
8. For larger groups the moderator can break the group into groups of 4 or 5 people.

REFERENCES

1. Clark , Charles Hutchinson. The Dynamic New Way to Create Successful Ideas Publisher: Classic Business Bookshelf (November 23, 2010) ISBN-10: 1608425614 ISBN-13: 978-1608425617
2. Rawlinson J. Geoffrey Creative Thinking and Brainstorming. Jaico Publishing House (April 30, 2005) ISBN-10: 8172243480 ISBN-13: 978-8172243487

out of the box

WHAT IS IT?

This is a method to perform out-of-the box brainstorming to generate outrageous and wild ideas.

WHY USE THIS METHOD?

1. To generate wild ideas
2. To promote creative thinking among participants.

RESOURCES

1. Pen
2. Paper
3. White board
4. Dry erase markers
5. Post-it-notes

CHALLENGES

1. Avoid persona representations that may be harmful.
2. Groupthink
3. Not enough good ideas
4. Taking turns
5. Freeloading
6. Inhibition
7. Lack of critical thinking
8. A group that is too large competes for attention.

WHEN TO USE THIS METHOD

1. Explore Ideas

HOW TO USE THIS METHOD

1. The moderator introduces this method.
2. The moderator shows the team several wild or out of the box ideas.
3. Participants Explore Ideas stressing that they must be wild and out of the box.
4. The moderator records the ideas on a white board.
5. The team reviews the ideas and selects some for further development and bringing back to reality.

RESOURCES

1. Pen
2. Paper
3. White board
4. Dry erase markers
5. Post-it-notes

REFERENCES

1. Clark , Charles Hutchinson. The Dynamic New Way to Create Successful Ideas Publisher: Classic Business Bookshelf (November 23, 2010) ISBN-10: 1608425614 ISBN-13: 978-1608425617
2. Rawlinson J. Geoffrey Creative Thinking and Brainstorming. Jaico Publishing House (April 30, 2005) ISBN-10: 8172243480 ISBN-13: 978-8172243487

pattern language

WHAT IS IT?

Pattern language is an approach to design that uses visual icons rather than words to stimulate and develop design concepts. Developed by Alexander to discover the design factors such as life, wholeness or spirit for architectural projects that he called design elements that give a community "the quality that has no name"

WHO INVENTED IT?

Christopher Alexander, Sara Ishikawa, Murray Silverstein 1977

WHY USE THIS METHOD?

1.   A non verbal approach to design.

RESOURCES

1.   Blank Index cards
2.   Pens
3.   Paper

WHEN TO USE THIS METHOD

1.   Explore Ideas

HOW TO USE THIS METHOD

1.   Write a list of about 250 words that are attributes or factors of your design problem.
2.   Create a series of iconic images to illustrate each word on a deck of blank index cards.
3.   Write the associated word on the back face of each icon card.
4.   Spread the cards on a table with the icons facing upwards and randomly associate two or three cards at a time.
5.   Explore Ideas based on these associations.
6.   Review the ideas with your team
7.   Prioritize the ideas.
8.   Develop preferred ideas.

REFERENCES

1.   Alexander, C., Ishikawa, S., Silverstein, Murray. (1977). A pattern language. New York: Oxford University Press.

personal

WHAT IS IT?

Recent research has suggested that some individuals are more creative working alone for brainstorming sessions rather than in groups. In this case the divergent idea generation is done by an individual and the convergent phase is done by the team.

WHO INVENTED IT?

Alex Faickney Osborn 1953

WHY USE THIS METHOD?

1. Leverages the diverse experiences of a team.
2. Uses the creativity of the individual free from distractions.
3. Helps build empathy.

CHALLENGES

1. Some ideas that you generate using the tool may be impractical.
2. Best used with other creativity methods

WHEN TO USE THIS METHOD

1. Explore Ideas

HOW TO USE THIS METHOD

1. Define a problem
2. Find a quiet place
3. Generate as many ideas as possible in 30 minutes.
4. Get the team together and present the ideas to them.
5. Get the team to vote on which ideas they like the most. Two votes per person.
6. Analyze results and prioritize.
7. Develop actionable ideas.

RESOURCES

1. Pens
2. Post-it-notes
3. A flip chart
4. White board or wall
5. Refreshments

REFERENCES

1. Clark , Charles Hutchinson. The Dynamic New Way to Create Successful Ideas Publisher: Classic Business Book-shelf (November 23, 2010) ISBN-10: 1608425614 ISBN-13: 978-1608425617
2. Rawlinson J. Geoffrey Creative Thinking and Brainstorming. Jaico Publishing House (April 30, 2005) ISBN-10: 8172243480 ISBN-13: 978-8172243487

persona brainstorming

WHAT IS IT?

This is a brainstorming method that uses the imagined perspectives of an identified persona or group identified as one of your client's customer groups such as students look at a design problem.

WHO INVENTED IT?

Alex Faickney Osborn 1953

WHY USE THIS METHOD?

1. Leverages the diverse experiences of a team.
2. Helps build empathy.
3. Makes group problem solving fun.
4. Helps build team cohesion.
5. Everyone can participate.

CHALLENGES

1. Some ideas that you generate using the tool may be impractical.
2. Best used with other creativity methods

WHEN TO USE THIS METHOD

1. Explore Ideas

HOW TO USE THIS METHOD

1. Define a problem
2. Select a diverse design team of 4 to 12 people and a moderator.
3. Identify a persona to focus on. See personas.
4. Ask the team how they would deal with the problem if they were the persona
5. Analyze results and prioritize.
6. Develop actionable ideas.

RESOURCES

1. Pens
2. Post-it-notes
3. A flip chart
4. White board or wall
5. Refreshments

REFERENCES

1. Clark , Charles Hutchinson. The Dynamic New Way to Create Successful Ideas Publisher: Classic Business Bookshelf (November 23, 2010) ISBN-10: 1608425614 ISBN-13: 978-1608425617
2. Rawlinson J. Geoffrey Creative Thinking and Brainstorming. Jaico Publishing House (April 30, 2005) ISBN-10: 8172243480 ISBN-13: 978-8172243487

objectstorming

WHAT IS IT?

A brainstorming technique that uses found objects for inspiration.

WHO INVENTED IT?

Alex Faickney Osborn 1953 is often credited with inventing brainstorming.

WHY USE THIS METHOD?

1. Leverages the diverse experiences of a team.
2. Makes group problem solving fun.
3. Helps build team cohesion.
4. Everyone can participate.

CHALLENGES

1. Groupthink
2. Not enough good ideas
3. Taking turns
4. Freeloading
5. Inhibition
6. Lack of critical thinking
7. A group that is too large competes for attention.

WHEN TO USE THIS METHOD

1. Explore Ideas

HOW TO USE THIS METHOD

1. The moderator introduces the method to the group.
2. The problem is defined by the moderator.
3. The larger group is broken down into groups of 4 or 5 participants. The moderator collects a diverse collection of objects before the brainstorming session.
4. Each participant is given two objects and asked to use them as inspiration to generate 10 ideas
5. Allow 20 minutes
6. The participants are asked to vote for their three preferred solutions.
7. Select the top ideas for further development.

RESOURCES

1. Pens
2. Post-it-notes
3. A flip chart
4. White board or wall
5. Refreshments

phillips 66 method

WHAT IS IT?

The Phillips 66 method is a method for stimulating interaction such as questions, ideas, or opinions from a large conference group.

WHO INVENTED IT?

Donald Phillips

WHY USE THIS METHOD?

1. Involves a large number of people in a process to share ideas.
2. May generate a large number of ideas.

CHALLENGES

1. The original Phillips 66 process called for the dividing of a large group into groups of 6 people each and to allow 6 minutes per small group for discussing a problem or generating ideas.
2. The small group size should be adjusted to suite the size of the larger group and the discussion time should be adjusted to suite the problem being addressed
3. Two or more teams will generate the same idea through different methods of reasoning.

WHEN TO USE THIS METHOD

1. Explore Ideas

HOW TO USE THIS METHOD

1. Divide the larger group into smaller groups of between 4 and 8 people.
2. The moderator presents a clearly defined problem to all of the groups.
3. Each smaller group should move to an area where they can discuss the problem.
4. Each small group should select a spokesperson to record and later present their conclusions.
5. Each group should discuss the problem for between 6 and 30 minutes.
6. The group spokesperson records the ideas.
7. Each group selects the top one to three ideas. The number selected depends on time available for the presentations to the larger group.
8. The selected ideas are recorded and passed on to the moderator. This can be done using index cards.
9. The selected ideas are reviewed by the moderator and discussed by the larger group or reviewed and discussed at a later time.

RESOURCES

1. Pens
2. Index cards
3. Post-it-notes
4. White board
5. Dry erase markers.

pictive

1. WHAT IS IT?

PICTIVE (Plastic Interface for Collaborative Technology Initiative through Video Exploration) is a low fidelity participatory design method used to develop graphical user interfaces. It allows users to participate in the development process. A PICTIVE prototype gives a user a sense of what a system or a piece of software will look like and how it will behave when completed.

WHO INVENTED IT?

Developed by Michael J. Muller and others at Bell Communications Research around 1990

WHY USE THIS METHOD?

2. Less development time.
3. Less development costs.
4. Involves users.
5. Gives quantifiable user feedback.
6. Facilitates system implementation since users know what to expect.
7. Results user oriented solutions.
8. Gets users with diverse experience involved.

CHALLENGES

1. Designers can become too attached to their prototypes and allow them to become jewelry that stands in the way of further refinement.
2. Don't worry about it being pretty.

WHEN TO USE THIS METHOD

1. Explore Ideas

HOW TO USE THIS METHOD

1. A PICTIVE is usually made from simple available tools and materials like pens, paper, Post-It stickers, paper clips and icons on cards.
2. Allow thirty minutes for initial design.
3. Allow ten minutes for user testing.
4. Ten minutes for modification.
5. Five minutes for user testing.
6. Create task scenario.
7. Anything that moves or changes should be a separate element.
8. The designer uses these materials to represent elements such as drop-down boxes, menu bars, and special icons. During a design session, users modify the mock up based on their own experience.
9. Take notes for later review.
10. Record the session with a video camera
11. The team then reviews the ideas and develops a strategy to apply them.
12. A PICTIVE enables non technical people to participate in the design process.

REFERENCES

1. Michael J. Muller PICTIVE an exploration in participatory design. Published in: · Proceeding CHI '91 Proceedings of the SIGCHI Conference on Human Factors in Computing Systems Pages 225-231 ACM New York, NY, USA ©1991 table of contents ISBN:0-89791-383-3 doi 10.1145/108844.108896

pin cards

WHAT IS IT?

The pin cards technique is a brainwriting process to generate ideas on colored cards that are sorted into groups and discussed. This method allows participants to think of more ideas during the writing process. This method can generate more ideas than some other brainstorming methods.

WHO INVENTED IT?

Wolfgang Schnelle

WHY USE THIS METHOD?

1. To generate ideas to solve a problem
2. To produce many ideas quickly and without filtering from other participants.

CHALLENGES

1. Cards need to be passed on quickly
2. Participants may feel time stressed.
3. Some participants may want to make their ideas confidential.

RESOURCES

1. Colored blank index cards
2. Pins
3. Pin Board
4. Pens
5. Markers

WHEN TO USE THIS METHOD

1. Explore Ideas

HOW TO USE THIS METHOD

1. The moderator writes the problem statement on a white board.
2. The participants should be seated around a large table.
3. The moderator distributes 10 cards of the same color to each participant.
4. Each participant receives different-colored cards.
5. Participants record one idea per card.
6. Ideas can be a cartoon sketch or a sentence
7. Completed cards are passed to the person on the participant's right hand side.
8. Participants can review cards from a person on their left hand side.
9. After 30 to 45 minutes all the participants pin the cards that they have to a wall.
10. Each participant should aim to produce at least 40 ideas.
11. The team sorts the cards into a number of groups by association. The type of association are determined by the group.
12. The participants prioritize the groups and combine the ideas in the favored group for further development.

pool method

WHAT IS IT?

Brainstorming is one of the oldest,fastest and most widely used creativity methods. Brainstorming does need to be undertaken by experts. It can be undertaken as a group or individually. Osborn believed that brainstorming as a group was most effective. Recent research has questioned this assumption.

It should be used to address a single problem. Brainstorming is worthwhile when it is part of a larger process of design.

WHO INVENTED IT?

Alex Faickney Osborn 1953

WHY USE THIS METHOD?

1. It is useful for generating new types of solutions to problems.
2. It can be used to overcome creative blocks.
3. There is group buy-in to a design direction.

CHALLENGES

1. Groupthink
2. Not enough good ideas
3. Taking turns
4. Freeloading
5. Inhibition
6. Lack of critical thinking
7. A group that is too large competes for attention.

WHEN TO USE THIS METHOD

1. Explore Ideas

HOW TO USE THIS METHOD

1. Define the problem
2. Moderator briefs the design team.
3. A group size of 4 to 20 people is optimum.
4. Supply each team member with a pile of 50 blank index cards
5. Give the team 30 minutes to create 10 ideas each.
6. Each team member describes their ideas and places the cards with the ideas, one per card in a central pool .
7. Give the team another 30 minutes. Each team members can select one or more ideas to develop which have been created by another team member from the central pool to develop in the second session.

post-it

WHAT IS IT?

It is a method that uses combinations of brainstormed words to generate ideas.

WHY USE THIS METHOD?

1. New ideas start with making new connections.

RESOURCES

1. Whiteboard
2. Dry erase markers
3. Post-it notes
4. Pens
5. Paper
6. Markers

WHEN TO USE THIS METHOD

1. Explore Ideas

HOW TO USE THIS METHOD

1. Ask your team to write all the words that they associate with the problem.
2. One word per post-it-note.
3. Spread the post-it-notes over a wall.
4. As the second level of brainstorming generate ideas based on combinations of words
5. Brainstorm a list of "how to" solutions based on the ideas.

related context

WHAT IS IT?

A method that involves discovering and projecting the thinking of another sector, brand, organization or context onto a design problem.

WHY USE THIS METHOD?

A method of discovering affinities that can facilitate innovative thinking and solutions.

1. Scenarios become a focus for discussion which helps evaluate and refine concepts.
2. Usability issues can be explored.
3. Scenarios help us create an end to end experience.
4. Personas give us a framework to evaluate possible solutions.

CHALLENGES

1. Strong personalities can influence the group in negative ways.
2. Include problem situations
3. Hard to envision misuse scenarios.

WHEN TO USE THIS METHOD

1. Explore Ideas

HOW TO USE THIS METHOD

1. Identify a design problem
2. Put together a design team of 4 to 12 members with a moderator.
3. Brainstorm a list of sectors, organizations, or contexts that may imply a different approach or thinking to your design problem.
4. Imagine your design problem with the associated list.
5. Explore Ideas for each relationship
6. Vote for favored directions using dot voting method.
7. Analyze and summarize insights.

RESOURCES

1. Post-it notes
2. White board
3. Paper
4. Pens
5. Dry-erase markers

REFERENCES

1. "Scenarios," IDEO Method Cards. ISBN 0-9544132-1-0
2. Carroll, John M. Making Use: Scenario-based design of human-computer interactions. MIT Press, 2000.
3. Carroll J. M. Five Reasons for Scenario Based Design. Elsevier Science B. V. 2000.

resources

WHAT IS IT?

This is a brainstorming method that uses the availability of resources to look at a design problem.

WHO INVENTED IT?

Alex Faickney Osborn 1953

WHY USE THIS METHOD?

1. Leverages the diverse experiences of a team.
2. Helps build empathy.
3. Makes group problem solving fun.
4. Helps build team cohesion.
5. Everyone can participate.

CHALLENGES

1. Some ideas that you generate using the tool may be impractical.
2. Best used with other creativity methods

REFERENCES

1. Clark , Charles Hutchinson. The Dynamic New Way to Create Successful Ideas Publisher: Classic Business Bookshelf (November 23, 2010) ISBN-10: 1608425614 ISBN-13: 978-1608425617
2. Rawlinson J. Geoffrey Creative Thinking and Brainstorming. Jaico Publishing House (April 30, 2005) ISBN-10: 8172243480 ISBN-13: 978-8172243487

WHEN TO USE THIS METHOD

1. Explore Ideas

HOW TO USE THIS METHOD

1. Define a problem
2. Select a diverse design team of 4 to 12 people and a moderator.
3. Identify a resource to limit or make more available such as finance, time, people, materials or process.
4. Ask the team how they would deal with the problem if the resource was changed as proposed
5. Analyze results and prioritize.
6. Develop actionable ideas.

RESOURCES

1. Pens
2. Post-it-notes
3. A flip chart
4. White board or wall
5. Refreshments

rolestorming

WHAT IS IT?
Rolestorming is a brainstorming method where participants adopt other people's identity while brainstorming.

WHO INVENTED IT?
Rick Griggs1980s

WHY USE THIS METHOD?
1. Helps reduce inhibitions which some team members may have in suggesting innovative solutions.

CHALLENGES
1. Avoid persona representations that may be harmful.
2. Groupthink
3. Not enough good ideas
4. Taking turns
5. Freeloading
6. Inhibition
7. Lack of critical thinking
8. A group that is too large competes for attention.

WHEN TO USE THIS METHOD
1. Explore Ideas

HOW TO USE THIS METHOD
1. Select moderator
2. Conduct a traditional brainstorming session
3. At the conclusion of the first brainstorming session the moderator identifies a number of identities to be used for the second session
4. The identities can be any person not in the brainstorming group such as a competitor, a famous person, a boss. They should be known to the team members.
5. The Moderator asks some questions
How would this identity solve the problem?
What would this persona see as the problem?
Where would this persona see the problem?
Why would the persona see a problem?
6. Brainstorm in character.
7. Use words such as "My persona"
8. Share ideas.

REFERENCES
1. Clark , Charles Hutchinson. The Dynamic New Way to Create Successful Ideas Publisher: Classic Business Bookshelf (November 23, 2010) ISBN-10: 1608425614 ISBN-13: 978-1608425617
2. Rawlinson J. Geoffrey Creative Thinking and Brainstorming. Jaico Publishing House (April 30, 2005) ISBN-10: 8172243480 ISBN-13: 978-8172243487

sensorial method

WHAT IS IT?

Design in northern Europe and the United States focuses on the visual sense which is only a component of the design experience. A design such as an Italian sports car gives greater consideration to other senses such as hearing, smell touch to give a consistent experience of through all senses to a product user.

WHO INVENTED IT?

Rob Curedale 1995

WHY USE THIS METHOD?

1. It gives a design a greater experience of quality than a design that focuses on the visual sense.
2. It gives a consistent experience.
3. It provides a more stimulating experience than a design that focuses on the visual experience.

CHALLENGES

1. Groupthink
2. Not enough good ideas
3. Taking turns
4. Freeloading
5. Inhibition
6. Lack of critical thinking
7. A group that is too large competes for attention.

WHEN TO USE THIS METHOD

1. Explore Ideas

HOW TO USE THIS METHOD

1. The moderator frames the design challenge.
2. Team members generate ideas on post-it notes.
3. The team works through 20 minute brainstorming sessions in each sense, Vision, smell, touch hearing, taste.
4. Ask team members to generate 6 to 10 ideas each under each category.
5. Use up to 25 words for non visual senses and simple sketches for the visual ideas.
6. Organise post-it notes into groups through discussion with five concepts in each group, one idea from each sense group or five different senses in each group.
7. Ask team to vote on which groups have the most potential for further development.

RESOURCES

1. Paper
2. Pens
3. White board
4. Dry-erase markers
5. Post-it-notes.

313

WORD LISTS

VERB LIST	ADJECTIVE LIST	ADVERB LIST	PRODUCT LIST
walk	adaptable	accidentally	GPS
stand	adventurous	anxiously	marine
reach	affable	beautifully	printer
sit	affectionate	blindly	copy
jump	agreeable	boldly	chair
fly	ambitious	bravely	sofa
accept	amiable	brightly	video
allow	amicable	calmly	game
advise	amusing	carefully	camera
answer	brave	carelessly	desk
arrive	bright	cautiously	tv
ask	broad-minded	clearly	music
avoid	calm	correctly	floor
stop	careful	courageously	bookcase
agree	charming	cruelly	tools
deliver	communicative	daringly	fence
depend	compassionate	deliberately	cart
describe	conscientious	doubtfully	car
deserve	considerate	eagerly	house
destroy	convivial	easily	bean bag
disappear	courageous	elegantly	audio

314

semantic intuition

WHAT IS IT?

Semantic intuition is a method of generating ideas based on word associations.

WHO INVENTED IT?

Warfield, Geschka, & Hamilton, 1975. Battelle Institute

WHY USE THIS METHOD?

1. To find new solutions to a problem.

WHEN TO USE THIS METHOD

1. Explore Ideas

RESOURCES

1. Pens
2. Paper
3. Post-it -notes
4. White board
5. Dry erase markers.

HOW TO USE THIS METHOD

1. Define the problem to be explored.
2. The team brainstorms two to four word lists that are related to the problem. They could be for example a list of nouns, a list of verbs and a list of adjectives.
3. The team makes a forth lists of associations of two or three words from the lists that can form the basis of new ideas.
4. Combine one word from one set with another word from the other set.
5. The team visualizes new products services or experiences based on the word associations.
6. Each team member produces five to ten ideas based on the word associations over a 30 minute period.
7. The ideas are prioritized by the group by voting.

REFERENCES

1. Warfield, J. N., H. Geschka, and R. Hamilton, Methods of Idea Management, Approaches to Problem Solving No. 4, Columbus: Academy for Contemporary Problems, August, 1975.

scenarios

WHAT IS IT?

A scenario is a narrative or story about how people may experience a design in a particular future context of use. They can be used to predict or explore future interactions with concept products or services. Scenarios can be presented by media such as storyboards or video or be written. They can feature single or multiple actors participating in product or service interactions.

WHO INVENTED IT?

Herman Kahn, Rand Corporation 1950, USA

WHY USE THIS METHOD?

1. Scenarios become a focus for discussion which helps evaluate and refine concepts.
2. Usability issues can be explored at a very early stage in the design process.
3. The are useful tool to align a team vision.
4. Scenarios help us create an end to end experience.
5. Interactive experiences involve the dimension of time.
6. Personas give us a framework to evaluate possible solutions.

CHALLENGES

1. Generate scenarios for a range of situations.
2. Include problem situations
3. Hard to envision misuse scenarios.

WHEN TO USE THIS METHOD

1. Frame insights
2. Explore Ideas
3. Create Solutions

HOW TO USE THIS METHOD

1. Identify the question to investigate.
2. Decide time and scope for the scenario process.
3. Identify stake holders and uncertainties.
4. Define the scenarios.
5. Create storyboards of users goals, activities, motivations and tasks.
6. Act out the scenarios.
7. The session can be videotaped.
8. Analyze the scenarios through discussion.
9. Summarize insights

RESOURCES

1. Storyboard templates
2. Pens
3. Video cameras
4. Props
5. White board
6. Dry-erase markers

REFERENCES

1. "Scenarios," IDEO Method Cards. ISBN 0-9544132-1-0
2. Carroll, John M. Making Use: Scenario-based design of human-computer interactions. MIT Press, 2000.
3. Carroll J. M. Five Reasons for Scenario Based Design. Elsevier Science B. V. 2000.
4. Carroll, John M. Scenario-Based Design: Envisioning Work and Technology in System Development.

up and down

WHAT IS IT?

This is a brainstorming method that creates ideas from the top and lowest employees of an organization

WHO INVENTED IT?

Alex Faickney Osborn 1953

WHY USE THIS METHOD?

1. It is useful for generating new types of solutions to problems.
2. Brainstorming allows each person in a group to better understand a problem.
3. It can be used to overcome creative blocks.
4. There is group buy-in to a design direction.

CHALLENGES

1. Groupthink
2. Not enough good ideas
3. Taking turns
4. Freeloading
5. Inhibition
6. Lack of critical thinking
7. A group that is too large competes for attention.

WHEN TO USE THIS METHOD

1. Explore Ideas

HOW TO USE THIS METHOD

1. Ask your team to brainstorm the viewpoint of the CEO
2. Ask your team to brainstorm the problem from the viewpoint of the lowest employee
3. How would the problem be different from their perspectives?
4. Formulate how to statements.

RESOURCES

1. Pens
2. Post-it-notes
3. A flip chart
4. White board or wall
5. Refreshments.

REFERENCES

1. Clark , Charles Hutchinson. The Dynamic New Way to Create Successful Ideas Publisher: Classic Business Book-shelf (November 23, 2010) ISBN-10: 1608425614 ISBN-13: 978-1608425617
2. Rawlinson J. Geoffrey Creative Thinking and Brainstorming. Jaico Publishing House (April 30, 2005) ISBN-10: 8172243480 ISBN-13: 978-8172243487

317

scamper

WHAT IS IT?

SCAMPER is a brainstorming technique and creativity method that uses seven words as prompts.

1. Substitute.
2. Combine.
3. Adapt.
4. Modify.
5. Put to another use.
6. Eliminate.
7. Reverse.

WHO INVENTED IT?

Bob Eberle based on work by Alex Osborne

WHY USE THIS METHOD?

1. Scamper is a method that can help generate innovative solutions to a problem.
2. Leverages the diverse experiences of a team.
3. Makes group problem solving fun.
4. Helps get buy in from all team members for solution chosen.
5. Helps build team cohesion.
6. Everyone can participate.

CHALLENGES

1. Some ideas that you generate using the tool may be impractical.
2. Best used with other creativity methods

SEE ALSO

1. Brainstorming

WHEN TO USE THIS METHOD

1. Explore Ideas

HOW TO USE THIS METHOD

1. Select a product or service to apply the method.
2. Select a diverse design team of 4 to 12 people and a moderator.
3. Ask questions about the product you identified, using the SCAMPER mnemonic to guide you.
4. Create as many ideas as you can.
5. Analyze
6. Prioritize.
7. Select the best single or several ideas to further brainstorm.

RESOURCES

1. Pens
2. Post-it-notes
3. A flip chart
4. White board or wall
5. Refreshments

REFERENCES

1. Scamper: Creative Games and Activities for Imagination Development. Bob Eberle April 1, 1997 ISBN-10: 1882664248 ISBN-13: 978-1882664245

SCAMPER QUESTIONS

SUBSTITUTE

1. What materials or resources can you substitute or swap to improve the product?
2. What other product or process could you substitute?
3. What rules could you use?
4. Can you use this product in another situation?

COMBINE

1. Could you combine this product with another product?
2. Could you combine several goals?
3. Could you combine the use of the product with another use?
4. Could you join resources with someone else?

ADAPT

1. How could you adapt or readjust this product to serve another purpose or use?
2. What else is the product like?
3. What could you imitate to adapt this product?
4. What exists that is like the product?
5. Could the product adapt to another context?

MODIFY

1. How could you change the appearance of the product?
2. What could you change ?
3. What could you focus on to create more return on investment?
4. Could you change part of the product?

PUT TO ANOTHER USE

1. Can you use this product in another situation?
2. Who would find this product useful?
3. How would this product function in a new context?
4. Could you recycle parts of this product to create a new product?

ELIMINATE

1. How could you make the product simpler?
2. What features, parts, could you eliminate?
3. What could you understate or tone down?
4. Could you make the product smaller or more efficient?
5. Would the product function differently if you removed part of the product?

REVERSE

1. What would happen if you changed the operation sequence?
2. What if you do the reverse of what you are trying to do?
3. What components could you substitute to change the order of this product?
4. What roles could you change?

STP CHART

SITUATION	TARGET	PROPOSAL

stp method

WHAT IS IT?

STP is a brainstorming method designed to help define ways of reaching a goal.

WHO INVENTED IT?

Ava S Butler 1996

WHY USE THIS METHOD?

1. To generate new ideas

CHALLENGES

1. Groupthink
2. Not enough good ideas
3. Taking turns
4. Freeloading
5. Inhibition
6. Lack of critical thinking
7. A group that is too large competes for attention.

RESOURCES

1. Pens
2. Post-it-notes
3. A flip chart
4. White board or wall
5. Refreshments.

REFERENCES

1. Butler, Ava S. (1996) Teamthink Publisher: Mcgraw Hill ISBN 0070094330
2. Clark, Charles Hutchinson. The Dynamic New Way to Create Successful Ideas Publisher: Classic Business Bookshelf (November 23, 2010) ISBN-10: 1608425614 ISBN-13: 978-1608425617

WHEN TO USE THIS METHOD

1. Explore Ideas

HOW TO USE THIS METHOD

1. The moderator writes three headings on a white board. Situation, target and proposal.
2. The moderator reviews the rules of brainstorming. Go for quantity.
3. The moderator asks the question "What do you see as the current situation?"
4. When all ideas have been recorded the moderator asks "Which comments need clarification?"
5. After team members provide clarification the moderator asks " What is our ideal goal?"
6. After all ideas have been recorded and clarifies the moderator asks" What is our preferred target?"
7. After the team votes and a preferred target is selected the moderator asks "How can we get from our current situation to our preferred target?"
8. After all ideas have been recorded and clarified the team selects a preferred way to get to the target by voting.

starbusting

WHAT IS IT?

Starbursting generates questions to clarify issues, probe for potential solutions, or verify resource requirements.

WHO INVENTED IT?

Alex Faickney Osborn 1953

WHY USE THIS METHOD?

1. To identify potential problem areas
2. Useful for generating new types of solutions to problems.

CHALLENGES

1. No evaluation of questions is allowed during the starbursting process.
2. Groupthink
3. Not enough good ideas
4. Taking turns
5. Freeloading
6. Inhibition
7. Lack of critical thinking
8. A group that is too large competes
9. for attention.

RESOURCES

1. Pens
2. Post-it-notes
3. A flip chart
4. White board or wall
5. Refreshments.

WHEN TO USE THIS METHOD

1. Explore Ideas

HOW TO USE THIS METHOD

1. The fist step is to define a problem to be explored or to review a set of previously brainstormed ideas.
2. The participants may ask as many questions as they would like without other participants judging them.
3. Participants write their questions on 3 × 5 inch index cards.
4. The moderator collects the questions and writes them on a white board.
5. The team organizes the questions into related groups and prioritizes them

RESOURCES

1. Pens
2. 3 x5 inch blank index cards
3. White board or wall
4. Refreshments.

REFERENCES

1. Clark , Charles Hutchinson. The Dynamic New Way to Create Successful Ideas Publisher: Classic Business Book-shelf (November 23, 2010) ISBN-10: 1608425614 ISBN-13: 978-1608425617
2. Rawlinson J. Geoffrey Creative Thinking and Brainstorming. Jaico Publishing House (April 30, 2005) ISBN-10: 8172243480 ISBN-13: 978-8172243487

synectics

WHAT IS IT?

Synectics is a structured creativity method that is based on analogy. Synectics is based on observations collected during thousands of hours of group process and group problem solving and decision making activities (Nolan 1989)The word synectics combines derives from Greek "the bringing together of diverse elements."

WHO INVENTED IT?

George Prince and William Gordon 1976

WHY USE THIS METHOD?

1. Use to stimulate creative thinking and generate new problem solving approaches.
2. Synectics provides an environment in which risk taking is validated.
3. Synectics can be fun and productive.

CHALLENGES

1. Synectics is more demanding than brainstorming,
2. If the analogy is too obvious, then it may not promote innovative thinking.
3. Synectics works best as a group process.

WHEN TO USE THIS METHOD

1. Frame insights
2. Explore Ideas

HOW TO USE THIS METHOD

1. Problem definition.
2. Create an analogy. Use ideas from the natural or man-made world, connections with historical events, your location, etc.
3. Use this Sentence Stem: An is a lot like a y because…
4. Use a syntectic trigger Mechanism like a picture, poem, song, drawing etc. to start your analogical reasoning.
5. The group generates as many solution approaches, called springboards, as possible.
6. Idea selection.
7. Excursions - Structured side trips.
8. Develop the selected ideas into concepts.
9. Analyze the connections in the analogy you have created.

RESOURCES

1. Paper
2. Pens
3. White board
4. Dry-erase markers

REFERENCES

1. Gordon, William J.J. Synectics: The Development of Creative Capacity. (New York: Harper and row, Publishers, 1961
2. Nolan, Vincent. "Whatever Happened to Synectics?" Creativity and Innovation Management, v. 21 n.1 (2003): 25.

thought leader

WHAT IS IT?

This is a brainstorming method that brainstorms imagined solutions that may be proposed by some of the most thoughtful people who have lived.

WHO INVENTED IT?

Alex Faickney Osborn 1953

WHY USE THIS METHOD?

1. Leverages the diverse experiences of a team.
2. Helps build empathy.
3. Makes group problem solving fun.
4. Helps build team cohesion.
5. Everyone can participate.

CHALLENGES

1. Some ideas that you generate using the tool may be impractical.
2. Best used with other creativity methods

REFERENCES

1. Clark , Charles Hutchinson. The Dynamic New Way to Create Successful Ideas Publisher: Classic Business Bookshelf (November 23, 2010) ISBN-10: 1608425614 ISBN-13: 978-1608425617
2. Rawlinson J. Geoffrey Creative Thinking and Brainstorming. Jaico Publishing House (April 30, 2005) ISBN-10: 8172243480 ISBN-13: 978-8172243487

WHEN TO USE THIS METHOD

1. Explore Ideas

HOW TO USE THIS METHOD

1. Define a problem
2. Select a diverse design team of 4 to 12 people and a moderator.
3. Identify a thought leader to focus on to explore the solutions such as Steve Jobs, James Dyson, Thomas Edison, Bill Gates, Henry Ford, Steven Spielberg, Albert Einstein, Richard Branson or Leonardo Da Vinci.
4. The moderator asks the group how they imagine that this person may solve the problem.
5. Analyze results and prioritize.
6. Develop actionable ideas.

RESOURCES

1. Pens
2. Post-it-notes
3. A flip chart
4. White board or wall
5. Refreshments

written scenario

WHAT IS IT?

Scenarios are stories that describe a possible future event. Scenarios are used by organizations to understand different ways that future events might unfold

WHO INVENTED THIS METHOD?

Herman Kahn RAND 1950s

WHY USE THIS METHOD?

1. A written scenario helps a designer understand interactions of an intended user with a product service or experience.
2. Scenarios can also be used for evaluating an intened design.

WHEN TO USE THIS METHOD

1. Define intent
2. Know Context
3. Know User
4. Frame insights
5. Explore Ideas
6. Make Plans

CHALLENGES

1. Work in small groups
2. Avoid identifying one solution
3. Keep focussed on the problem.

HOW TO USE THIS METHOD

1. Decide on the key question to be answered.
2. Determine the time and scope of the scenario.
3. Determine the stakeholders or actors.
4. Determine the goals the actor has to complete.
5. Map basic trends and driving forces.
6. Consider key uncertainties.
7. Determine a starting point of the scenario: a trigger or an event.
8. You need to have an understanding of the users and the context of use.
9. Brainstorm possible solutions.
10. Produce 7 to 9 initial mini-scenarios
11. Reduce to 2 to 3 scenarios
12. You can use story boarding.
13. In simple language describe the interactions.
14. Assess the scenarios. Identify the issues arising.

RESOURCES

1. Paper
2. Pens

REFERENCES

1. Schoemaker, Paul J.H. "Scenario Planning: A Tool for Strategic Thinking," Sloan Management Review. Winter: 1995, pp. 25-40.
2. M. Lindgren & H. Bandhold, Scenario planning – the link between future and strategy, Palgrave Macmillan, 2003

time machine

WHAT IS IT?

This is a brainstorming method that uses flexible time perspectives to look at a design problem.

WHO INVENTED IT?

Alex Faickney Osborn 1953

WHY USE THIS METHOD?

1. Leverages the diverse experiences of a team.
2. Makes group problem solving fun.
3. Helps build team cohesion.
4. Everyone can participate.

CHALLENGES

1. Some ideas that you generate using the tool may be impractical.
2. Best used with other creativity methods

REFERENCES

1. Clark , Charles Hutchinson. The Dynamic New Way to Create Successful Ideas Publisher: Classic Business Book-shelf (November 23, 2010) ISBN-10: 1608425614 ISBN-13: 978-1608425617
2. Rawlinson J. Geoffrey Creative Thinking and Brainstorming. Jaico Publish-ing House (April 30, 2005) ISBN-10: 8172243480 ISBN-13: 978-8172243487

WHEN TO USE THIS METHOD

1. Explore Ideas

HOW TO USE THIS METHOD

1. Define a problem
2. Select a diverse design team of 4 to 12 people and a moderator.
3. Ask team how they would deal with the problem if they were living 10 years ago, 1000 years ago, 10,000 years ago?
4. Ask the team how they would dal with the problem if they were living 5 years in the future, ten years, 100 years 1,000 years in the future?
5. Analyze results and prioritize.
6. Develop actionable ideas.

RESOURCES

1. Pens
2. Post-it-notes
3. A flip chart
4. White board or wall
5. Refreshments

trigger method

WHAT IS IT?

Iteration is important at all stages of the design process. This method takes the ideas of an initial brainstorming session and uses these ideas to build upon in a second session.

WHO INVENTED IT?

Alex Faickney Osborn 1953

WHY USE THIS METHOD?

1. Leverages the diverse experiences of a team.
2. Iteration allows refinement or ideas.
3. Makes group problem solving fun.
4. Helps build team cohesion.
5. Everyone can participate.

CHALLENGES

1. Some ideas that you generate using the tool may be impractical.
2. Best used with other creativity methods

REFERENCES

1. Clark , Charles Hutchinson. The Dynamic New Way to Create Successful Ideas Publisher: Classic Business Bookshelf (November 23, 2010) ISBN-10: 1608425614 ISBN-13: 978-1608425617
2. Rawlinson J. Geoffrey Creative Thinking and Brainstorming. Jaico Publishing House (April 30, 2005) ISBN-10: 8172243480 ISBN-13: 978-8172243487

WHEN TO USE THIS METHOD

1. Explore Ideas

HOW TO USE THIS METHOD

1. Ideas from a first brainstorming session are presented to the group.
2. The group creates a hierarchy by voting for the favored ideas.
3. The one or 3 ideas are selected as the basis for the brainstorming session.
4. Analyze results and prioritize.
5. Develop actionable ideas.

RESOURCES

1. Pens
2. Post-it-notes
3. A flip chart
4. White board or wall
5. Refreshments

327

wishful thinking

WHAT IS IT?

This method gives your team members an opportunity to propose possible outcomes that they would like to see and the team to brainstorm each team member's wish.

WHY USE THIS METHOD?

1. It is useful for generating new types of solutions to problems.
2. Brainstorming allows each person in a group to better understand a problem.
3. It can be used to overcome creative blocks.
4. There is group buy-in to a design direction.

CHALLENGES

1. Some team members may find the initial wishes challenging.

WHEN TO USE THIS METHOD

2. Frame insights
3. Explore Ideas

RESOURCES

1. Pens
2. Post-it-notes
3. A flip chart
4. White board or wall
5. Refreshments.

HOW TO USE THIS METHOD

1. Define the problem.
2. Moderator provides an overview of the method.
3. The participants each generate one wish. An example may be : 'We should have more flexible work hours"
4. The moderator records the statements on a white board
5. In a second stage of the brainstorm which can be called "reality check" The participants review the wish list and suggest how each wish may be actualized in a practical way. Ask: "How can we really do this?" "What resource could be used?" "What could happen if we try this?"
6. The team reviews the second list and votes on their preferred directions for further development.

REFERENCES

1. Clark , Charles Hutchinson. The Dynamic New Way to Create Successful Ideas Publisher: Classic Business Book-shelf (November 23, 2010) ISBN-10: 1608425614 ISBN-13: 978-1608425617
2. Rawlinson J. Geoffrey Creative Thinking and Brainstorming. Jaico Publishing House (April 30, 2005) ISBN-10: 8172243480 ISBN-13: 978-8172243487

camera journal

WHAT IS IT?

The research subjects record their activities with a camera and notes. The researcher reviews the images and discusses them with the participants.

WHO INVENTED IT?
WHY USE THIS METHOD?

1. Helps develop empathy for the participants.
2. Participants are involved in the research process.
3. Helps establish rapport with participants.
4. May reveal aspects of life that are seldom seen by outsiders.

CHALLENGES

1. Should obtain informed consent.
2. May not be ideal for research among particularly vulnerable people.
3. May be a relatively expensive research method.
4. May be time consuming.
5. Best used with other methods.
6. Technology may be unreliable.
7. Method may be unpredictable'.
8. Has to be carefully analyzed

WHEN TO USE THIS METHOD

1. Know Context
2. Know User
3. Frame insights

HOW TO USE THIS METHOD

1. Define subject of study
2. Define participants
3. Gather data images and insight statements.
4. Analyze data.
5. Identify insights
6. Rank insights
7. Produce criteria for concept generation from insights.
8. Explore Ideas to meet needs of users.

RESOURCES

1. Cameras
2. Voice recorder
3. Video camera
4. Note pad
5. Pens

REFERENCES

1. Latham, A. (2003). Researching and Writing Everyday Accounts ofthe City: An Introduction to the Diary-Photo Diary-interview Method in Knowles, C and Sweetmen, P (eds) Picturing the Social Landscape: Visual Methods and the Sociological Imagination. London, Routledge.
2. Latham,A.R.(2003)'Research, performance, and doing human geography: some reflections on the diary-photo diary-interview method', Environment and Planning A,35(11),1993-2017

C-BOX

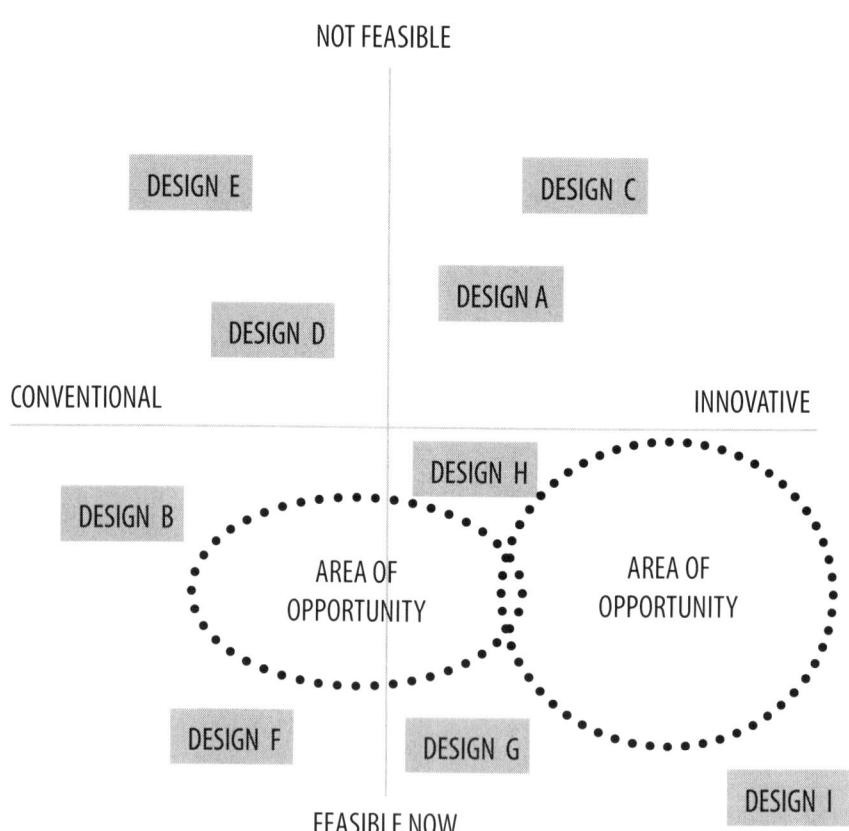

c-box

WHAT IS IT?

A c-box is a type of perceptual map that allows comparison and evaluation of a large number of ideas generated in a brainstorming session by a design team. The method allows everyone to contribute in a democratic way. It can be used to identify the most feasible and innovative ideas. It is up to your team to decide the level of innovation that they would like to carry forward from the idea generation or divergent phase of the project to the convergent or refinement and implementation phases.

WHO INVENTED IT?

Marc Tassoul, Delft 2009

WHY USE THIS METHOD?

1. It is democratic
2. It is quick and productive
3. It is inexpensive

WHEN TO USE THIS METHOD

1. Frame insights
2. Explore Ideas

REFERENCES

Tassoul, M. (2006) Creative Facilitation: a Delft Approach, Delft: VSSD.

HOW TO USE THIS METHOD

1. The moderator defines the design problem
2. You group can be optimally from 4 to 20 people.
3. On a white board or large sheet of paper create two axes. You can also use tape on a large wall.
4. The team should sit around a table facing the wall.
5. Innovation on the horizontal and feasibility on the vertical axes creating 4 quadrants
6. The scale on the innovation ranges from not innovative at the left hand to highly innovative on the right hand end.
7. Alternative axes are attractiveness and functionality.
8. The scale for feasibility runs from not feasible now at the bottom to immediately feasible at the top.
9. Hand out ten post-it-notes to each member of your team.
10. Brainstorm concepts. Each team member to generate 5 to 10 concepts over 30 minutes. One idea per post-it note. Hand out more post-it notes if required.
11. Each team member then presents each idea taking one to three minutes per idea depending on time available.
12. With the group's input discuss the ideas and precise position on the map.
13. Position each post-it-note according to the group consensus.

further reading

Alonso-Regardo, M., Thompson G. & Dannemark O. (2004). State of the art in service design and modelling vivace. University of Manchester.

Arnould & Price, (1993). River magic: extraordinary experience and the extended-service encounter, Journal of Consumer Research, Vol. 20.

Bechmann, Søren (2010): "Servicedesign", Gyldendal Akademisk.

Berry, L.L, Zeithaml V. A. & Parasuraman A. (1990). Five imperatives for improving service quality, Sloan Management Review, Vol. 31, No. 4, Summer, 29–38.

Berry, L.L. & Parasuraman, A. (1993). Building a new academic field – the case of services marketing, Journal of Retailing, 69, 1, 13–60.

Barabási, Albert-László (2002). Linked. How Everything Is Connected to Everything Else and what It Means for Business, Science, and Everyday Life. Cambridge, MA, Perseus.

Bell, Michael (2008). Service-Oriented Modeling. Service Analysis, Design and Architecture. Hoboken, NJ, John Wiley & Sons

Bell, Daniel (1974). The Coming of Post-Industrial Society. New York, Harper Colophon Books.

Brown, Tim (2009). Change by Design: How Design Thinking Transforms Organizations and Inspires Innovation. New York, HarperCollins.

Buur, J., T. Binder, et al. (2000). "Taking Video beyond "Hard Data" in User Centred Design." Design. Participatory Design Conference (PDC 2000).

Buchenau, M., & Suri, J. F. (2000). Experience prototyping. Symposium on designing interactive systems. In Conference Proceedings on designing interactive systems: processes, practices, and techniques, 424–433. New York: ACM Press.

Buur, J. and A. Soendergaard (2000). "Video Card Game: An augmented environment for User Centred Design discussions." Designing Augmented Reality Environments (DARE 2000), Helsingør.

Eiglier, P., Langeard,P (1977). Marketing Consumer Services: New Insights. Cambridge, Mass.

Marketing Science Institute, 1977. 128 P.

Bitner, M. J. (1990). Evaluating Service Encounters: The Effects of Physical Surroundings and Employee Responses. The Journal of Marketing , 54 (2), 69 - 82.

Blomkvist, J., Holmlid, S., & Segelström, F. (2010). This is Service Design Research. In M.Stickdorn, & J. Schneider (Eds.), This is Service Design Thinking. Amsterdam, Netherlands: BIS Publishers

Buera, Francisco & Kaboski, Joseph P. (2006). The Rise of the Service Economy. Proceedings in USC FBE, Macroeconomics & International finance workshop, Nov. 17 2006.

Chase, R.B. and Dasu, S. (2001), ""Want to perfect your company's service? Use behavioral science", Harvard Business Review , Vol. 79 No. 6, pp. 78-84.

Christensen, Clayton M. & Anthony, Scott D. (2004). Cheaper, faster, easier: disruption in the service sector. Harvard Business Review Publishing.

Diana, C., Pacenti, E., & Tassi, R. (2009). Visualtiles Communication tools for (service) design . First Nordic Conference on Service Design and Service Innovation.Oslo, Norway.

Dougherty, D. (2004). Organizing practices in services: capturing practice-based knowledge for innovation, Strategic Organization, 2, 1, 35–64.

Firat & Venkatesh (1995). Emancipatory postmodernism and the enchantment of con-sumption, Journal of Consumer Research, Vol. 22.

Fitzsimmons, J. A. & Fitzsimmons, M. J. (2000). New service development: creating memorable experiences. Thousand Oaks, CA: Sage Publications.

Fleiß, S. & Kleinaltenkamp, M. (2004). Blueprinting the service company: managing service processes efficiently, Journal of Business Research, 57, 392–404.

Florida, Richard (2002). The Rise of the Creative Class. And How It's Transforming Work, Leisure, Community, and Everyday Life. New York, Basic Books.

Frayling, C. (1993). Research in Art and Design. Royal College of Art Research Papers . Royal

further reading

College of Art Research Papers, 1(1):1--5.

Froehle, C.M., Roth, A. V., Chase, R. B. & Voss, C. A. (2000). Antecedents of new service development effectiveness. An exploratory examination of strategic oper-ations choices, Journal of Service Research, Vol. 3, No. 1, 3–17.

Fuad-Luke, Alastair (2012). Co-Designing Services in the Co-futured City. In Kuosa, Tuomo & Westerlund, Leo (eds.), Service Design: On the Evolution of Design Expertise. Lahti University of Applied Sciences Series A, Research reports, part 16, pp. 101—120.

Fullerton, B. (2009). Co Creation in Service Design. interactions , 6 9

Gabbott & Hogg (2000). An empirical investigation of the impact of non-verbalcom-munication on service evaluation, European Journal of Marketing, Vol. 34, No. 3/4.

Gaver B., Dunne T., Pacenti E., (1999). "Design: Cultural Probes." Interaction 6(1): 21–29.

Goldstein, Susan M. & Johnston, Robert & Duffy, JoAnn & Rao Jay (2002). The service concept: the missing link in service design research? Journal of Operations Management. 20 (2), pp. 121—134

Gronroos, C. (2000). Service management & marketing: a customer relationship man-agement approach. 2nd edition, Wiley.

Haksever, C., Render, B., Russell R. & Murdick, R. (2000). Service management and operations. Prentice-Hall.

Hart, S. (1996). New product development: a reader (especially the section: The devel-opment of new services by Lynn Shostack, Axel Johne, and Ulrike de Brentani). Thomson.

Hefley, Bill & Murphy, Wendy (eds.) (2008). Service Science, Management, and Engineering: Education for the 21st Century. (Service Research and Innovation Initiative). New York, Springer.

Hollins, G., Hollins, Bill (1991). Total Design : Managing the design process in the service sector. London, Pitman.

Hollins, W. & Shinkins, S. (2006). Managing service operations: design and implemen-tation. Sage.

Holmlid, S., & Evenson, S. (2007). Prototyping and enacting services: Lessons learned from human-centered methods. 10th Quality in Services conference. Orlando, Florida.

Kaivo-oja, Jari (2012). Service Science, Service Architectures, Service Designs, and Dynamic Service Business Development. In Kuosa, Tuomo & Westerlund, Leo (eds.). Service Design: On the Evolution of Design Expertise. Lahti University of Applied Sciences Series A, Research reports, part 16, pp. 69—82.

Kimbell, L. (2009b). Insights from Service Design Practice. 8th European Academy of Design Conference, (pp. 249-253). Aberdeen.

Kimbell, L. (2009c). The turn to service design. In G. Julier, & L. Moor, Design and Creativity: Policy, Management and Practice (pp. 157-173). Oxford: Berg.

Kimbell, L., & Siedel, P. (Eds.). (2008). Designing for Services - Multidisciplinary Perspectives: Exploratory Project on Designing for Services in Science and Technology-based Enterprises,. Oxford: Saïd Business School.

Koskinen, Jari (2009). Ambience Design — Future-Oriented Viewpoints, Service Development and Some Notions about Changing Communicational Identities. Web: http://www.service-design-network.org/system/files/media/8_Koskinen_Ambience%20Design_0. pdf Retrieved 12-06-30.

Koskinen, Jari (2012). Ambience Design Notes. In Kuosa, Tuomo & Westerlund, Leo (eds.). Service Design: On the Evolution of Design Expertise. Lahti University of Applied Sciences Series A, Research reports, part 16, pp. 155—165.

Leadbeater, C. and H. Cottam (2008). The User Generated State: Public Services 2.0.

Levitt, T. (1976). Industrialization of services, Harvard Business Review, 54, 5, 63—74.

Lim, Y.-K., Stolterman, E., & Tenenberg, J. (2008). The Anatomy of Prototypes: Prototypes as Filters, Prototypes as Manifestations of Design Ideas. ACM Trans. Comput.-Hum. Interact , 15 (2).

further reading

Lindsay, C. and S. Rocchi (2003). "'Highly Customerised Solutions' – The Context of Use Co-Research Methodology". Innovating for Sustainability. 11th International Conference of Greening of Industry Network, San Francisco.

Lovelock, C. & Gummesson, E. (2004). Whither services marketing?: in search of a new paradigm and fresh perspectives, Journal of Services Research, 7, 1, 20–41.

Mager, Birgit & Gais, Michael (2009). Service Design: Design studieren. Stuttgart, UTB.

Mager, Birgit & Sung, Tung–Jung (2011). Special issue editorial: Designing for services. International Journal of Design. 5 (2), pp. 1–3.

Makkula, Sami & Kaikonen, Hannu (2012). International Insights on Service Design. In Service Design Magazine. Lahti University of Applied Sciences Series C, Articles, reports and other current publications, part 107, pp. 20–25

Manzini, E., L. Collina, et al. (2004). Solution Oriented Partnership. How to Design Industrialised Sustainable Solutions. Cranfield, Cranfield University. European Commission GROWTH Programme.

Mannervick, U. & Ramirez, R. (2006). Customers as co-innovators: an initial explora-tion of its strategic importance. In Edvardsson, B., Gustaofsson, A., Kristensson, P., Magnusson, P. & Matthing, J. (Eds.), Involving customers in new service devel-opment (pp. 57–75). Imperial College Press, Series on Technology Management.

Meyer Goldstein, S., Johnston, R. Duffy, J. A. & Rao, J. (2002). The service concept: the missing link in service design research? Journal of Operations Management, Vol. 20, No. 2, 121–134.

Miettinen, S. (2009). Prototyping Social Design in Finland and In Namibia Service Design as a Method for Designing Services for Wellbeing. IASDR 2009: Rigor and Relevance. Seoul.

Moggridge, B. (2006). Designing Interactions. Cambridge, MA: MIT Press.

Morelli, N., (2002). Designing product/service systems: a methodological explora-tion, Design Issues, Vol. 18, No. 3, 3–17.

Morelli, N. (2006). "Developing new PSS, Methodologies and Operational Tools." Journal of Cleaner Production 14(17): 1495–1501.

Morelli, N. (2002). "Designing product/service systems. A methodological exploration." Design Issues 18(3): 3–17.

Normann, R. (2000). Service management : strategy and leadership in service business. Chichester ; New York, Wiley.

Normann, R. and R. Ramirez (1994). Designing Interactive Strategy. From Value Chain to Value Constellation. New York, John Wiley and Sons.

Osterwalder, A. and Pigneur, Y. (2010). Business Model Generation: A Handbook for Visionaries, Game Changers, and Challengers. New Jersey, John Wiley and Sons.

Ostrom, A. L., Bitner, M. J., Brown, S. W., Burkhard, K. A., Goul, M., Smith-Daniels, V., et al. (2010). Moving Forward and Making a Difference: Research Priorities for the Science of Service. Journal of Service Research , 13 (1), 4-36.

Parker, S. and J. Heapy (2006). The Journey to the Interface – How public service design can connect users to reform, Demos. Public Administration Select Committee (2008). User Involvement in Public Services, House of Commons: 37.

Parasuraman, A., Zeithaml, V. A. & Berry, L. L. (1988). SERVQUAL: a multi-item scale measuring consumer perceptions of service quality, Journal of Retailing, Vol. 64, No. 1, 12–37.

Pine II, B. J. & Gilmore, J. H. (2011). The Experience Economy: Work Is Theatre & Every Business a Stage. Updated Edition. Boston, MA, Harvard University Press.

Rae, J. (2007, September 12). Seek the magic with service prototypes. Retrieved 05 25, 2010, from Bloomberg Busienssweek: http://www.businessweek.com/innovate/content/sep2007/id20070912_418827.htm

Ramaswamy, R. (1996). Design and management of service processes: keeping custom-ers for life. Reading, MA: Addison-Wesley Publishing Company, Inc.

Sako, M. (2006). Outsourcing and offshoring: implications for productivity of busi-ness services,

further reading

Oxford Review of Economic Policy, Vol. 22, No. 4.

Samalionis, F. (2009). Can designers help deliver better services? In S. Miettinen, & M. Koivisto (Eds.), Designing Services with Innovative Methods (pp. 124-135). Keuruu: Otava Book Printing LTD.

Segelström, F. (2009). Communicating through Visualizations: Service Designers on Visualizing User Research. The First Nordic Conference on Service Design and Service Innovation. Oslo.

Segelström, F., & Holmlid, S. (2009). Visualization as tools for research: Service designers on visualizations. Nordic Design Research Conference. Oslo.

ServiceD (2011) = ServiceD: Interim report for project's work package two. Service design project. Lahti University of Applied Sciences. (unpublished).

Service Design Tools: Communication Methods Supporting Design Processes. (2009). Retrieved 08 17, 2009, from Service Design Tools: http://www.servicedesigntools.org/repository

Sawhney, M., Balasubramanian, S. & Krishnan, V. V. (2004). Creating growth with services, MIT Sloan Management Review.

Shostack, L. G. (1982). "How to Design a Service." European Journal of Marketing 16(1): 49–63.

Shostack, L. G. (1984). "Design Services that Deliver." Harvard Business Review(84115): 133-139.

Schneider, Benjamin & Bowen, David E. (1984). New Service Design, Development and Implementation. In George, William R. & Marshall, Claudia (eds.). Developing New Services. Chicago, American Marketing Association Proceedings Series, pp. 82—102.

Stickdorn, M. and Schneider, J. (2010). This is Service Design Thinking. Amsterdam, BIS Publishers. United Kingdom Prime Minister Strategy Unit (2007). [1]. HM Government Policy Review, Government of United Kingdom.

Tether, B. S. (2005). Do services innovate (differently)? Insights from the european innobarometer survey, Industry and Innovation, 12, 2, 153–184.

Tether, B. (2008). Service design: time to bring in the professionals? In L. Kimbell, & V. P. Siedel (Eds.), Designing for Services - Multidisciplinary Perspectives: Proceedings from the Exploratory Project on Designing for Services in Science and Technology-based Enterprises (pp. 7-9). Oxford, UK: Saïd Business School.
Tidd, J. & Hull, F. M. (Eds.) (2003). Service innovation: organizational responses to technological opportunities and market imperatives. Imperial College Press.

T Toivonen, M. (2004). Expertise as Business. Long-term Development and Future Prospects of Knowledgeintensive Business Services. Dissertation. Helsinki, Helsinki University of Technology, Department of Industrial Engineering and Management

Ulwick, Anthony W. (2005). What Customers Want: Using Outcome-Driven Innovation to Create Breakthrough Products and Services. New York, McGrawHill

Vandermerwe, S. and Rada, J. (1988) "Servitization of business: Adding value by adding services", European Management Journal, vol. 6, no. 4, 1988.

Voss, C., & Zomerdijk, L. (2007). Innovation in Experiential Services – An Empirical View. In DTI (Ed.), Innovation in Services (pp. 97-134). London: DTI.

Watson, Richard (2010). Future Files: A Brief History of the Next 50 Years. London, Nicholas Brealey Publishing. Wheeler, Kevin (2010). T-Shaped People, Jobs, and Recruiting. Web: http://www.ere.net/2010/02/11/t-shaped-people-jobs-and-recruiting Retrieved 12-06-01.

Westerlund, Leo & Kaivo-oja, Jari (2012). Digital evolution — From Information Society to Ubiquitous Society. In Kuosa, Tuomo & Westerlund, Leo (eds.). Service Design: On the Evolution of Design Expertise. Lahti University of Applied Sciences Series A, Research reports, part 16, pp. 137–153.

Zomerdijk, L. G., & Voss, C. A. (2010). Service Design for Experience-Centric Services. Journal of Service Research , 13 (1), 67-82.

de Reuver, M.; Bouwman, H.; Haaker, T.: Mobile business models: organizational and financial design issues that matter, in: Electronic Markets, 19, 1, 2009, pp. 3–13.

van de Kar, E.; den Hengst, M.: Involving users early on in the design process: closing the gap between mobile information services and their users, in: Electronic Markets, 19, 1, 2009, pp. 31–42.

index

index

index

index

index

index

index

index

other titles from this author

Design Thinking
Process and methods manual
Author: Curedale, Robert A
Publisher: Design Community College.
Edition 1 Feb 2013
ISBN-13: 978-0988236240
ISBN-10: 0988236249

Design Thinking
Pocket Guide
Author: Curedale, Robert A
Publisher: Design Community College.
Edition 1 Jun 2013
ISBN-13: 978-0-9892468-5-9
ISBN-10: 098924685X

Design Methods 1
200 ways to apply design thinking
Author: Curedale, Robert A
Publisher: Design Community College.
Edition 1 November 2012
ISBN-10:0988236206 ISBN-13:978-0-9882362-0-2

Design Methods 2
200 more ways to apply design thinking
Author: Curedale, Robert A Publisher: Design
Community College.
Edition 1 January 2013
ISBN-13: 978-0988236240
ISBN-10: 0988236249

Design Research Methods
150 ways to inform design
Author: Curedale, Robert A
Publisher: Design Community College.
Edition 1 January 2013
ISBN-10: 0988236257
ISBN-13: 978-0-988-2362-5-7

50 Brainstorming Methods
for team and individual ideation
Author: Curedale, Robert A
Publisher: Design Community College.
Edition 1 January 2013
ISBN-10: 0988236230
ISBN-13: 978-0-9882362-3-3

50 Selected Design Methods
to inform your design
Author: Curedale, Robert A
Publisher: Design Community College.
Edition 1 January 2013
ISBN-10:0988236265 ISBN-13:978-0-9882362-6-4

Mapping Methods
for design and strategy
Curedale, Robert A
Publisher: Design Community College.
Edition 1 April 2013
ISBN-10: 0989246817
ISBN-13: 978-0-9892468-1-1

Interviews Observation and Focus Groups: 110
methods for user-centered design
Curedale, Robert A
Publisher: Design Community College.
Design Community College Inc
ISBN-13: 978-0989246835
ISBN-10: 0989246833

about the author

Rob Curedale was born in Australia and worked as a designer, director and educator in leading design offices in London, Sydney, Switzerland, Portugal, Los Angeles, Silicon Valley, Detroit, and China. He designed and managed over 1,000 products and experiences as a consultant and in-house design leader for the world's most respected brands. Rob has three decades experience in every aspect of product development, leading design teams to achieve transformational improvements in operating and financial results. He has extensive experience in forging strategic growth, competitive advantage, and a background in expanding business into emerging markets through user advocacy and extensive cross cultural expertise. Rob's designs can be found in millions of homes and workplaces around the world.

Rob works currently as a Adjunct Professor at Art Center College of Design in Pasadena and consults to organizations in the United States and internationally and presents workshops related to design. He has taught as a member of staff and presented lectures and workshops at many respected design schools and universities throughout the world including Yale, Pepperdine University, Art Center Pasadena, Loyola University, Cranbrook, Pratt, Art Center Europe; a faculty member at SCA and UTS Sydney; as Chair of Product Design and Furniture Design at the College for Creative Studies in Detroit, then the largest product design school in North America, Art Institute Hollywood, Cal State San Jose, Escola De Artes e Design in Oporto Portugal, Instituto De Artes Visuals, Design e Marketing, Lisbon, Southern Yangtze University, Jiao Tong University in Shanghai and Nanjing Arts Institute in China.

Rob's design practice experience includes projects for HP, Philips, GEC, Nokia, Sun, Apple, Canon, Motorola, Nissan, Audi VW, Disney, RTKL, Governments of the UAE,UK, Australia, Steelcase, Hon, Castelli, Hamilton Medical, Zyliss, Belkin, Gensler, Haworth, Honeywell, NEC, Hoover, Packard Bell, Dell, Black & Decker, Coleman and Harmon Kardon. Categories including furniture, healthcare, consumer electronics, sporting, homewares, military, exhibits, packaging. His products and experiences can be found in millions of homes and businesses throughout the world.

Rob established and manages the largest network of designers and architects in the world with more than 300,000 professional members working in every field of design.

Printed in Great Britain
by Amazon